Southern Literary Studies

SOUTHERN LITERARY STUDIES

Louis D. Rubin, Jr., Editor

A Season of Dreams: The Fiction of Eudora Welty
ALFRED APPEL, JR.

The Hero with the Private Parts
ANDREW LYTLE

Hunting in the Old South: Original Narratives of the Hunters
EDITED BY CLARENCE GOHDES

Joel Chandler Harris: A Biography
PAUL M. COUSINS

John Crowe Ransom: Critical Essays and a Bibliography
EDITED BY THOMAS DANIEL YOUNG

A Bibliographical Guide to the Study of Southern Literature
EDITED BY LOUIS D. RUBIN, JR.

Poe: Journalist and Critic
ROBERT D. JACOBS

Love, Boy: The Letters of Mac Hyman
EDITED BY WILLIAM BLACKBURN

The Complete Works of Kate Chopin
EDITED BY PER SEYERSTED

Kate Chopin: A Critical Biography
PER SEYERSTED

Without Shelter: The Early Career of Ellen Glasgow
J. R. RAPER

Southern Excursions: Essays on Mark Twain and Others
LEWIS LEARY

The Poetry of Randall Jarrell
SUZANNE FERGUSON

Death by Melancholy: Essays on Modern Southern Fiction
WALTER SULLIVAN

The Sovereign Wayfarer: Walker Percy's Diagnosis of the Malaise
MARTIN LUSCHEI

Literature and Society in Early Virginia, 1608–1840
RICHARD BEALE DAVIS

The Question of Flannery O'Connor
MARTHA STEPHENS

Grace King of New Orleans: A Selection of Her Writings
EDITED BY ROBERT BUSH

The Loneliness at the Core: Studies in Thomas Wolfe
C. HUGH HOLMAN

The Loneliness at the Core

The

Louisiana State University Press / *Baton Rouge*

Loneliness

 at the Core

Studies in Thomas Wolfe

C. Hugh Holman

ISBN 0-8071-0085-4
Library of Congress Catalog Card Number 74-77325
Copyright © 1975 by Louisiana State University Press
All rights reserved
Manufactured in the United States of America

This book was designed by Dwight Agner. It was set in Linotype Janson and printed on Warren Olde Style paper by Moran Industries, Inc., Baton Rouge, Louisiana.

For permission to quote copyrighted material from works and letters by Thomas Wolfe, acknowledgment is made to Paul Gitlin, Administrator C.T.A. of the Estate of Thomas Wolfe, and to the following publishers and persons:

Look Homeward, Angel, copyright © 1929 by Charles Scribner's Sons; renewal copyright © 1957 by Edward C. Aswell, Administrator C.T.A. of the Estate of Thomas Wolfe, and/or Fred Wolfe. *Of Time and the River,* copyright © 1935 by Charles Scribner's Sons. *From Death to Morning,* copyright © 1935 by Charles Scribner's Sons. *The Story of a Novel,* copyright © 1936 by Charles Scribner's Sons. *The Letters of Thomas Wolfe,* edited by Elizabeth Nowell, copyright © 1956 by Edward C. Aswell, Administrator C.T.A. of the Estate of Thomas Wolfe. *The Short Novels of Thomas Wolfe,* edited by C. Hugh Holman, copyright © 1961 by Charles Scribner's Sons.

Acknowledgment is also made to Harper & Row for *The Web and the Rock,* copyright © 1938 by Maxwell E. Perkins as Executor; *You Can't Go Home Again,* copyright © 1940 by Maxwell E. Perkins as Executor; and *The Hills Beyond,* copyright © 1941 by Maxwell E. Perkins as Executor.

To
LOUIS D. RUBIN, JR.
who got there first with the most

Contents

Acknowledgments   *xi*

Introduction   *xv*

I   The Loneliness at the Core   *1*

II   The Stigma of Autobiography   *37*

III   "The Blest *Nouvelle*"   *47*

IV   The Problem of Point of View   *72*

V   Rhetorical Hope and Dramatic Despair   *86*

VI   The Web of the South   *107*

VII   Europe as His Catalyst   *138*

VIII   The Epic Impulse   *155*

Notes   *168*

Index   *179*

Acknowledgments

MOST OF THE EIGHT STUDIES that make up this volume result from the merging, rewriting, and reorganizing of both new material and previously published pieces. I am deeply grateful to the original publishers for permission to reprint the essays cited below.

"The Loneliness at the Core" is a revised version of *Thomas Wolfe*, University of Minnesota Pamphlets on American Writers, No. 6. Minneapolis: University of Minnesota Press. Copyright © 1960 by the University of Minnesota.

"The Stigma of Autobiography" appeared in slightly different form in the *Virginia Quarterly Review*, Autumn, 1964.

" 'The Blest *Nouvelle*' " appeared in somewhat different states as the introduction to *The Short Novels of Thomas Wolfe*, ed. C. Hugh Holman. New York: Charles Scribner's Sons, 1961, and as "Thomas Wolfe, Scribner's Magazine, and 'the Blest *Nouvelle*,' " in *Essays Mostly on Periodical Publishing in America: A Collection in Honor of Clarence Gohdes*. Durham, N.C.: Duke University Press, 1973.

"Rhetorical Hope and Dramatic Despair" was adapted from portions of two essays: "Focus on Thomas Wolfe's *You Can't Go Home Again*: Agrarian Dream and Industrial Nightmare," in *American Dreams, American Nightmares*, ed. David Madden. Carbondale: Southern Illinois University Press, 1970; and "Thomas Wolfe: Rhetorical Hope and Dramatic Despair," in *Thomas Wolfe and the*

Acknowledgments ❈ ❈ ❈ ❈ ❈ ❈ ❈ ❈ ❈ ❈ ❈ ❈ ❈ ❈

Glass of Time, ed. Paschal Reeves. Athens: University of Georgia Press, 1971.

"The Web of the South" was adapted from portions of two essays: " 'The Dark, Ruined Helen of His Blood': Thomas Wolfe and the South," in *South: Modern Southern Literature in Its Cultural Setting*, ed. Louis D. Rubin, Jr., and Robert D. Jacobs. Garden City, N.Y.: Doubleday & Company, 1961; and "Thomas Wolfe: The Epic of the National Self," in C. Hugh Holman, *Three Modes of Modern Southern Fiction: Ellen Glasgow, William Faulkner, Thomas Wolfe*. Athens: University of Georgia Press, 1966.

"Europe as His Catalyst" was adapted from portions of two essays: "Europe as Catalyst for Thomas Wolfe," in *Essays in American and English Literature Presented to Bruce Robert McElderry, Jr.*, ed. Max F. Schulz. Athens: Ohio University Press, 1967; and "Thomas Wolfe's Berlin" in *Saturday Review*, March, 11, 1967.

"The Epic Impulse" appeared in somewhat different form in *Literatur und Sprache der Vereinigten Staaten: Aufsätze zu Ehren von Hans Galinsky*, ed. Hans Helmcke *et al*. Heidelberg: Carl Winter Universitätsverlag, 1969.

I am grateful to many people who have encouraged these explorations by asking me, under different circumstances, to present studies or papers. Heading this list must be Louis D. Rubin, Jr., whose work *Thomas Wolfe: The Weather of His Youth* was an inspiriting experience for me when it appeared in 1955 and who certainly encouraged substantially my further interest in exploring Wolfe by asking me to contribute an essay to his volume *South*. To William Van O'Connor, who was responsible for my doing the University of Minnesota pamphlet, my debt is very great. To Robert Evett, who was responsible for the "Reappraisal: 1955" essay in the *New Republic*; to James W. Webb, who asked me to deliver the Christopher Longest Lectures at the University of Mississippi; to Paschal Reeves, who invited me to participate in the University of Georgia's Thomas Wolfe Symposium; to David Madden, who asked me to contribute to his volume *American Dreams, American Nightmares*;

※ ※ ※ ※ ※ ※ ※ ※ ※ ※ ※ ※ ※ ※ *Acknowledgments*

to William Templeman, who invited me to contribute to the Mc-
Elderry *Festschrift*; to the editors of the *Saturday Review*, who
asked me to explore Thomas Wolfe in Berlin; to Benjamin W. Grif-
fith, who invited me to deliver the Lamar Lectures at Mercer University; and to Hans Helmcke, who asked me to contribute to the
Galinsky *Festschrift*, my thanks are great. Without the encourage-
ment which these and other people gave me, the thief procrastina-
tion would have stolen from me the will to produce these essays,
despite the thought which I have given to this matter in repeated
readings and studies of Wolfe over the years. I am also indebted to
the John Simon Guggenheim Memorial Foundation for a fellowship and to the Research Council of the University of North Carolina at Chapel Hill for grants which made possible some of the research behind these studies.

I should like to add a special word of gratitude to Richard Kennedy, whose knowledge of Wolfe has informed my efforts at almost
every turn and whose thoughtful criticism of my work I have sometimes disagreed with but always respected. I also owe a deep debt to
the late Andrew Turnbull, who shared his hard-earned understanding of Wolfe with generosity and grace.

In the preparation of this volume I owe particular thanks to several people: to John McLean, who checked my references and footnotes; to Charmian Green, who taught me much about Wolfe and
did yeoman work in the preparation of the final manuscript; to Ruth
Laney of Louisiana State University Press, whose editorial skill and
thoroughness substantially improved the book; and especially to Mrs.
Dinah S. Lloyd, whose excellent and cheerful aid was indispensable
in getting the book together—to all these my debts are large and my
gratitude great.

C. Hugh Holman

Introduction

TO THE GENERATIONS that grew up during the Depression and the Second World War, Thomas Wolfe had a special and highly personal meaning. It seemed to us that he alone articulated our inchoate longings, understood our secret and hungry desires, and had suffered as we had the anguish of what, until we read him, we had thought to be our unique and painful loneliness. Mark Schorer, an undergraduate when *Look Homeward, Angel* was published, wrote to its author: "It is the most magnificent book I know. This is the sort of book I have always wanted to write."

Look Homeward, Angel, in 1929, was the record of the collective childhood and young manhood of every sensitive provincial American boy. *Of Time and the River*, in 1935, took that provincial boy on the archetypal American adventure, storming the bastions of the city and its sophisticates, conquering the endlessly expanding, complex world. Our hopes, dreams, and fears rode with Eugene Gant on that fabulous Joycean train into the enchanted North—to Harvard, to New York, to England, to Paris, to Orléans—in an ever-widening sequence of concentric circles, remote from the home to which we could never return and always haunted, as its subtitle said, by "Man's Hunger in His Youth."

Before his death in 1938 Wolfe published a collection of short stories and short novels, *From Death to Morning*, and an essay in literary criticism, *The Story of a Novel*, which described in great and passionate detail his concept of fiction and how he came to write

Of Time and the River. Following his death Edward Aswell, his editor at his new publisher, Harper and Brothers, assembled from the huge mass of manuscript which Wolfe had left two more novels, *The Web and the Rock* and *You Can't Go Home Again,* and one collection of short stories and the fragment of a novel in the volume *The Hills Beyond.* All, however ostensibly changed, are basically the same intense record of an exploring self.

"This," we felt, suffused, as Wolfe was, with youthful *Weltschmerz,* "is it. This is what we have felt but could not say. And this man has said it." William Styron wrote in 1968: "It would be hard to exaggerate the overwhelming effect that reading Wolfe had upon so many of us. . . . the sudden exposure to a book like *Look Homeward, Angel,* with its . . . sense of youthful ache and promise and hunger and ecstasy which so corresponded to that of its eighteen-year-old reader . . . was like being born again into a world as fresh and wondrous as that seen through the eyes of Adam."

Most exciting of all was the example that Wolfe the author set of having made what seemed to us high art out of the materials of a young man's daily life. Styron says that Wolfe made the writer's life a possibility for him, as he did for hundreds of others. To live in Wolfe's natal state and to teach, as I do, at Wolfe's university (Chapel Hill—"Pulpit Hill"), and to have written about him, makes one realize, through his contact with visiting Wolfe enthusiasts, the force that Wolfe was upon generations of Americans, Germans, and more recently Japanese. The force is that of the writer rather than of his books.

To people approaching a novel in this way, it is an experience and not a work of art. Questions of style, of form, of structure seem remote and finally impertinent. These young, experiential readers were largely oblivious to artistic issues that would later be of commanding importance to them. Mark Schorer (his own life very much on the Wolfe pattern: Sauk Centre, Minnesota, to Madison, Wisconsin, to Harvard) by 1948 had lost his enthusiasm and wrote, "Thomas Wolfe apparently assumed that by the mere disgorging of the raw material of his experience he would give us at last our epic. ... For the crucial act of the artist, the unique act which is composition, a sympathetic editorial blue pencil and scissors were substituted."

But almost from the beginning of Wolfe's career, the praise which was lavished upon him as a young man of tremendous promise had major qualifications. Robert Penn Warren called *Of Time and the River* "a novel possessing no structure in the ordinary sense of the word." Malcolm Cowley, in the *New Republic*, pointed out the inadequacy of the form of *Of Time and the River* to its theme: "The best passages are scattered ... they occur without logic or pattern." And Bernard De Voto informed the young novelist that "Genius Is Not Enough" and accused him of keeping both baby and placental matter, making for a messy delivery. Most of his readers who had seen Wolfe's work as the impassioned, almost inspired expression of a diviner and better "one of us" began as they grew older, like Mark Schorer, to have their serious doubts.

Certainly I have been one of that group. I greeted Wolfe's work originally with a tremendous sense of its authority and power. I came by the late forties to feel when I looked back upon the Wolfe novels for which I had had such enthusiasm a faint sense of embarrassment that my artistic judgment had not been better and that I had swallowed so many badly conceived, bombastically expressed passages and poorly constructed works with the belief that they were wonderful art. This feeling persisted even after I had moved to Chapel Hill and begun to work at the University of North Carolina, on the Wolfean "sacred soil."

It was not until I had the opportunity to reexamine *Look Homeward, Angel* for a "Reappraisal: 1955" series for the *New Republic* that I was led seriously to look again at Wolfe as an artist. What I saw persuaded me that he had been a writer of enormous talent and substantial accomplishment without blinding me to the fact that he was also a writer of remarkably limited self-criticism and poor artistic judgment. Over the years, he has been increasingly a challenge to me. I have spent almost twenty years exploring that challenge, and the book which follows this introduction is a series of summary reports on that exploration.

It requires some special explanation. The long introductory essay was originally written at the suggestion of William Van O'Connor to be published in the University of Minnesota Pamphlets on American Writers series. It says in summary outline most of what I have to say about Thomas Wolfe. The ideas that are first advanced in that long tentative statement I have explored in expanded form in the studies which follow it in this volume.

The next section, "The Stigma of Autobiography," published in the *Virginia Quarterly Review* in 1964, attempts to examine the basis for the reader's feeling that Thomas Wolfe is an autobiographical writer. The long section on " 'The Blest *Nouvelle*' " is a merging and, to a certain extent, a rewriting of the introduction to the collection of Thomas Wolfe's short novels which I edited for Scribner's in 1961, and an essay on Wolfe and the short novel which was prepared for a *Festschrift* volume for my friend Clarence Gohdes, published in 1973. In it I establish a pattern which I follow in most of the other sections: I select and define an angle of approach and then look at Wolfe from that angle and through that definition. Thus, I try to describe what the short novel is, then examine Wolfe's experience with it, then evaluate its meaning for an understanding of his work and his career.

The same method is followed in the next section, "The Problem of Point of View." This essay was delivered as one of the Christopher Longest Lectures at the University of Mississippi in 1972. The following piece, "Rhetorical Hope and Dramatic Despair," is a merging and partial rewriting of a talk given at the Thomas Wolfe Symposium at the University of Georgia in 1969 and published by the University of Georgia Press in a transcript of that conference, *Thomas Wolfe and the Glass of Time*, and an essay on *You Can't Go Home Again*, written for David Madden's 1970 collection, *American Dreams, American Nightmares*. It attempts to examine the imperfect fusion of two modes of writing in Wolfe's work, particularly in the posthumous novels.

"The Web of the South" was adapted from an essay prepared in 1960 for the volume *South: Modern Southern Literature and Its Cultural Setting*, edited by Louis D. Rubin, Jr., and Robert D. Jacobs, and a lecture on Wolfe and the South given as a part of the Lamar Lectures at Mercer University and published in my volume *Three Modes of Modern Southern Fiction*. The piece following it, "Europe as His Catalyst," was rewritten from two essays, one prepared for a *Festschrift* volume for Bruce McElderry and the other prepared for a special travel issue of the *Saturday Review*. It explores the impact of Europe on Wolfe, particularly the impact of Nazi Germany and of Berlin.

The final section, "The Epic Impulse," was prepared for a *Festschrift* volume for Hans Galinsky. It is included here in the final position because it contains in succinct form a restatement of almost all the ideas that have been expressed in this collection of essays. That it is repetitious is, I believe, justified in the extent to which it tries to tie together the materials of the preceding works. Thus, as I see this volume of studies in Thomas Wolfe, it opens with a long general statement presenting my essential critical positions about Wolfe; it takes up several of those positions and explores them in depth; and it concludes with a summary of this material in terms of Wolfe's impulse toward epic creation.

A caveat should be issued about repetition. These several studies explore the same man and the same six books, approaching them from various points of view. In fitting twelve essays into eight studies, I have tried to keep the studies' integrity as separate essays, although I, of course, hope that they meld well enough to make at least a semibook. But maintaining their separateness has resulted in my occasionally saying the same thing in different contexts. I hope the reader will understand that this is not unintentional self-plagiarism.

It seems to me that in Thomas Wolfe's total work there is a strong, persistent, and largely unresolved conflict between the introspective, internal, deeply emotional, and very lonely self of the writer and the almost equally compelling impulse to unite that self with a larger social and national theme and to produce not merely the record of a lonely boy and man but somehow to see that boy and man as indicative of the national rather than the personal self.

I hope that it will be obvious to anyone examining this book that, although I have devoted almost twenty years to exploring the issues here briefly presented, my statements remain tentative, and I do not believe that I have solved the riddle of what is right and what is wrong about this writer of great talent, great achievements, and great failures.

The Loneliness at the Core

I   The Loneliness at the Core

A UNION OF OPPOSITES

Thomas Wolfe grappled in frustrated and de-
monic fury with what he called "the strange and bitter miracle of
life," a miracle which he saw in patterns of opposites. The elements
of life and of art seem to have existed for him as a congeries of contradictions, and he could not understand a thing until its negation
had been brought forth. The setting down of these opposites is the
most obvious single characteristic of his work, the significant parts
of which are four vast novels, seven or eight short novels (depend-
ing on definition), two collections of short stories, and an essay in
criticism—all fragments of an incomplete whole, only the most shadowy outlines of which are discernible.

Even the titles of his books—*Look Homeward, Angel*, with its
suggestion of near and far; *Of Time and the River*; *From Death to
Morning*; *The Web and the Rock*; *You Can't Go Home Again*, with
its idea of home and exile; *The Hills Beyond*, with its suggestion of
movement, of extension—reflect this view of experience. So do his
geographical oppositions—South and North, country and city, plain
and "enfabled rock," America and Europe—and the contrasting pairs
into which he regularly grouped his characters—father and mother,
Jew and Gentile, South and North Carolinian, poor and rich, true
artist and pretentious aesthete. Wolfe's vision of himself carried the
same pattern of oppositions; in *The Web and the Rock* Esther Jack
sums up the autobiographical hero with these words: "He has the
face of a demented angel . . . and there is madness and darkness and

1

evil in his brain. He is more cruel than death, and more lovely than a flower. His heart was made for love, and it is full of hate and darkness."[1]

There is also a basic conflict of themes in Wolfe's work. He declared, "I have at last discovered my own America. . . . And I shall wreak out my vision of this life, this way, this world and this America, to the top of my bent, to the height of my ability, but with an unswerving devotion, integrity and purity of purpose." He saw himself as one with Walt Whitman, Mark Twain, and Sherwood Anderson, whom he called "men who have seen America with a poet's vision."[2] The "epic impulse," the desire to define in fiction the American character and to typify the American experience, was obsessively present in his work. Yet another theme, contradictory but equally persistent in his work, was loneliness and the isolation of the incommunicable self. In a major sense, his subject matter was himself, his self-discovery and his groping toward self-knowledge; his forte was the lyrical expression of personal emotion and the rhetorical expression of personal attitudes. Aside from Whitman, no other major American writer ever celebrated himself at such length, with such intensity, or with so great a sense of his own importance as Wolfe did. The private self and the public seer were roles that he was never quite able to harmonize, and yet he persisted in playing them both.

This fundamental concern with opposites is reflected in Wolfe's literary style itself—in the balanced antitheses that abound in his writing, in his shocking juxtaposition of images, in his use of oxymoron, such as "changeless change," and of contradictory phrases, such as "splendid and fierce and weak and strong and foolish," "of wandering forever and the earth again," and "the web and the rock." In fact, Wolfe was a writer with two distinctive and contrasting styles. On one level he wrought with lyrical intensity a web of sensuous images capable of evoking from his readers a response almost as intense as that resulting from direct experience. Of American writers in this century, Ernest Hemingway is Wolfe's only equal at the evocative representation of the physical world through images so startlingly direct that they seem to rub against the reader's raw nerve ends. Wolfe said, "The quality of my memory is characterized, I believe, in a more than ordinary degree by the intensity of its sense impressions, its power to evoke and bring back the odors, sounds, colors, shapes, and feel of things with concrete vividness." [3] At its best his style was superbly suited for transferring this concrete vividness to the reader.

Yet Wolfe was seldom content to let the scene or the senses speak for themselves; rather, he felt an obligation to define the emotion which he associated with the scene and to suggest a meaning, a universality, a significance through rhetorical exhortation. The resulting passages are marked by extravagant verbal pyrotechnics—by apostrophe, by incantation, by exhortation, by rhapsodic assertion, and, all too often, by rant and bombast. The lyric style evokes in the reader the ineffable emotion called forth in Wolfe by the scene; then the rhetorical assertion attempts to utter the ineffable and to articulate the transcendent aspects of the scene which Wolfe fears that the reader otherwise may miss. While passages in this second style often succeed magnificently with their cadenced chants in lifting the reader to glimpse Wolfe's ultimate visions, it is also true that such passages sometimes degenerate into dithyrambic incantations that become strident, false, and meaningless. Few writers have been so clearly at the same time both the masters and the slaves of language.

The same contrasts are apparent in the structural qualities of Wolfe's fiction. On the level of dramatic scene, fully realized and impacted with immediacy, Wolfe could construct magnificently. Single episodes of his work, published separately as short stories, are powerful narrative units. "The Child by Tiger," first a short story in the *Saturday Evening Post* and later an episode in *The Web and the Rock*, is a clear example; so are "Only the Dead Know Brooklyn," "The Lost Boy," and "Chickamauga." In the middle length of the short novel he worked with perhaps his greatest effectiveness. He produced seven or eight pieces in this middle length, all of them originally published in magazines as independent entities, although five were later fragmented and distributed through the full-length novels. These short novels represent strong dramatic and narrative writing, rich in subject matter, firm in control, often objective in point of view. (This aspect of Wolfe's work is examined in detail in Chapter III.)

Furthermore, Wolfe projected ambitious plans for his books. Out of the experiences which were to be the material of his fiction he wished to weave a myth of his native land, an embodiment of its nature and its spirit. At a time when the American critic was just beginning to be concerned with the newer concepts of myth, Wolfe wrote, in the manuscript later published as the title piece of *The Hills Beyond*: "The Myth is founded on *extorted* fact: wrenched from the context of ten thousand days. . . . For it is not a question of having faith, or lack of it. It is a simple fact of seeing."[4] In order to contain and define this mythic aspect of human experience, Wolfe sought in old myths and in fable, as well as in the structure of his own experience, the enclosing form for his utterance. *Of Time and the River* in one of its earlier projections was to be called *Antaeus*, and its characters were to symbolize Heracles, Poseidon, Gaea, Helen, Demeter, Kronos, Rhea, Orestes, Faustus, Telemachus, Jason. After outlining the proposed plot in a letter to his editor Maxwell Perkins, he wrote: "Now, don't get alarmed at all this and think I'm writing a Greek myth. All of this is never mentioned once the story gets under way, but . . . it gives the most magnificent plot and unity to my book."[5] Such projects are one of the staples of Wolfe's correspondence with the editors at Scribner's and at Harper's and with his agent.

Yet, in sharp contrast to the dramatic power in individual scenes and the magnificent and mythic scope in plan, the realized larger units of his work show a formlessness and plotlessness that have baffled and perplexed the critic of Wolfe since he first published a novel. The structure of his works, at least on the surface, seems to be the simple chronological pattern of his own life, their incidents reflecting those he participated in or witnessed. Scholars and critics have explored the close relationship of Wolfe's work to his life, and they have found that, despite his frequent disclaimers that his work is no more autobiographical than that of other novelists, the use of direct experience and the representation of actual persons and events are very great in his novels. Floyd C. Watkins, who examined Wolfe's use of materials drawn from his home town, Asheville, concluded, "There are many more than 300 characters and places mentioned by name or described in *Look Homeward, Angel*, and probably there is not an entirely fictitious person, place, or incident in the whole novel."[6] Wolfe's disarming statement, "Dr. Johnson remarked that a man would turn over half a library to make a single book: in the same way, a novelist may turn over half the people in a town to make a single figure in his novel,"[7] is no defense at all when the people of the town are merely represented under the thinnest and most transparent disguises, and when the changes in name are as slight as Chapel Hill to Pulpit Hill, Raleigh to Sydney, Woodfin Street to Woodson Street, or Reuben Rawls to Ralph Rolls. His father's name is changed from W. O. Wolfe to W. O. Gant, his mother's from Julia Elizabeth Westall Wolfe to Eliza Pentland Gant, his brother's from Ben Wolfe to Ben Gant.

Wolfe's artistic method was a combination of realistic representation and romantic declaration; and it seems to have reflected accurately a contradictory—or perhaps double—view of the nature of art. On one hand, he was committed to the detailed, exact, accurate picturing of the actual world—committed to such an extent that he found it hard to represent anything that he had not personally experienced. On the other hand, his view of the nature and function of art was essentially that of the nineteenth-century Romantic poets and critics.

In one sense this aesthetic view was a natural outgrowth of his education. Six teachers had major influences on Wolfe, and five of them were clear-cut romantics. Margaret Roberts, who taught him for four years in a boys' preparatory school, made an indelible impression upon him with her love for the English poets; Mrs. Roberts, represented in *Look Homeward, Angel* as Margaret Leonard, filled the boy with a love of Wordsworth, Burns, Coleridge, Herrick, Carew, Jonson, Shakespeare, Poe, Hawthorne, Melville, and Scott. At the University of North Carolina he studied under Horace Williams, a philosophy professor whom he represented as Vergil Weldon and whom he called "Hegel in the Cotton Belt." Williams, who was a mystic, taught him a rather loose form of the Hegelian dialectic, in which a concept, or thesis, inevitably generates its opposite, or antithesis, and the interaction of the two produces a new concept, or synthesis. He also studied under Frederick Koch, who was beginning his work with the Carolina Playmakers and was encouraging his students to write folk plays, finding and underscoring the strange in the commonplace. Wolfe's first successful literary efforts were one-act plays written for Koch and produced by the Playmakers with Wolfe acting in them. At Chapel Hill he was also greatly influenced by the teaching of the Spenserian scholar Edwin A. Greenlaw and by his theories of the inseparable relationship of "literature and life." At Harvard an important influence was John Livingston Lowes, who was writing *The Road to Xanadu* while Wolfe was a graduate student in his classes and whose view of the nature of Coleridge's imagination remained for Wolfe until his death a truthful picture of the workings of the artist's mind. At Harvard, too, he was influenced by George Pierce Baker, famous as the director of the "47 Workshop" in drama, although he later broke with Baker, at least partially as a result of dissatisfaction with the brittle and essentially antiromantic views of students whom Baker applauded.

The marked romanticism of his aesthetic theory, with its pronounced distrust of almost all forms of intellectualism and its emphasis on the expression of the artist's feelings as the highest objective of a work of art, was at a polar extreme from the view Wolfe later developed of the novelist as a national prophet obligated to represent the social scene; and his own novels are caught between the tug of the representation of the nation and the expression of the self. (This problem in Wolfe's later work is discussed in Chapter V.) Wolfe's tendency to see and to express things in terms of oppositions may have been learned from Horace Williams; it is possible that, as some critics have asserted, it represented a failure of his mind adequately to grapple with the problems before it; certainly it was, to some extent, an expression of his southern qualities, for the typical native of the southern states is fascinated by paradox, enamored of ambiguity, devoted to the particular and the concrete, and, although a dreamer of grandiose dreams, seldom the articulator of effective larger structures. The men of Wolfe's region were, like Wolfe himself, caught between the romantic view of their own past and the realistic fact of their present poverty. And over the years they have proved themselves capable of living with unresolved contradictions. (For an elaboration on this point, see Chapter VI.) Yet Thomas Wolfe was marked almost from his birth by certain unique paradoxes that formed a peculiar aspect of his life and, therefore, an inevitable aspect of his autobiographic art.

"THE STRANGE AND BITTER MIRACLE OF LIFE"

Thomas Wolfe was born in Asheville, North Carolina (which he was to call Altamont and Libya Hill in his novels) on October 3, 1900. He was, therefore, a southerner, yet his native state in 1900 was in the midst of the espousal of its form of the Populist movement that has left a heritage of liberalism in educational, social, and economic matters quite different from that in most of the rest of the South. Furthermore, Wolfe came from a mountain town far removed from even the dream of a South of tall white columns and banjo-strumming darkies. Asheville was soon to be caught in a real-estate fever and go on a middle-class speculative binge, keyed, as Wolfe lamented, to Yankee materialism and dollar greed. In *You Can't Go Home Again* he described that binge and its painful aftermath in coruscating detail. It would have been hard to find a south-

7

ern town more thoroughly middle class than Asheville in the years of Wolfe's childhood; yet it was a town still of its region, tasting on its tongue the bitterness of defeat, the sharp sting of southern poverty, and the acrid flavor of racial injustice. This middle-class world was his particular subject throughout his career, although he qualified its customary "booster" optimism by the more pessimistic approach natural to a poverty-stricken region still conscious—as no other part of America is—of defeat.

His mother was Julia Elizabeth Westall Wolfe, a member of a mountain clan memorialized by her son as the "time-devouring" Joyners and Pentlands, and she symbolized for him the protean texture of the South, which was always feminine in his view, "the dark, ruined Helen of his blood." The Westalls were people of some prominence in their region, men and women of medium standing in Asheville and its encircling hills. His mother had been a schoolteacher and a bookseller before she became the third wife of William Oliver Wolfe, a native of Pennsylvania. W. O. Wolfe was a stonecutter by profession, owning his own business, and he was a powerful man of great gusto, vast appetites, and a torturing need to assert himself vividly against his drab world. Wolfe's representations of his parents as Eliza and W. O. Gant are among his greatest portraits, and their chance meeting and marriage in a southern hill town were central to his view of the "bitter mystery" of his life. He opens his first novel, *Look Homeward, Angel,* with a speculation on "that dark miracle of chance which makes new magic in a dusty world" and symbolized it through "a destiny that leads ... from Epsom into Pennsylvania, and thence into the hills that shut in Altamont." He saw Eugene Gant, the hero of that novel, as "the fusion of two strong egotisms, Eliza's in-brooding and Gant's expanding outward."[8]

Thomas was the youngest of the Wolfes' eight children, of whom two died in infancy. During his childhood his mother bought a boardinghouse and moved into it, taking Thomas and his brother Ben with her and leaving W. O. Wolfe and their daughter Mabel in the old house. (The other two sons and a daughter were no longer living at home.) Wolfe's childhood was spent in a family divided between two home establishments, with itinerant boarders as his closest companions, except for his brother Ben, whom he idolized and whose death left upon Thomas' spirit a scar that never healed. Wolfe regarded himself in later life as "God's Lonely Man," and he attributed that loneliness to the experiences of his childhood. In 1933 he wrote his sister, "I think I learned about being alone when I was a child about eight years old and I think that I have known about it ever since."[9]

He attended public school until he was eleven; then he entered a small private school operated by Mr. and Mrs. J. M. Roberts. Wolfe was a bright and perceptive boy, and during the four years he spent at the Roberts' school he was almost totally absorbed in learning. At the age of fifteen—three years ahead of his contemporaries—he entered the University of North Carolina at Chapel Hill; at that time he was the only one of his family to have reached so high an educational level.

When he entered it, the university was undergoing the changes that converted it from a leisurely undergraduate liberal arts college into a university engaged in research and graduate instruction and that made it the focal point of the New South movement, the center of southern liberalism. Once more the southern boy was caught up in the fabric of change, confronted by the oppositions of the old and the new. In the university Wolfe proved to be a good student and a "big man on campus," being active in debate, publications, and fraternities, as well as working with the Carolina Playmakers. He was graduated at the age of twenty, with an urge to study further and the desire to become a playwright.

Borrowing from his mother against his anticipated share in his father's estate, Wolfe went to Harvard, where he studied for three years, and earned the master of arts degree in English literature. But the central interest of his Harvard years was in the "47 Workshop" in drama and the furtherance of his projected career as a playwright.

The picture he paints of the workshop in *Of Time and the River* is a satiric attack on pretension and lifeless aestheticism, although his portrait of Professor Baker as "Professor Hatcher" (in the original notes for the novel he had called him "Butcher"), while tainted with malice, is still drawn with respect.

Although teachers as eminent as John Livingston Lowes praised Wolfe's "very distinct ability" as a scholar, he had chosen playwriting for his career, and he vainly tried his fortunes peddling his plays in New York City in the fall of 1923 before he accepted an appointment as instructor in English at New York University in January, 1924. Wolfe taught at the university, satirically represented as the School of Utility Cultures in *Of Time and the River*, intermittently until the spring of 1930. During this period he made several European tours; he also met and had a violent love affair with Mrs. Aline Bernstein, a scene and costume designer eighteen years his senior and a married woman with two children. She is the "Esther Jack" of his later novels.

In London in the autumn of 1926 Wolfe began committing to paper in the form of a huge novel the steadily accelerating flood of his childhood memories. The mounting manuscript bore the stamp of the immersion in literature and poetry which had been a major element of Wolfe's life up to that point, but above all it bore, by his own testimony,[10] the mark of Joyce's *Ulysses*. Discernible in it too were the influences of H. G. Wells, particularly his novel *The Undying Fire*, and Sinclair Lewis. When Wolfe returned to New York, he continued writing the book, while his love affair with Mrs. Bernstein waxed and waned and waxed again. Both have left records of the affair, Mrs. Bernstein in *The Journey Down*, an autobiographical novel, and in the story "Eugene" in *Three Blue Suits*, and Wolfe in *The Web and the Rock*. The exact measure of Mrs. Bernstein's influence in disciplining Wolfe's monumental flow of memory, energy, and words into the form which *Look Homeward, Angel* had taken by its completion in first draft in March, 1928, is a matter of debate, but it was certainly great. The manuscript of the book was

complete, in any case, when, after a violent quarrel with Mrs. Bernstein, Wolfe went again to Europe in July, leaving it with an agent.
When he returned to New York in January, 1929, it was to find a
letter from Maxwell E. Perkins, editor of Charles Scribner's Sons,
expressing an interest in the novel, if it could "be worked into a form
publishable by us."[11]

Wolfe renewed the affair with Mrs. Bernstein, to whom *Look
Homeward, Angel* is dedicated, and worked desperately to cut and
arrange the material of his manuscript into a publishable book. In its
original form, *Look Homeward, Angel* was the detailed and intense
record of the ancestry, birth, childhood, adolescence, and youth of
Eugene Gant. It began with a ninety-page sequence on Eugene's
father's life, and it concluded when, after graduating from college,
Eugene discovers, in an imaginary conversation with the ghost of his
brother, that "*You* are your world," and, leaving home, "turns his
eyes upon the distant soaring ranges." Perkins insisted on the dele-
tion of the historical opening, on the removal of some extraneous
material, and on minor rearrangements, but the novel when it was
published on October 18, 1929, probably had undergone little more
editorial supervision than long manuscripts by exuberant but talented
first novelists generally undergo. As it was to work out, *Look Homeward, Angel* was more unqualifiedly Wolfe's in conception, writing,
arrangement, and execution than any other work of long fiction that
was ever to be published under his name.

Its lyric intensity and its dramatic power were immediately recognized and hailed; even before Sinclair Lewis, in accepting the
Nobel Prize in 1930, praised him highly, Wolfe was recognized as
a figure to be reckoned with in the literary world. His native Asheville paid him the tribute of being collectively indignant at the portrait of itself in the novel. A novelistic career of great promise was
launched, and Wolfe, who had hungered for fame, suddenly found
that he didn't want it. Not only were the members of his family hurt
and the people of Asheville angry, but he also felt the obligation of
producing a second work that represented an advance over the first.
This proved to be one of the major struggles of his life.

11

He resigned from New York University, ended the affair with Mrs. Bernstein, and went to Europe for a year on a Guggenheim fellowship. When he returned to America, he established himself in an apartment in Brooklyn and took up the lonely vigil with himself and his writing which he describes in *The Story of a Novel* and portrays in *You Can't Go Home Again*. Before *Look Homeward, Angel* was published, he had begun planning the new novel and writing parts of it. During the lonely years in Brooklyn, he struggled in growing desperation to produce the second book. The short novel *A Portrait of Bascom Hawke* in 1932 shared a short-novel contest prize of five thousand dollars offered by *Scribner's Magazine*. He published several short novels and short stories during this period. (See Chapter III.) Despite the fact that Wolfe was living almost entirely on the rather slender proceeds from the sale to magazines of his stories and short novels, when he was approached by a representative of Metro-Goldwyn-Mayer about the possibility of his doing motion picture writing at a thousand to fifteen hundred dollars a week, he declined it on the grounds that he had "a lot of books to write."

He was struggling with a vast novel, to be entitled "The October Fair," which would be in at least four volumes and would have a time span from the Civil War to the present, with hundreds of characters and a new protagonist, David Hawke, replacing Eugene Gant. Maxwell Perkins was working with Wolfe every night and on weekends in an attempt to give the new work an acceptable structure and symmetry. It is difficult to separate in Wolfe's letters what is defensible judgment based on fact and what is the frenzied product of his febrile imagination; yet, if his versions are to be trusted even in minor part, Maxwell Perkins had a truly major role to play in the formulation of his second novel. Seemingly it was Perkins who turned him back to Eugene Gant and away from David Hawke; it was Perkins who discouraged his attempts at formulations of his vision of America in other terms than those of the autobiographical "apprenticeship novel," for Wolfe had worked out a number of elaborate schemes for his new novel. (For additional data on the matter of Perkins' editing, see Chapter IV.) And it was Perkins who insisted that *Of Time and the River* was ready to be published and in 1935 sent it to the printers despite Wolfe's protest.

Of Time and the River is a mammoth book, continuing the chronicle of Eugene Gant's sensibility. It opens as he leaves Altamont for Harvard, follows him there, to New York City where he teaches in the School of Utility Cultures, to Europe, where he begins the writing of a novel and has a frustrating love affair with a girl named Ann, and concludes as he meets Esther on the boat back to America. *Look Homeward, Angel*, although it had lacked the traditional novelistic structure, had a certain unity through its concentration on a family, a mountain town, and a way of life. In reading it one was caught up in the sharp impressions of youth and somehow rushed along to that moment of self-realization with which it ended. *Of Time and the River* had less plot, more introspection, less structural cohesion, more rhetoric. Large segments of the book exist without thematic or plot relevance; some of the best scenes and most effective portraits seem to be dramatic intrusions; and it is only when one knows the rest of the story as it is revealed in *The Web and the Rock* that one is able to appreciate the climactic significance of the meeting with Esther with which the book closes.

That these events have meaning for Wolfe beyond their merely personal expression—indeed, that Eugene Gant is in an undefined way the generic Everyman of Whitman's poems or the racial hero of the national epic (see Chapter VIII)—one senses from the amount of rhetorical extrapolation by which the hero becomes one with the world, his experiences one with the national experience. Sometimes the rhetoric is wonderfully handled. Indeed, *Of Time and the River* is unusually rich in Wolfe's "poetic passages," but the organization of the materials of the story so that they speak a national myth through self-sufficient action is not attempted with any consistency in the book. (See Chapter IV.)

It was greeted with mixed reactions. Many hailed it as a fulfill-

ment of the earnest given by *Look Homeward, Angel*; but its formlessness, its lack of story, and its rhapsodic extravagance were also
inescapable, and the really serious critical questions which have been
debated about Wolfe's work ever since were first clearly expressed
about this novel. These questions are whether it is legitimate in fiction to substitute autobiography (see Chapter II) and reporting for
creation; whether rhetorical assertion, however poetic, can be an
acceptable substitute for dramatic representation (see Chapter V);
whether immediacy can ever be properly bought at the expense of
aesthetic distance; and, inevitably, what constitutes form.

In the fall of 1935 a group of stories and sketches originally written as parts of the novel but published in periodicals and excluded
from the completed work was assembled and published under the
title *From Death to Morning*. This volume, which was attacked
by the critics when it appeared and which sold poorly, has never
received the attention it deserves. The stories reprinted in it are
extremely uneven in quality, but they show Wolfe as a serious ex-
perimenter in fiction. His mastery of the short and middle forms
of fiction is demonstrated here in such works as *Death the Proud
Brother*, "Only the Dead Know Brooklyn," "In the Park," and *The
Web of Earth*. Wolfe knew that the book would take a critical
pounding, but he said, "I believe that as good writing as I have ever
done is in this book."[12] The judgment is startlingly accurate.

Yet if this volume demonstrated a technical virtuosity with which
Wolfe is seldom credited, it also showed through its characters and
incidents the essential unity and hence the basic autobiographical
tendency in his total work. When, in 1936, Wolfe published an
essay in criticism, *The Story of a Novel*, originally a lecture given
at a writers' conference at Boulder, Colorado, this record of how
he wrote *Of Time and the River*, told with humility and straightforward honesty, seemed to many critics to prove that he simply
was not a novelist: in two long novels and a volume of short stories,
Wolfe had written out of his direct experience, seemingly without a
sense of form and under the direction of the editors at Scribner's.

More than one critic found this situation less than admirable. Robert Penn Warren summed up the case: "Despite his admirable energies and his powerful literary endowments, his work illustrates once more the limitations, perhaps the necessary limitations, of an attempt to exploit directly and naively the personal experience and the self-defined personality in art."[13] And Bernard De Voto, in a savage attack, declared Wolfe to possess great narrative and dramatic talents but to be unable to realize them in novelistic form; he was guilty of leaving coexisting with true fictional materials too much "placental" matter "which nature and most novelists discard." De Voto also charged that Wolfe's novels were put together by "Mr. Perkins and the assembly-line at Scribner's." That Wolfe was a genius he conceded, but he added that "genius is not enough."[14]

The De Voto article hurt Wolfe deeply. In 1936 a desire to prove De Voto wrong (perhaps heightened by an unconscious awareness that in certain respects at least he was right) joined with many other factors to make Wolfe wish to change his publisher. Among the reasons were a dispute with Perkins about Wolfe's representation of Scribner's people in a story, a disagreement over the cost of corrections in *Of Time and the River*, a libel suit which Scribner's wanted to settle out of court, and, most important of all, Wolfe's awareness that his attitudes were incompatible with those of Perkins and that he wanted to go in directions in which Perkins did not wish him to travel. The long and agonizing break with Scribner's, begun in mid-1936, was finally effected in 1937, when Wolfe formed a publishing arrangement with Harper and Brothers, with Edward C. Aswell to act as his editor.

In 1935 and 1936 he made two visits to Berlin, where he was greeted as a literary hero and lionized because of the tremendous success of the translation of *Look Homeward, Angel*. There, too, however, he saw through the orderly mask of Naziism to the terrible realities behind it, and his social and political conscience was deeply aroused. (See Chapter VII.)

He spent the summer of 1937 working in a cabin in the North

Carolina mountains and was happy to find that he was received by his people with pride and pleasure, that they had forgiven him; but he also learned from the experience that "you can't go home again," an idea that loomed large in his thinking and which symbolized for him the fact that we move onward not backward. He was working hard, with the frenzied expenditure of energy of which he was capable, getting material ready to show his publishers as the beginning of a book. At that time he was again projecting a story of great magnitude in at least four volumes, and he was seeking forms and structures through which it could be made into a mythic record of "an innocent man's discovery of life and the world." At one time the book was to be called "The Vision of Spangler's Paul," with the subtitle "The Story of His Birth, His Life, His Going To and Fro in the Earth, His Walking Up and Down in It: His Vision Also of the Lost, the Never-Found, the Ever-Here America." At another time he changed the protagonist's name to Doaks, in an effort to symbolize his typical nature, and wrote "The Doaksology," a history of his family. Finally, he selected George Webber as his protagonist—a character physically very much like the David Hawke whom he had wished to make the hero of *Of Time and the River*—and wrote of him: "The protagonist becomes significant not as the tragic victim of circumstances, the romantic hero in conflict and revolt against his environment, but as a kind of polar instrument round which the events of life are grouped, by means of which they are touched, explained, and apprehended, by means of which they are seen and ordered."[15]

In May, 1938, he delivered a great mass of manuscript, perhaps a million words, to Aswell. It represented an ordering of the materials on which he was working, but not a book ready for the press. He himself estimated that more than a year's work remained to be done before the first volume of the new work would be ready. Then he left on a tour of the West which ended with his serious illness from pneumonia in Vancouver, followed by a worsening of his condition in Seattle, and the discovery, after he had been moved to the Johns

Hopkins hospital in Baltimore, that the pneumonia had released old sealed-off tuberculosis bacteria in his lungs and that these bacteria had gone to his brain. On September 15, 1938, eighteen days before his thirty-eighth birthday, he died.

Edward Aswell extracted the materials for three books from the mountain of manuscript which Wolfe left. The first, *The Web and the Rock* (1939), is apparently in a form not too different from that which Wolfe had planned, although the last four hundred pages of it are still in the earlier and more extravagant style of *Of Time and the River*, rather than the sparser and more controlled style of the opening sections. The new protagonist, George Webber, is surprisingly like Eugene Gant, although his physical characteristics and his family life have changed. The early sections of the book take him through childhood, to college, and then to New York City. There he meets Esther Jack and the novel becomes the record of a tempestuous love affair. Then Webber goes to Germany, is badly beaten in a riot at the *Oktoberfest* in Munich, and, through a monologue between his body and his soul, Webber understands that he must turn from his immersion in himself and his past. "He knew and accepted now its limitations [and] . . . looked calmly and sanely forth upon the earth for the first time in ten years."[16] *The Web and the Rock* is a very imperfect book, seeming to be the forced union of two inharmonious parts. Yet it is much more nearly a novel than *Of Time and the River*, and in the early parts, prepared for publication during the last year of Wolfe's life, it shows a groping toward the control of material and a desire to represent dramatically rather than to assert rhetorically. Wolfe was still grappling with the problem of novelistic form and language, and grappling with at least limited success.

The second of the books which Aswell assembled is much less a novel than *The Web and the Rock. You Can't Go Home Again* (1940) brings together in a narrative frame large units of material which Wolfe had completed but only partially arranged at the time of his death. It continues the story of George Webber, but in it what Wolfe meant when he said that the protagonist was to be a "kind of

17

polar instrument, round which the events of life are grouped,"[17] becomes clearer. The book—it is hardly a novel at all—has the very loose narrative structure of George Webber's life: he returns from Europe, writes his book, goes to Libya Hill (Asheville) for his aunt's funeral, travels in Europe, sees the emptiness of fame in the person of Lloyd McHarg (Sinclair Lewis), travels in Germany and comprehends the horror of the Nazi regime, and writes a long letter setting forth his credo. Yet what gives the book vitality is not George and his experiences—although those dealing with the publication and reception of his novel *Home to Our Mountains* are extremely interesting to the Wolfe student—but the view of life which is seen through George. Mr. Katamoto, Mr. Jack and the party at his house, Judge Rumford Bland and the satiric picture of the moral and material collapse of Libya Hill, Daisy Purvis, Lloyd McHarg, Foxhall Edwards and his family, Mr. C. Green, who jumps from the twelfth story of the Admiral Francis Drake Hotel, the frightened little Jew on the train out of Germany—it is in such materials as these that the dramatic strength of the book resides.

You Can't Go Home Again is freer than his other books of the rhapsodic assertion that so often replaces dramatic statement. (For a study of this aspect of the novel, see Chapter V.) Those who have found Wolfe's strength in his ability to depict character and to invest scenes with life and movement are likely to find in *You Can't Go Home Again* both his best writing and a discernible promise of greater work and greater control to come. On the other hand, those who see Wolfe's strength to be peculiarly his power with words are likely to feel that the dramatic and narrative success of *You Can't Go Home Again* was bought at the price of his most distinctive qualities. As a novel it is the least satisfactory of his works, yet in its pages are to be seen, dimly and afar off it is true, the faint outline of what he was striving for in his vast and unrealized plans for the "big book."

The third volume that Aswell mined from the manuscript was *The Hills Beyond* (1941), a collection of fragments and sketches. A few of the stories were published in magazines after 1935, but most of them were previously unpublished units of the manuscript. Two distinguished short stories are here, "The Lost Boy" and "Chickamauga," together with a 150-page fragment, "The Hills Beyond," which is a narrative of the Joyners and would have been the early introductory material to the big book. "The Hills Beyond" parallels, in subject matter, material which Wolfe tried to introduce at the beginning of each of his major works. In this fragment Wolfe's efforts at being an objective novelist have more immediately apparent success than they do elsewhere, and he seems to be moving much more toward the realism of the southern frontier and away from the romanticism of his early career. Valuable though it is to have as many of the self-contained fragments of the Wolfe manuscripts as we can get, *The Hills Beyond* adds very little to Wolfe's stature as a novelist.

In 1948 *Mannerhouse*, one of the plays which Wolfe had tried very hard to peddle to professional producers without success, was published from the manuscript. An abbreviated version of his ten-scene play *Welcome to Our City* was published in *Esquire* magazine in 1957. Both documents are primarily of historical importance, as is also Pat M. Ryan's edition of both the one-act and the three-act versions of Wolfe's play *The Mountains*, published in 1970. With the publication of *The Hills Beyond* most of Wolfe's significant work was in print, and, incomplete though it is as a record of his vast and ambitious project, it is all that remains of his efforts to formulate in fiction a vision of himself and his world. The manuscripts out of which Aswell quarried the last three books are now in the William B. Wisdom Collection at Harvard. They contain many scenes, characters, and sections that have never been published, but the unpublished materials will probably have to await a completely new editing of the total manuscripts before they will find an audience. Wolfe's notebooks, which are also in the Wisdom Collection, have been edited in two volumes by Richard S. Kennedy and Paschal Reeves, in 1971. They are basically of biographical value.

19

THE BROKEN CIRCLE

Wolfe's career, like his works, became a matter of debate before his death; and his untimely demise, when seemingly the world was all before him and his prodigious talent was still groping toward an adequate mode of expression, increased the debate without giving appreciable weight to any of the answers. He remains, despite his thirty-seven years, a "golden boy" cut off in the moment of the flowering of his talent, and the issue of whether he had already done all that he was capable of and was, therefore, saved by death from tasting the fruits of a certain diminution of power or whether a major talent went unrealized through the cruel accident of time will remain as unsolved with him as it has been with all the other "golden boys" who tasted too early "the bitter briefness of our days."

The remark of William Faulkner, "I rated Wolfe first [among modern American writers] because we had all failed but Wolfe had made the best failure because he had tried hardest to say the most," is a peculiarly unsatisfying and unrewarding comment which merely restates the question; although his added remark, "He may have had the best talent of us, he may have been 'the greatest American writer' if he had lived longer, though I have never held much with the 'mute inglorious Milton' theory,"[18] helps a little.

One of the principal facts of Wolfe's career is his extension of interest from himself to the surrounding world, to "life," from the time of the publication of *Look Homeward, Angel* to his death. In 1929, when the new book was to be "The October Fair," he described it to the Guggenheim Foundation: "It tries to find out why Americans are a nomad race (as this writer believes); why they are touched with a powerful and obscure homesickness wherever they go, both at home and abroad."[19] In 1930 he wrote Perkins: "I believe I am at last beginning to have a proper use of a writer's material: for it seems to me he ought to see in what has happened to him the elements of the universal experience." He wrote John Hall Wheelock, another editor at Scribner's, enthusiastically about a section of "The October Fair" which he had just completed: "In *An-*

taeus, in a dozen short scenes, told in their own language, we see people of all sorts *constantly in movement,* going somewhere." But in the same letter he also says, "God knows what Maxwell Perkins will say when he sees it." He was always toying with ideas like his largely unwritten "The Hound of Darkness," of which he said, "It will be a great tone-symphony of night—railway yards, engines, freights, dynamos, bridges, men and women, the wilderness, plains, rivers, deserts, a clopping hoof, etc.—seen *not by a definite personality,* but haunted throughout by a *consciousness* of personality."[20]

The struggle by which *Of Time and the River* achieved publication over Wolfe's protest is well known; but the depth of Wolfe's dissatisfaction with the book became clear only with the publication of the *Letters* in 1956. When *Of Time and the River* appeared, he wrote Perkins, "As I told you many times, I did not care whether the final length of the book was 300, 500, or a 1000 pages, so long as I had realized completely and finally my full intention—and that was not realized. I still sweat with anguish—with a sense of irremediable loss—at the thought of what another six months would have done to that book—how much more whole and perfect it would have been. Then there would have been no criticism of its episodic character— for, by God, in purpose and in spirit, that book was not episodic, but a living whole and I could have made it so."[21]

There is certainly the possibility that Wolfe was too completely lost in the deluge of his own memories and words to form them into an intelligent large whole in the years between 1930 and 1935—although his most distinguished short and middle-length fiction was done in this period—and the sometimes violent midwifery of Perkins may have been essential to getting anything publishable from the laboring author. On the other hand, when one examines the first three hundred pages of *The Web and the Rock* and recalls that it is Wolfe's own work done without editorial assistance or thinks of the power and directness of the first two books of *You Can't Go Home Again,* it is difficult not to wish that Wolfe had been free to try.

To the imponderable *ifs* which haunt the mind in the case of an artist too youthfully dead must be added in Wolfe's case this one:

what might his career have been if he had struggled through toward the realization of form without the assistance of Perkins? Certainly if Wolfe had written *Of Time and the River* without Perkins' aid, it would have been a radically different book and possibly a much better one. But he did not, and so the fact remains that only as the lyric recorder of his youth was Wolfe truly successful in the longer fictional forms. His great vision of being the critic of his society and the definer of his nation can be seen in fragments but its large outline is shadowy and incomplete.

It is for this reason that the central problems concerning Wolfe as a writer are as intimately tied up in his personality and his career as they are in his work. Louis D. Rubin, Jr., in an excellent critical study of Wolfe, has asked that the autobiographical quality of the novels be accepted as clear fact and that they then be examined as novels, as works of art.[22] When this is done—and Mr. Rubin does it with great skill—*Look Homeward, Angel* emerges as Wolfe's only satisfactory full-length novel, and in his other book-length works one almost has the feeling of an expense of talent in a waste of form-lessness. Perhaps such a conclusion is proper—certainly it is the one reached by many of the best and most rigorous of American critics— but it leaves untouched the question of Wolfe's power and the success which he has with readers.

Wolfe's failure to write his own books as he wanted them written cannot ultimately be laid at any door other than his own. The causes of this failure are complex: they include his own lack of security (his extreme sensitivity to reviews shows that such a lack was there), his desire to achieve publication at whatever cost (there is evidence of this quality in his letters), and a deep-seated affection for Perkins and gratitude to him. As William Faulkner once declared, "The writer's only responsibility is to his art. He will be completely ruthless if he is a good one . . . If a writer has to rob his mother, he will not hesitate."[23] Paradoxically, Thomas Wolfe devoted his life and his energies to the creation of art with a singlemindedness not surpassed in this century—he is almost archetypally the "dedicated writer"—and yet he lacked that ultimate ruthlessness of which Faulkner speaks. For a writer whose talent is of the magnitude of Wolfe's and whose plans have the scope and importance that his do, such a failing cannot be easily brushed aside. On this point he was highly culpable—he did not make the longer forms of fiction, at whatever cost, the adequate vehicles of his vision and his talent; he did not subject his ego to the discipline of his own creative imagination—and the price he has paid for the failure has been very great indeed. It is the price of being a writer of inspired fragments and of only one satisfying larger work—and that an imperfect one.

Here the oppositions in Wolfe reach a crucial test. He seemed always to feel that when the contrasting opposites were defined the synthesis would result automatically; he was always stating a thing and its opposite and allowing the "miracle" of their coexistence to stand. Here in his own work the fact of his great talent and the fact of his ambitious projects were never submitted to the discipline which would have made a synthesis of them; they were allowed to coexist without serious efforts at fusion.

This aspect of Wolfe's work points to its essential romanticism, to the extent to which it is imbedded in the doctrine of self-expression and self-realization. Wolfe's work is not, therefore, of primary value as a group of novels, or even in terms of his shadowy larger plan. His total work stands, as do so many other monuments of romantic art, as a group of fragments imperfectly bodying forth a seemingly ineffable cosmic vision in terms of the self of the artist. Although it contains large areas of poor and even bad writing, scenes that do not come off or that bear no relevance to what has gone before, and rhapsodies that fail utterly to communicate, it also contains some of the best writing done by an American this century, and it merits our thoughtful examination.

THE SEARCH FOR A LANGUAGE

The most obvious of Wolfe's strengths is his ability with language. The word has for him unique powers; he was fascinated by language, enchanted with rhythms and cadences, enamored of rhetorical devices. Language was the key he sought to unlock mysteries and to unloose vast forces; he approached it almost in the spirit of primitive magic. This aspect of language he expressed in the paragraph printed as a prologue to *The Web and the Rock*: "Could I make tongue say more than tongue could utter! Could I make brain grasp more than brain could think! Could I weave into immortal denseness some small brede of words, pluck out of sunken depths the roots of living, some hundred thousand magic words that were as great as all my hunger, and hurl the sum of all my living out upon three hundred pages—then death could take my life, for I had lived it ere he took it: I had slain hunger, beaten death!"[24]

Another aspect of his effective use of language is his accurate and vivid dialogue. Wolfe had a remarkable ear for folk speech, and his people speak personal dialects set down with great verisimilitude. His characters sometimes seem to talk forever, but their speech is always marked by distinctiveness in diction, syntax, and cadence. Accuracy, however, is a less obvious quality of their speech than gusto and vigor are. There is a feeling of great energy in the speech of most of them. The clearest example of Wolfe's mastery of the spoken language is to be seen in *The Web of Earth*, but it is apparent in almost everything that he wrote.

He declared that he sought a language, an articulation. He sought this language, this tool of communication, not only in the rolling periods of rhetoric but also in the sensuous image drawn from the "world's body," which is a distinctive aspect of the language of lyric and dramatic writing. And here, in the concrete and particularized representation of the sensory world, he was triumphantly the master. It is Wolfe's ability to evoke the world's body which is responsible for the sense of total reality which his work produces in the young and impressionable, and it is this seeming immersion in the sensuous which makes him sometimes appear to be more the poet of the senses than of sense.

This concern with language, one so great that he might have said of his total work, as Whitman said of *Leaves of Grass*, that it was "only a language experiment," is the logical expression of one of Wolfe's major themes, the loneliness at the core of all human experience. He saw each individual in the world as living in a compartment in isolation from his fellows and unable to communicate adequately with them. This tragedy of loneliness is at the heart of Eugene Gant's experience and makes *Look Homeward, Angel* a book which can appropriately bear the subtitle "A Story of the Buried Life." The desire to break down the walls keeping him from communion with others is at least a part of "man's hunger in his youth" in *Of Time and the River*. The need Wolfe's characters have for a language with which to breach the isolating walls is very great. In a scene in *Of Time and the River*, Helen, Eugene Gant's sister, is lying awake in the darkness: "And suddenly, with a feeling of terrible revelation, she saw the strangeness and mystery of man's life; she felt about her in the darkness the presence of ten thousand people, each lying in his bed, naked and alone, united at the heart of night and darkness, and listening, as she, to the sounds of silence and of sleep. ... And it seemed to her that if men would only listen in the darkness, and send the language of their naked lonely spirits across the silence of the night, all of the error, falseness and confusion of their lives would vanish, they would no longer be strangers, and each would find the life he sought and never yet had found."[25] There are few lonelier people in fiction than W. O. and Eliza Gant. Each is lost in an envelope of private experience and each tries vainly to express himself—W. O. through rhetoric, invective, alcohol, and lust; Eliza through garrulity, money, and real estate. The terrible incompatibility in which they live reaches its almost shocking climax when, in the last moments of Gant's life, they finally speak across the void to each other, and Gant's expression of kindness dissolves Eliza into tears.

Wolfe described the controlling theme of all his books as "the search for a father"—the theme he said he consciously made central in *Of Time and the River* at Perkins' suggestion. Perkins had intended merely to suggest a type of plot, but Wolfe took the suggestion as a statement of philosophical theme, and he defined that search as a search for certainty, an "image of strength and wisdom external to his [man's] need and superior to his hunger."[26] In one sense, this search is the seeking for an individual with whom communication can be established and maintained. The search grows out of Eugene's loneliness in his childhood and the sense of isolation which he has in his world. It is intensified by his inability to communicate his love to his brother Ben. In his later life, whether for Gant or for George Webber, it finds expression in the relationships established and broken with Francis Starwick, Esther Jack, and Foxhall Edwards, to name only the major figures. About all these relationships there is a recurrent pattern: the new person is approached with eagerness; an intense relationship is established; then a failure of communication and understanding occurs; and Gant-Webber rejects the friendship. The affair with Esther Jack is, perhaps, the clearest example of this pattern. It is debatable whether the idea of the search for the father, with its suggestion of myth and of fable, defines as well as does the representation of loneliness the fundamental theme of Thomas Wolfe, whether that loneliness he described as the search for "a stone, a leaf, an unfound door," as the urge to wandering and the counter tug of home (so well articulated in *The Web of Earth* and parts of *Of Time and the River*), or as the desire vicariously to be one with and to understand "ten thousand men" in the cities, towns, and hamlets of America.

Here Wolfe's concern with oppositions takes on its tragic overtone. The essentially contradictory aspect of life creates barriers of race, of place, of heritage, of language, and as he portrays these barriers, he tries to lead us to say at the end of the Gant-Webber chronicle, as he says at its beginning: "Naked and alone we came into exile. In her dark womb we did not know our mother's face; from the prison of her flesh have we come into the unspeakable and incommunicable prison of this earth." Thus, as Wolfe sees it, all human experience seeks the "great forgotten language, the lost lane-end into heaven."[27] Certainly, as several critics have pointed out, there are Wordsworthian suggestions here. Out of some transcendent glory of childhood, we gradually are hemmed in by the growing prison house of the world, the luster and glory of life are gradually tarnished, and we are forced further away from communion. But there are also suggestions of a book which Wolfe knew and praised and whose formlessness he defended, Laurence Sterne's *Tristram Shandy*.

THE MYSTERY OF TIME, DARK TIME

For while the Wolfean character cannot find a language through which to speak, cannot break through "the incommunicable prison of this earth," he is the victim of more than silence and the lack of a language—he is also the victim of time. And the entity time is for Wolfe the great factor in life and in his books and the only really serious philosophical concept which he uses in his fiction. One of the structural problems with which he grappled seriously throughout his novelistic career was the finding of a means by which to represent adequately his views of time, which he saw as threefold.

The first and most obvious element of time, he believed, is that of simple chronology, the element that carries a narrative forward; this may be called "clock time." The second element is past time, the "accumulated impact of man's experience so that each moment of their lives was conditioned not only by what they experienced in that moment, but by all that they had experienced up to that moment." This past time exists in the present principally through the action of the memory, being triggered by a concrete sensory impression which in some way recalls the past. However, as Margaret Church has pointed out,[28] memory in Wolfe merely recalls this past; it does not recreate it or actually assert its continued existence, as Bergson's and Proust's theories of time tend to do. All this action— the present and the recollections of the past in the present—takes place against what Wolfe calls "time immutable, the time of rivers, mountains, oceans, and the earth; a kind of eternal and unchanging universe of time against which would be projected the transience of man's life, the bitter briefness of his day." [29] It is this inexorable forward flow of time, pictured as a river or more often as a train, which constantly carries man away from his golden youth, which is "lost and far" and can exist again only in memory. It is Wolfe's repeated representation of his protagonist as a narrator reporting his present emotions as he remembers the past in sensuous detail which, at least in part, creates the nostalgic quality of his writing. (See Chapter II.)

Wolfe's problem was the picturing of scenes so that an awareness of these three elements of time was created. In a given situation a man caught in his particular instant in time has it enriched and rendered more meaningful as the past impinges upon him through memory, and he gets thereby a sense of the absolute time within which his days are painfully brief. Wolfe gives this concept fictional expression in his four-part story "The Lost Boy." In the first part, a boy, Grover, passes an initiation point in life, as his father intercedes for him with a candy store keeper. " 'This is Time,' thought Grover. 'Here is the Square, here is my father's shop, and here am I.' " The second part is the mother's reminiscence years later about Grover on a train trip to the St. Louis Fair. Her monologue ends, "It was so long ago, but when I think of it, it all comes back . . . I can still see Grover just the way he was, the way he looked that morning when we went down through Indiana, by the river, to the Fair." The third part is a monologue by the sister, recounting Grover's death. It ends, "It all comes back as if it happened yesterday. And then it goes away again, and seems farther off and stranger than if it happened in a dream." In the fourth part, the brother, who was a very small boy when Grover died, goes to the house in St. Louis where it happened and tries by the use of memory to bring back "the lost boy." This section ends: "And out of the enchanted wood, that thicket of man's memory, Eugene knew that the dark eye and the quiet face of his friend and brother—poor child, life's stranger, and life's exile, lost like all of us, a cipher in blind mazes, long ago—the lost boy was gone forever and would not return." [30] The ultimate meaning of the statement "you can't go home again," which Wolfe used over and over in the last year of his life, is to be found here. "Home" is a symbol of the past, of what has been lost; for the holder of a romantic view of childhood, it is a peculiarly effective and revealing symbol. None of us, it says, can return to the lost childhood, the lost community, the fading glory; for time carries us inexorably away. We can't go home again.

In Wolfe's work this vision of time is always associated with the sense of being alone, isolated. In *Of Time and the River* he tries to enumerate the concrete memories which taken together make up the remembered past for America, and then he says: "But this was the reason why these things could never be forgotten—because we are so lost, so naked and so lonely in America. Immense and cruel skies bend over us, and all of us are driven on forever and we have no home. Therefore, it is not the slow, the punctual sanded drip of the unnumbered days that we remember best, the ash of time; nor is it the huge monotone of the lost years, the unswerving schedules of the lost life and the well-known faces, that we remember best. It is a face seen once and lost forever in a crowd, an eye that looked, a face that smiled and vanished on a passing train." And a little later, he describes the way in which the past almost forcefully entered the present for him: "Always when that lost world would come back, it came at once, like a sword thrust through the entrails, in all its panoply of past time, living, whole, and magic as it had always been."[31] It is like a sword because it cuts sharply and deeply and hurts very much. Perhaps the one emotion which Wolfe describes most effectively is this pain from which comes the sudden hunger for a lost and almost forgotten aspect of life, for "the apple tree, the singing, and the gold." Wolfe succeeds in giving us this sense of the onward rush of time and the death of the morning's gold, an awareness of the price that is paid before the "years of philosophic calm" can come. Since this feeling is very much a part of youth and its pain and *Weltschmerz*, its inarticulate melancholy, he speaks with peculiar authority to the very young and to those older chiefly through their memories of having been very young.

Wolfe did not theorize about these concepts of time, or, except in passing, discuss them. He probably did not know the works of Proust at all well, despite the degree to which the sense impressions in the present restored the lost past for both of them. Karin Pfister has suggested that Wolfe's time theories may owe something to those of Bergson, to whom Proust was also a debtor.[32] As a novelist Wolfe seemingly was fascinated by the mystery rather than the metaphysics of time. In *The Web and the Rock* he wrote: "Time is a fable and a mystery . . . it broods on all the images of earth . . . Time is collected in great clocks and hung in towers . . . and each man has his own, a different time."[33]

The river and the ocean he used as large symbols for "time immutable," yet his clearest figure for the ceaseless motion and the inexorable passage of time is the train. No American in the past fifty years has been more the poet of trains. Their rushing across the face of the earth, the glimpses of life to be seen flashing past their speeding windows, the nostalgic and lonely wail of their whistles in the night, even their sounds echoing in depots, which in *Of Time and the River* he imagines to be the very sounds of time itself—all these characteristics Wolfe associates with loneliness and movement and the sad passage of time.

THE PARADOX OF THE SELF AND THE LARGER WORLD

In one sense Wolfe's characters transcend his themes. The paradox here is a very great one: Wolfe, who asserted that no man could know his brother, described his fellowmen with deep understanding; Wolfe, whose subject seemed always to be himself, whose characters are drawn in large measure from real life rather than imagined, and who presented his world chiefly through the consciousness of an autobiographical hero, created a group of characters so fully realized that they live with great vigor in the reader's mind. *Look Homeward, Angel* is perhaps the most autobiographical novel ever written by an American, yet the protagonist, Eugene Gant, is a much less vivid person than the members of his family. It is W. O. Gant, Eliza, Helen, and brother Ben who glow with life and absorb our imaginations. Eugene himself is more a "web of sensibility" and a communicating vehicle than a person, or perhaps it is that he seems to us more nearly ourselves and less someone whom we are observing. In *Of Time and the River* the Gant family, Bascom Pentland, Francis Starwick, Abraham Jones, and Ann are more convincingly persons than the hero is. *The Web and the Rock* is less centered in the consciousness of the protagonist, and George Webber exists more as an individual than Eugene does. As a result, the other characters of this novel and of *You Can't Go Home Again* are seen in relation to the protagonist rather than through him. Yet in these books too Wolfe's gift for creating believable people of unbelievable gusto is impressive. Certainly among all his memorable creations Esther Jack, Dick Prosser, Nebraska Crane, Judge Rumford Bland, and Foxhall Edwards stand high.

Wolfe's concentration upon people of excessive vigor may be the result of his vitalism, his worship of life as a pervasive force and a supreme value in itself. Certainly, whether as the result of philosophical attitude or of mere artistic excess, the characters in Wolfe's work loom larger than life and are possessed of an awesome and sometimes awful dynamism. They are large in body, appetite, feeling, disease, and suffering. They crowd the canvas to the exclusion of the background and even of the context of action. Possibly this lack of aesthetic distance, which is one of the most obvious qualities of Wolfe's work, results from his extreme subjectivity, but it is also attributable in part to his view of life. Bella Kussy thinks that the example of vitalism run rampant which Wolfe saw in Nazi Germany cured him, and that the German experience caused his concern in his last years with social rather than personal consequences. (For Wolfe's experiences in Germany and Miss Kussy's comments in more detail, see Chapter VII.) The tendency toward social criticism, however, was present in his work some time before he was made shockingly aware of the direction that Nazi Germany was taking.

Among the important influences on the social aspect of Wolfe's work was that of Sinclair Lewis, whose satiric condemnation of a materialistic society dedicated to bulk, glitter, and the conscious disregard of beauty made a powerful impact on the young writer. As early as 1923 Wolfe wrote his mother contemptuously of "those people who shout 'Progress, Progress, Progress'—when what they mean is more Ford automobiles, more Rotary Clubs, more Baptist Ladies Social unions."[34] This attitude is just about the extent of the social criticism in *Look Homeward, Angel*, although it is often expressed in that novel. Wolfe's tendency toward satire is clearly present in the book, but it is satire aimed at Main Street and Boosters' Club targets; in the name of beauty it is attacking blatant commercialism and its attendant ugliness.

The years that Wolfe spent in Brooklyn during the depths of the Depression were filled with social lessons for him. "Everywhere around me," he wrote later, "during these years, I saw the evidence of an incalculable ruin and suffering. ... Universal calamity had somehow struck the life of almost every one I knew."[35] He became convinced that something was basically wrong with such a social order. His letters show that he had wanted to make what he and Perkins regarded as a Marxist interpretation of the social scene in *Of Time and the River*, although Perkins dissuaded him from doing it. The egalitarianism and the essentially middle-class economic radicalism of his native region reasserted themselves in his thinking during this period, and in *You Can't Go Home Again* they find expression. A sense of primary social injustice in the world is an operative force in Book II, "The World That Jack Built," which was originally published as the short novel *The Party at Jack's* and which contrasts the world of the very wealthy with that of the laboring classes that serve it; in the section "The Hollow Men," dealing with the suicide of C. Green and asserting the primary worth of the individual in a society that would reduce him to a mere statistic; in Book IV, " 'I Have a Thing to Tell You,' " also originally a short novel, with its angry picture of Nazi Germany; and in the revised segments from the short novel "Boom Town," with its satiric pictures of

Libya Hill in the grip of the real-estate boom and in the disaster of the crash, where ignoble motives of little men play destructively upon the common greed of their fellow citizens.

One of the repeated charges that Wolfe made against Perkins was that he was a "conservative," whereas Wolfe had become what he called a "revolutionary." Yet his social thinking is lacking in depth and significance. Pamela Hansford Johnson is probably too harsh when she says, "His is a young man's socialism, based on the generous rage, the infuriated, baffled pity; like the majority of young, middle-class intellectuals, he looked for 'the people' in the dosshouse and upon the benches of the midnight parks."[36] But, as E. B. Burgum has noted, "He was so constituted that he must fight alone."[37] In that aloneness he was unable to act as a part of any coordinated social scheme. The future of America which he asserts at the conclusion of *You Can't Go Home Again* is really an act of faith—and of a faith still based on the spiritual as opposed to the material, on the reawakening of "our own democracy" within us. (See Chapter V.) Here, as a social critic, he again reminds us most of Whitman. For Whitman in *Democratic Vistas* saw with mounting alarm the pattern that his nation was following and opposed it to the expanding realization of the self, of "Personalism," which it was the poet's program to advance. This is a defensible and even an admirable position, but the work of those who hold it can seldom bear the logical scrutiny of those who espouse specific social programs. As contrasted with Maxwell Perkins, Wolfe properly regarded himself as a "revolutionary," yet he remained the most persuasive advocate of an enlightened middle-class democracy that America has produced in this century.

It was inevitable that the centrality of loneliness and separateness in Wolfe's experience and his writing, coupled with the social problems and the human suffering of the years of his active career, should have fostered in him a sense of evil in the world and have given a tragic quality to his writing. His very method of oppositions would lead him to a Manichaean cosmic view. Furthermore, he was a product of a region steeped in defeat, suffering, and the acceptance of an unthinkable inevitability. As C. Vann Woodward has stated it, "Nothing about [its] history is conducive to the theory that the South was the darling of divine providence."[38] Something of this attitude—which, in Wolfe, E. B. Burgum inaccurately called "reconciliation with despair"—is a part of the heritage of all southerners, even in the liberal areas of the South such as the one in which Wolfe grew up.

Wolfe wrote of the shock he experienced in Brooklyn during the Depression at the "black picture of man's inhumanity to his fellow man ... of suffering, violence, oppression, hunger, cold, and filth and poverty," and added, "And from it all, there has come the final deposit, a burning memory, a certain evidence of the fortitude of man, his ability to suffer and somehow to survive."[39] Loneliness and suffering and pain and death—these are the things which man—frail, weak, hauntingly mortal—can expect. Yet man, for Wolfe, is also a noble creature. The despair of the literary naturalist, so common in America in the twentieth century, is not a part of his thinking. In a too obvious extension of speeches by Hamlet and by Jaques in *As You Like It*, in the twenty-seventh chapter of *You Can't Go Home Again*, Wolfe attempts to answer the question "What is man?" and in his answer states as clearly as he was ever to do the basic contradiction and the tragic magnitude of the earthly experience. Man is "a foul, wretched, abominable creature ... it is impossible to say the worst of him ... this travesty of waste and sterile breath." Yet his accomplishments are magnificent. The individual, viewed as physical animal, is a "frail and petty thing who lives his days and dies like all other animals and is forgotten. And yet, he is immortal, too, for both the good and the evil that he does live after him."[40] In the teeming, uneven pages of Wolfe's work this vision of man possessed of tragic grandeur—essentially the vision of the nineteenth-century Romantic—is presented with great intensity.

Wolfe believed that the American experience demanded a new art form and a new language for the expression of this view, however. Like Whitman, he too invited the Muse to "migrate from Greece and Ionia," and

Making directly for this rendezvous, vigorously clearing a path
  for herself, striding through the confusion,
By thud of machinery and shrill steam-whistle undismay'd,
Bluff'd not a bit by drain-pipe, gasometers, artificial fertilizers,
Smiling and pleas'd with palpable intent to stay,
She's here, install'd amid the kitchen ware! [41]

In his attempt to accomplish that task Wolfe strove with unceasing diligence. That he failed to realize the full structural plan of his
work in the years in which he lived is obvious; that he made no
whole articulation of the space and energy of American life is obvious; that he failed to formulate a completely adequate language for
the singer of America in fiction is also obvious. What he might have
done and even why he did not accomplish more of it become finally
unanswerable questions; they tease the mind without enlightening it.
We must ultimately accept or reject what he did accomplish.

Wolfe's kind of imagination and his artistic attitudes and methods
equipped him well for the depiction of character and the portrayal
of action in self-contained but isolated sequences. He seems to have
functioned most naturally and best when he was depicting his recollections of individual people and specific actions, when he was making an effort which F. Scott Fitzgerald praised in him and called "the
attempt . . . to recapture the exact feel of a moment in time and space,
exemplified by people rather than by things . . . an attempt at a mature memory of a deep experience." [42]

Hence he showed a control and objectivity in his short stories
and his short novels that effectively belie the charge of formlessness.
Yet his desire to find a new "structural plan" and as a kind of national epic-maker to create the "complete and whole articulation"
of America led him to fragment these effective short fictions and use
them as portions of the record of the total experience by which his
Whitmanesque narrator knows and expresses his native land. (See
Chapter VIII.) He never succeeded completely in this effort, and the
result is that the parts of his books are often better than the wholes
which they go together to create. Despite his bardic effort and his
epic intention, his total work—however flawed, imperfect, fragmen-

tary—is ultimately the record of a self and only very partially that of a nation. Wolfe himself described its strength and suggested its great weakness when he called it "a giant web in which I was caught, the product of my huge inheritance—the torrential recollectiveness, derived out of my mother's stock, which became a living, million-fibered integument that bound me to the past, not only of my own life, but of the very earth from which I came, so that nothing in the end escaped from its inrooted and all-feeling explorativeness."[43] To the end Thomas Wolfe retained a childlike, pristine delight in the manifold shapes, colors, odors, sounds, and textures of experience and his work communicates this delight—shadowed with a nostalgia for things past—with almost total authority.

The measure of this accomplishment is not small. *Look Homeward, Angel* is a richly evocative account of the pains and joys of childhood and youth, peopled with a host of living characters. With all its flaws, it is a fine novel, and one that gives promise of enduring. In Wolfe's total work a personality is set down with a thoroughness and honesty, an intensity and beauty of language unsurpassed by any other American prose writer, even though, aside from *Look Homeward, Angel*, it is only in the short novels that we find really sure artistic control, and sprinkled through the other books are passages of very bad writing and of irrelevant action.

Wolfe was always obsessed with paradox and contradiction; the shape of his whole career reflects startling contrast. He who would have written the definition of his nation left primarily the definition of a self; he who would have asserted that though we "are lost here in America . . . we shall be found" was from birth to death a lonely man, vainly seeking communion. He survives—and probably will continue to survive—as the chronicler of a lost childhood, a vanished glory, the portrayer of an individual American outlined, stark and lonely, beneath a cruel sky.

II   The Stigma of Autobiography

IT WAS INEVITABLE that the problem of autobiography would develop in twentieth-century fiction, for three tendencies of the nineteenth century were moving inexorably toward it. One was the Romantic doctrine of self-definition as a goal of the artist. A second was the epistemological concern which first shattered the transcendental intuition and then dissolved the real world of men and things into the impressions it created in its perceivers—resulting in impressionism in painting and elaborate concerns with problems of perception and points of view in realistic fiction. A third was the murky subterrain explored by the depth psychologists inquiring searchingly backward in time and inward into the self for the mainsprings of motive and meaning.

A recurrent twentieth-century protagonist has been the novelist-hero engaged in a search for a meaning which he finally discovers in the artistic process itself—a kind of aesthetic solipsism. A comparison may be illuminating. In the 1840s, Charles Dickens embarked upon a fictional autobiography; the result was David Copperfield, whose novels are all written offstage. In the second decade of this century, James Joyce's fictional autobiography was *A Portrait of the Artist as a Young Man,* where one of the crises is the composition of a villanelle and the climax is reached in Stephen's adoption of an aesthetic position. Many other major novels of our century are similarly autobiographical, such as Samuel Butler's *The Way of All Flesh,* D. H. Lawrence's *Sons and Lovers,* Somerset Maugham's *Of*

Human Bondage, and Marcel Proust's *Remembrance of Things Past*. In the face of this widespread practice and praise of autobiographical fiction in our time, it is, at first glance, a little surprising that against the American novelist Thomas Wolfe a charge should be often leveled that he failed because he was "autobiographical," that he was weak because he had no subject except himself. Philip Rahv contemptuously declared that "Thomas Wolfe plunged into a chaotic recapitulation of the cult of experience as a whole," [1] and Mark Schorer flatly stated, "The books of Thomas Wolfe were, of course, journals." [2] Louis D. Rubin, Jr., asserted: "What we have in Thomas Wolfe's work is the problem of the shape of autobiographical fiction, and of the steps in working it out. When we talk about Wolfe's career, we are in a real sense explicating the text of the novels." [3] And Floyd C. Watkins, who admires Wolfe almost extravagantly, says: "Life had for him the innate integrity that other writers find only after they have made great alterations." [4]

The evidence that Wolfe used the materials of experience very directly is great. Hayden Norwood's conversations with Wolfe's mother, *The Marble Man's Wife*, demonstrate it on one level. His sister Mabel Wolfe Wheaton's reminiscences, *Thomas Wolfe and His Family*, demonstrate it on another. And Elizabeth Nowell, in her biography, literally—and perhaps unwisely—used the events and emotions of the novels as biographical data. Clearly, Wolfe was an autobiographical writer—and it has usually been held an error and against him proved. [5]

But if Wolfe embraced the cult of experience, he did not differ greatly in this respect from Ernest Hemingway, whose Nick Adams, a protagonist with a father like Dr. Hemingway, has a life whose pattern parallels his author's in close detail. Frederic Henry, in *A Farewell to Arms*, like Hemingway, is an ambulance driver in the Italian army and shares with his creator the experience of almost being blown to bits. The events and characters of *The Sun Also Rises* so closely parallel those of Hemingway's own experience that the book was a celebrated *roman à clef* and one of its major charac-

ters, Harold Loeb (the Robert Cohn of the novel), has written a fac-
tual account, entitled *The Way It Was,* "to set the record straight."
Colonel Cantwell, of *Across the River and Into the Trees,* resem-
bled Hemingway in so many aspects, even of age and illness, that the
unpleasant qualities of his portrait were extended in the popular reaction to his creator and to the quality of the book. And there were
those who maintained that Santiago, the aged fisherman of *The Old
Man and the Sea,* was a thinly veiled picture of Hemingway's encounter with the destructive, sharklike critics.

Hemingway was frank about his insistence on direct experience.
In *Death in the Afternoon*—in many ways a study in aesthetic
theory—he says: "The great thing is to last and get your work done
and see and hear and learn and understand; and write when there is
something that you know; and not before; and not too damned much
after." And at another place he says: "Whoever reads this can only
truly make such a judgment [of its validity] when he, or she, has
seen the things that are spoken of and knows truly what their reactions to them would be."[6]

Few writers have worked more completely from their personal
experience than Hemingway, and if we set his few recurrent actions,
based in large measure on personal events and private emotions,
against the complexity of character and action in Wolfe, Hemingway appears—at first glance at least—as by far the more autobiographical writer of the two. Yet such a charge was leveled against
him infrequently and then usually by unfriendly critics about a book
of his that they considered to be a failure, such as *Across the River
and Into the Trees.*

Let us consider a third example. James Joyce's *A Portrait of
the Artist as a Young Man,* a book which served in part as a model
for Wolfe's *Look Homeward, Angel,* is clearly autobiographical,
although the term is not too often applied to it. This account of
the emotional and intellectual life of Stephen Dedalus, presented
through an intensely subjective treatment of the emotions of the boy
at the immediate time of action of the story, gives the impression

that, although the author's experiences are the subject of the book, the author's feelings about these past actions are not only irrelevant but have been carefully excluded. Stephen in the novel decides: "The personality of the artist, at first a cry or a cadence or a mood and then a fluid and lambent narrative, finally refines itself out of existence.... The artist, like the God of the creation, remains within or behind or beyond or above his handiwork, invisible, refined out of existence, indifferent, paring his fingernails."[7] And this quality— which Wayne Booth in *The Rhetoric of Fiction* calls "distance"— has, in the minds of most critics, "redeemed" *A Portrait of the Artist* from the charge of autobiography, although, as Booth brilliantly points out, its "distance" is bought at the price of our certainty about the basic meaning of the book and about the author's attitude toward his youthful self.

It becomes clear, I believe, that autobiography is, in fact, a pejorative term, employed by the critic not to describe an author's use of personal experience or of himself as subject or of his immersion in experience, but rather to denominate a special use of such material, usually one of which the critic disapproves.

One obvious reason that Wolfe's work is considered autobiographical is that he himself raised the issue of autobiography often. Half truculently, he addressed the reader of his first novel, *Look Homeward, Angel*, with the declaration: "This is a first book, and in it the author has written of experience which is now far and lost, but which was once part of the fabric of his life. If any reader, therefore, should say that the book is 'autobiographical' the writer has no answer for him: it seems to him that all serious work in fiction is autobiographical."[8] By contrast, Hemingway's address to the reader in *In Our Time* takes the form of an objective, dramatic account of experiences of cruelty in the Greco-Turkish war, an account that makes an impersonal presentation of the author. The people of Asheville announced in public outrage that Wolfe had not written fiction but had maliciously distorted fact; on the other hand, Hemingway's first book was obviously objective.

Hemingway's novel *The Sun Also Rises* was plainly based on actual people, such as Donald Ogden Stewart, Harold Stearns, Ford Madox Ford, Harold Loeb, Niño de la Palma, Lady Duff Cooper, and others; and it recounted an actual event with great faithfulness. Yet, although the matching of the characters with their prototypes became a favorite game of café society in the 1920s, the book seemed then and seems now to be a symbolic vignette of a generation and not a confession by its author.

Wolfe, however, persisted in discussing the issue of autobiography in public. In *The Story of a Novel* he said:

A man must use the materials and experience of his own life if he is to create anything that has substantial value. But I also believe now that the young writer is often led through inexperience to a use of the materials of life which are, perhaps, somewhat too naked and direct for the purpose of a work of art. The thing a young writer is likely to do is to confuse the limits between actuality and reality. He tends unconsciously to describe an event in such a way because it actually happened that way and from an artistic point of view, I can now see that this is wrong.[9]

Such a statement, although close in fundamental meaning to Hemingway's many insistences on the necessity of writing from experience, actually invites the critic to seek autobiographical flaws in Wolfe's work. And this naïve, almost disingenuous, approach to the public has proved costly for Wolfe's reputation.

Equally costly was the widespread knowledge of the relationship between Wolfe and his editors. The common image of Wolfe during his lifetime and since has been of a spontaneous genius producing in a wild frenzy great formless masses of material which his editors shaped into publishable form. In this picture, Wolfe functions as the amanuensis to a memory of imposing magnitude and intensity but he hardly appears as a conscious craftsman. Wolfe also put the materials for this attack into the hands of his critics: Bernard De Voto's infamous "Genius Is Not Enough,"[10] with its condescending admonition to desert "the assembly-line at Scribner's" and develop "simple competence in the use of tools," was a review of *The Story of a Novel*.

I think there is little doubt that Wolfe was too plastic an author in the hands of an able editor, and yet the evidence of his serious and continuing struggle toward form is present in his correspondence and in the manuscripts at Harvard and the University of North Carolina; and Richard Kennedy's long, detailed, and thoroughly convincing study, *The Window of Memory*, should go a long way toward forcing a reassessment of this issue. Nevertheless, the common view of Wolfe is that his editors shaped his books. By contrast, Hemingway is, in Carlos Baker's words, "the writer as artist," [11] laboring endlessly toward a uniquely personal and permanently valid aesthetic expression. As a result Wolfe and Hemingway stand in the popular mind almost as archetypes of the undisciplined and the disciplined writer.

The special formal qualities of Wolfe's works have also encouraged their being attacked as formless personal recollection. Somewhere at or near the perceptive center of most of Wolfe's writing is a protagonist notably similar to the author, whether he be Eugene Gant or George Webber or David Hawke or Joseph Doaks. And everything that happens in the many parts of Wolfe's fictional writings plays a part in and has a definable chronological relationship to the life of this protagonist. Furthermore, Wolfe's writing habits seem to have allowed him to work on separate units of this "life-story" without worrying about the chronological links. To take an overview of the four long novels and the two volumes of short fiction makes them appear to be fragments of one vast and incomplete work. When the letters and *The Story of a Novel* are added, they, too, have their place in the autobiographical whole. Wolfe's subject seems, in retrospect, always to have been the author himself.

One of the principal reasons for the sense we have in Wolfe of reading autobiography rather than fiction is the absence of a controlling action such as the Cohn-Brett relationship in *The Sun Also Rises* or the effort at a separate peace in *A Farewell to Arms*. In fact, only *Look Homeward, Angel* has a clearly defined and unified structure and it is the simple one of the apprenticeship novel. *Of Time and the River* is an anthology of fictions rather than a novel. *The*

Web and the Rock has very little unity of tone, and *You Can't Go Home Again* is a loosely assembled collection of episodes.

Wolfe, in fact, was not really a novelist. He could organize magnificently single episodes and closely related sequences of events. Scenes like the death of Ben in *Look Homeward, Angel* and the death of W. O. Gant in *Of Time and the River* are fully and dramatically realized. Episodes such as "The Child by Tiger" in *The Web and the Rock* or "In the Park" in *From Death to Morning* function brilliantly to dramatize an event and define a feeling. Short novels, such as "*I Have a Thing to Tell You*" and *The Party at Jack's*, are telling social criticism. Most of these fictions, and many others like them, come to us through the control of Gant-Webber but are significant primarily for themselves rather than for what they tell us of the protagonist's development. Yet when Wolfe put them in large books, the controlling action of the large work into which they were fitted was the development of the protagonist, and there was a resulting subtle but significant shift of interest from the actors to the perceiving and remembering teller or center.

Those who would see and defend Wolfe as a writer of controlled and nonpersonal fiction must, it seems to me, turn away from the big sprawling books and center their attention on these relatively self-contained units—units which Wolfe often initially fashioned as long stories or short novels. I believe that Wolfe *as artist* is best seen in the early versions of these self-contained units. If a fictional event is viewed as an objective experience that is perceived and later recalled by a perceiver who knew it first directly, this event, as both fact and memory, becomes a dual part of the totality of experience that defines the perceiver. Wolfe's short fictions represent the portion of this process in which the self remembers, isolates, organizes, and understands the event. The inclusion of these short fictions in the long novels represents the perceiver's attempt to absorb them into his total experience of the complexity of life and to use them as elements in his search for ultimate meaning. (See Chapter III.) The elements in Wolfe's work that are usually designated as "autobio-

43

graphical" are attributes of the large works rather than of their self-contained parts. They represent attempts to use objective experience in finding subjective meanings.

This autobiographical quality in Wolfe's writings is further enhanced by his tendency to use lyrical and rhetorical passages to interpret and to integrate the dramatic portions of his work. A very large percentage of Wolfe's writing consists of the author's attempt to reinforce the significance of a narrative passage by rhapsodic comment or declamatory assertion. With the power to evoke a particular object, scene, or character with remarkable clarity, he is unwilling to let these creations speak for themselves, but must try by the sheer force of rhetoric to give expression to the peculiar meanings that they suggest, to define ineffable feelings, to formulate the inchoate longings and the uncertain stirrings of spirit which he feels that all men share. Such passages represent pretty clearly that rhetorical groping toward understanding and expression which is a very large element in Wolfe's work. He is fascinated by language, enchanted by words, carried away by rhetorical devices. A kind of primitive logomania is in him: if the word can be found and uttered, vast forces are unleashed and great truths miraculously uncovered. The artist's search, Wolfe declared in *The Story of a Novel*, is the search for a language, for an articulation. Yet clearly the consciousness operating in these rhetorical passages is that of the author rather than of his characters, and to the extent to which the rhetoric finds itself bound to the actor in the story it makes the actor and the author one in the reader's mind. This aspect of Wolfe's work finds no parallel in Hemingway's, for rhetorical expression has no place in the work of a man whose intention was, as he expressed it in *Death in the Afternoon*, "to put down what really happened in action; what the actual things were which produced the emotion that you experienced."[12]

Wolfe's work is obsessively concerned with time and memory. In *The Story of a Novel*, he described the problem of presenting concurrently three time elements—present, past, and "time immutable"—

as "the tremendous problem ... that almost defeated me and that cost me countless hours of anguish." This persistent sense of the reality of the past was associated for Wolfe with an unusually keen memory. He declared: "Now my memory was at work night and day, in a way that I could at first neither check nor control and that swarmed unbidden in a stream of blazing pageantry across my mind, with the million forms and substances of the life that I had left, which was my own, America."[13] This view of time and memory resulted in Wolfe's world being one of heightened sensory response recollected in nostalgia and defined in rhetoric. Wolfe tries to say how it felt at a specific moment in the recollected past. In contrast, Hemingway tries to show what is literally happening now to produce a real but undescribed feeling in you. Hemingway described this process when he was discussing how to present the emotion experienced on witnessing a matador being gored by a bull:

For myself, not being a bullfighter, and being much interested in suicides, the problem was one of depiction and waking in the night I tried to remember what it was that seemed just out of my remembering and that was the thing that I had really seen and, finally, remembering all around it, I got it. When he stood up, his face white and dirty and the silk of his breeches opened from waist to knee, it was the dirtiness of the rent breeches, the dirtiness of his slit underwear and the clean, clean, unbearably clean whiteness of the thigh bone that I had seen, and it was that which was important.[14]

Here Hemingway is worrying about making the reader experience an emotion vicariously, whereas Wolfe in his apostrophes tries to describe an emotion which he felt and which he and the reader must share with the character. For example, following Ben's death in *Look Homeward, Angel*, the author addresses this apostrophe to him and to a still persistent grief:

Wind pressed the boughs, the withered leaves were shaking. It was October, but the leaves were shaking. A star was shaking. A light was waking. Wind was quaking. The star was far. The night, the light. The light was bright. A chant, a song, the slow dance of the little things within him. The star over the town, the light over the hill, the sod over Ben, night over all. His mind fumbled with little things. Over us all is something. Star, night, earth, light ... light ... O lost! ... a stone ... a leaf ... a door ... O ghost! ... a light ... a song ... a light ... a light swings over the hill ... over us all ... a star shines over the town ... over us all ... a light.

We shall not come again. We never shall come back again. But over us all, over us all, over us all is—something. . . .

The laurel, the lizard, and the stone will come no more. The women weeping at the gate have gone and will not come again. And pain and pride and death will pass, and will not come again. And light and dawn will pass, and the star and the cry of a lark will pass, and will not come again. And we shall pass, and shall not come again.[15]

Wolfe has stepped through the fictional mask and has asked us to step with him. The carefully constructed fictional world has been torn apart and the author has spoken directly for himself rather than for his character. Essentially it is this linking of author and character in a single emotion that we mean when we talk of "autobiography." The problem is one of technique, not of subject matter: thus we can say that Wolfe is autobiographical in one important sense in which Hemingway is not, although both value and write from personal experience and in themselves constitute their principal subject matter.

III   "The Blest *Nouvelle*"

THOMAS WOLFE exists in the popular fancy and even in the opinion of many of his most devoted admirers as the fury-driven author of a vast but incomplete saga of one man's pilgrimage on earth, a saga so formless that the term *novel* can be applied to its parts only with extreme caution and so monumental that it exploded the covers of six vast books in which its portions were imprisoned. Of the work upon which he embarked after *Look Homeward, Angel*, Wolfe wrote: "What I had to deal with was material which covered almost 150 years in history, demanded the action of more than 2000 characters, and would in its final design include almost every racial type and social class of American life."[1] In a letter in 1932 he said, "The book on which I have been working for the last two or three years is not a volume but a library."[2]

In the nine years that remained in his career after the publication of *Look Homeward, Angel*, he never found an adequate structure for imprisoning and ordering his experience, although he grappled mightily with the problem, projecting vast schemes, borrowing organizational principles from mythology, and attempting to substitute theme or leitmotif for plot and causal development.[3] For him event was seldom as important as the impact of event on his protagonist; the emotion aroused in Eugene Gant or George Webber was as important as the action producing the emotion. The failure to find a satisfactory form for the representation of his protagonist's experiences is, then, major and overwhelming and cannot be explained

47

away either by his verbal success or the effectiveness of many of his individual scenes.

Even his severest critics have recognized his ability to realize fully and intensely a dramatic scene or situation. Bernard De Voto, perhaps Wolfe's harshest attacker, praised his "ability to realize all three [intuition, understanding, and ecstasy] in character and scene, whose equal it would have been hard to point out anywhere in the fiction of the time. ... [Such scenes] seemed to exist on both a higher and a deeper level of realization than any of Mr. Wolfe's contemporaries had attained."[4] John Peale Bishop, in an early and brilliant analysis of Wolfe's failure to give objective structure to his work, asserted that "the most striking passages in Wolfe's novels always represent these moments of comprehension. For a moment, but a moment only, there is a sudden release of compassion, when some aspect of suffering and bewildered humanity is seized, when the other's emotion is in a timeless completion known. Then the moment passes, and compassion fails."[5] When this essay was first published, Bishop did not have the evidence from the manuscripts and the publishing history of Wolfe's work that at least a portion of the responsibility for the fleeting quality of these moments of awareness of others resulted not from how Wolfe originally wrote the scenes, but from how he later fragmented and assembled them in making the larger works.

Clearly it was how Wolfe wrote that is one key to the success of his scenes and the weakness of his larger structures. Much has been written about Wolfe's methods, and most of it has been romanticized or has so centered on quantity and frenzy rather than artistry that a seemingly permanent picture of Wolfe as the eternal *naïf* has emerged. In fact, his method seems to have been to deal with individual scenes, characters, actions, or emotions in depth and at length and then later to fit them into the larger composition. One example, which is typical of his method, will illustrate this aspect of his work. The first thing published by Wolfe after *Look Homeward, Angel* was a short novel, *A Portrait of Bascom Hawke*. It was consciously written as a unit,[6] and as late as March, 1934, he thought of it as independent of the "work in progress," *Of Time and the River.*[7] Yet when the novel appeared in 1935, Wolfe had found a place for the episodes of *Bascom Hawke* among the adventures of Eugene Gant. But it is fragmented into eight separate parts and distributed among Eugene's varied experiences.[8] Before his death thirty-eight stories or sketches by Wolfe had been published in magazines.[9] Of these, twenty reappear as parts of the novels, with portions of a number being in more than one book. The twelve-thousand-word story "The Train and the City," for example, is distributed among *Of Time and the River, The Web and the Rock,* and *You Can't Go Home Again.*[10] Those not utilized in the novels are reprinted in *From Death to Morning* and *The Hills Beyond.* While in many cases editors like Maxwell Perkins or agents like Elizabeth Nowell independently selected from the larger manuscripts episodes sufficiently self-contained to be given separate life, this fact does not invalidate the claim that Wolfe's natural method of writing was in reasonably brief and self-contained units.

Wolfe's whole career was an endless search for a language and a form in which to communicate his vision of reality. This passion to find a mode of expression was coupled in Wolfe with a thoroughly organic view of art, one in which the thing to be said dictates the form in which it is uttered. He once wrote to Hamilton Basso: "There is no accepted way: there are as many art forms as there are forms of art, and the artist will continue to create new ones and to enrich life with new creations as long as there is either life or art. So many of these forms that so many academic people consider as masterly and final definitions derived from the primeval source of all things beautiful or handed Apollo-wise from Mount Olympus, are really worn out already, will work no more, are already dead and stale as hell."[11]

Look Homeward, Angel had almost automatically assumed a simple but effective narrative form. The record of childhood and youth, cast at least semiconsciously in the *Bildungsroman* pattern of James

Joyce's *A Portrait of the Artist as a Young Man,* it had found its theme and taken its shape from the sequential flow of lyric feeling which it expressed. After its publication, Wolfe began a desperate search for another form into which to pour his materials. His letters between 1930 and 1934 are crowded with ambitious plans, nebulous projections of structure, plot, and myth—all pointed toward forming his next book. Increasingly its matter grew and the problems of the control of that matter enlarged.

Here a case can be made (and I believe should be made) that Maxwell Perkins' insistence that *Look Homeward, Angel* should be followed by a "big book" was injurious to Wolfe's career. He wanted to follow it with a brief novel, *K-19,* which was actually put in production by Scribner's and a salesman's "dummy" containing boards, jacket, and the first signature was prepared before Perkins decided against going ahead with publication.[12] To speculate on the effect such publication might have had on the shape of Wolfe's career, although interesting, is futile. Kennedy is probably correct in his judgment that *K-19* was simply a bad book.[13] However, it is difficult to read *The Story of a Novel* without believing that the agony which he describes there of struggling over the years to make the "big book" in the face of growing critical skepticism was fundamentally injurious to his work.[14] Certainly the effect of this urging by his editor was to center Wolfe's attention on a large work for which he had no clearly defined organizational principle.[15]

By the fall of 1931 Wolfe found himself immersed in a struggle for form whose magnitude and difficulty, as well as spiritual and emotional anguish, he recorded touchingly in *The Story of a Novel.* In November, badly in need of money and in black despair over "the book," he turned to a body of materials on which he had earlier worked and began shaping them into a short novel. These materials dealt with his experiences in Cambridge and with his uncle, Henry Westall. In its finished form the short novel, *A Portrait of Bascom Hawke,* pictured an old man resigned to the death of dreams as he is seen through the eyes of a youth still half blinded by the visions of glory which the old man has given up. The two points of view, the youth's and the old man's, together gave a sense of the flow and corrosion of time. The result was a portrait in depth, done with irony, poignance, and tolerant laughter, of an eccentric who might have stepped from the pages of Dickens.

Thus Wolfe stumbled, almost by accident, upon a congenial form. For the short novel was remarkably well suited to Wolfe's method of writing. Many of the incidents that were the bases of Wolfe's short, separate compositions were incidents that he had witnessed rather than participated in or involved characters other than himself who had fascinated him. In producing them both his natural inclination for the dramatic scene and his considerable experience in writing for the theater helped in the creation of an objective world of great specificity and integrity. The novella seems, indeed, to have built into it some safeguards that Wolfe's approach to writing made desirable, while at the same time it allowed him some of the expansiveness of attitude which his special concerns made imperative. And just what special qualities or virtues exist for the writer in the short novel that do not exist for him in the short story or the full-length novel? A definitive answer would, of course, chop up the protean form of the short novel and force it to fit the Procrustean bed of the particular critic's special attitudes. Yet it is possible to suggest some of the distinctive qualities of the form.

The short novel, declares Howard Nemerov in the most courageous and persuasive attempt that I know of to get at its essence, is "neither a lengthily written short story nor the refurbished attempt at a novel sent out into the world with its hat clapped on at the eightieth page."[16] Yet it can best be discussed with reference to these two things which it is not. The strength of the short story lies in its power of concentration. Like a lyric poem it places a premium on preciseness and control, and it demands some sharply realized principle around which its materials are organized. That principle may be quite varied, ranging from the neatness of a well-made plot, to the presentation of a single character, to the explication of a theme or a

symbol, to Poe's famed "effect." But in all cases the focusing principle is there, and through its operation the short story shares with
the lyric poem the quality of exclusion, of shutting out in order to
arrange, concentrate, and unify. But this quality of exclusion and
concentration in the short story is bought for a price, that of giving
up the showing of a scene in a continuum of action, of the development as opposed to the revelation of character, and the adjudication
among conflicting themes or the exploration of complexities of symbol. The short story reveals, discloses, shows a person, an action, a
situation as it is at the moment of the story. This revelatory quality
in the short story probably was in James Joyce's mind when he
called his short stories "epiphanies." An epiphany gives us immediate—and unexpected—access to the heart of a mystery, but it does
not show the development of that mystery. It is beautifully suited
to showing an event or a person at a special time; but it is poorly
equipped to show an event or a person *in* time. It is, perhaps, this inability of the short story to deal with "time in process" that yielded
it a generally unfruitful form for Wolfe, whose obsession with time
was deep and pervasive.

The novel, on the other hand, is primarily characterized by the
quality of expansiveness, of inclusion. As Howard Nemerov suggests, readers "tend to live in novels, and sometimes they live there
very comfortably indeed: thus you have descriptions which are
nothing but description, thus you have philosophical excursions, set
pieces, summaries, double-plot and full orchestration, not to mention that all the chairs are heavily upholstered and even the walls
padded." [17] Mr. Nemerov is clearly exaggerating, but the thrust of
his remarks is right. The special forte of the novel is not revelation
but development, not comment or demonstration but presentation
in the fullest possible sense. For this reason we accept and believe in
characters and actions in a novel which would be incredible to us if
presented in the same way in a short story. The novel is remarkably
well adapted to the demonstration of the effects of time on character,
to seeing the meaning of an incident in terms of the continuum of

events within which it exists. Perhaps no other literary medium is as immediately suited to showing the corrosive effects of the passage of time as the novel. The events of a novel picture a growth and they demand—and, when they succeed, receive—a concurrent growth in the reader's mind. This evolving process gives a novel a sense of depth in experience and a quality of richness in interpretation that even the finest short story at best can merely suggest, although a few masters of the short story craft have made their suggestions remarkably powerful. Thus, when Wolfe incorporated his short episodes into his novels, they tended to lose their separate integrity and to become a part of the protagonist's experience; hence their value underwent a shift from objective reality to subjective interpretation, and the apparent self-centeredness of the protagonist cast over them an often unpleasant autobiographical light.[18]

The short novel at its best unites the concentrated focus of the short story with the expansiveness and the scope of the novel. It tends toward the concentration and unity of the short story, working within more obvious limits more consciously imposed than those of the full-length novel. One of the reasons that Wolfe's short novels took on extra wordage and diffuseness and often were fragmented when they became part of his long novels was that in the longer form they lost some of their artistic and inherent right to the unifying exclusiveness of the short form. Yet within the short-novel form, the author has—always within fairly strict limits—the privilege of developing and creating rather than revealing and demonstrating his materials. Henry James had this quality in mind when, in the preface to *The Author of Beltraffio* volume in the New York edition, he characterized the short story as "the concise anecdote" and found it suitable for material where it was possible "to follow it as much as possible from the outer edge in." The short novel, which he called the *nouvelle*, resulted, he thought, from the opposite method of pursuing its subject "from the centre outward." He set the short story against the short novel, of which, he declared, "the subject treated would perhaps seem one demanding 'developments,' " and added,

"There is of course neither close nor fixed measure of the reach of a development which in some connexions [the short story] seems almost superfluous and then in others [the short novel] to represent the whole sense of the matter."[19]

Howard Nemerov defined the short novel as well as that impossible task has ever been done: "What are short novels? For the writer who is by habit of mind a novelist, they must represent not simply a compression but a corresponding rhythmic intensification, a more refined criterion of relevance than the one he usually enjoys, an austerity and economy perhaps somewhat compulsive in the intention itself. For the writer who habitually thinks in short stories—a bad habit, by the way—the challenge is probably greater: he will have to learn as never before about the interstices of his action, he will have to think about a fairly large space which must be filled, not with everything (his complaint against the novelist), but with something definite which must be made to yield in a quite explicit way its most reserved and recondite ranges of feeling; he will have to think, for once, of design and not merely of plot."[20]

Such terms as "the effect of time on character," "rhythmic intensification," "the interstices of his action," "recondite ranges of feeling," and "design and not merely ... plot" point to those intrinsic qualities of the short novel that are well adapted to Wolfe's special kinds of creative problems. Although he was skilled at the revelatory vignette—a fact demonstrated repeatedly in his novels and a few times in such stories as "Only the Dead Know Brooklyn"—those characters and actions that were central to his interpretation of experience he saw in relation to the expanding pattern of life. One of the distinctive aspects of his imagination is the tendency to see life as a process of "becoming." He saw time—"dark time"—as being at the center of the mystery of existence, and its representation on three complex levels as a major philosophical and technical concern. The individual scene or person had little permanent value to him; it had to be put back into time—the complex time which he described as tripartite in *The Story of a Novel*: present chronological time;

past time impinging upon, making, and modifying the present; and "time immutable."[21] Hence the ultimate use he had made of the apparently self-contained materials of his art was to make them portions of the continuum of experience of his protagonist, and thus to strip them of the unity and independence which they enjoyed in their first forms.

Yet the fact remains that one of Wolfe's most effective mediums was the short novel. Such a fact made him by no means unusual among the world's writers of fiction. On the Continent fiction in the intermediate length—what Henry James called "the beautiful and blest *nouvelle*"—enjoyed critical acclaim and reader acceptance. "It was," James asserted, "under the star of the *nouvelle* that, in other languages, a hundred interesting and charming results, such studies on the minor scale as the best of Turgenieff's, of Balzac's, of Maupassant's, of Bourget's ... has been, all economically arrived at."[22] Other distinguished names rush to mind to join James's examples: Goethe, Voltaire, Thomas Mann, Anatole France, Anton Chekhov, André Gide, François Mauriac, Albert Camus, and Franz Kafka.

Perhaps the earliest decisive English example is Laurence Sterne's *A Sentimental Journey*, and few schoolboys will forget such differing short novels as Stevenson's *Dr. Jekyll and Mr. Hyde* and George Eliot's *Silas Marner*. The distinguished work of Joseph Conrad cannot be overlooked. Virginia Woolf wrote short novels, as did John Galsworthy, notably in *The Apple Tree* and even in *The Forstye Saga*, where his use of the *nouvelle* for *Indian Summer of a Forsyte* represents the use of the short novel as an element in a vast work somewhat like Wolfe's use of it in *A Portrait of Bascom Hawke* and *The Party at Jack's*.

The short novel can almost be said to be a natural mode for the American writer. Melville's finest accomplishments after *Moby-Dick* are short novels, *Benito Cereno* and *Billy Budd*. Stephen Crane was at his best in this length, as witness *Maggie, A Girl of the Streets* and *The Red Badge of Courage*. Simms, Cooper, and Howells used the short novel, as did Mark Twain in *The Mysterious Stranger* and

The Man That Corrupted Hadleyburg. Edith Wharton, in such works as *Ethan Frome, False Dawn,* and *The Old Maid,* and Willa Cather, in *A Lost Lady* and *My Mortal Enemy,* found the form congenial. John Steinbeck in *Of Mice and Men, The Pearl,* and *The Red Pony;* Thornton Wilder in *The Bridge of San Luis Rey;* Eudora Welty in *The Robber Bridegroom, The Ponder Heart,* and *The Optimist's Daughter;* Katherine Anne Porter in *Pale Horse, Pale Rider* and *Noon Wine;* William Faulkner in *The Bear* and *Knight's Gambit;* DuBose Heyward in *Porgy;* and Ernest Hemingway in *The Old Man and the Sea,* have all employed the short novel effectively and successfully. And such distinguished—and different—craftsmen as Gertrude Stein, Truman Capote, Robert Nathan, and Nathanael West have used it as their characteristic mode of expression.

The American novelist Henry James was also the major American practitioner of the short novel. He brought to it "an awareness of its technical possibilities, a consciousness of its ideal balance between development of idea and economy of execution, and the full measure of his craftsmanship."[23] Yet James, whose short novels include such distinguished work as *Madame de Mauves, The Aspern Papers, The Turn of the Screw, Daisy Miller, The Lesson of the Master,* and *The Beast in the Jungle,* complained bitterly of "the blank misery of our Anglo-Saxon sense . . . [that] a 'short story' was a 'short story,' and that was the end of it," and sadly pictured the American writer forced to compress a *nouvelle* to a standard length as "the anxious effort of some warden of the insane engaged at a critical moment in making fast a victim's straight-jacket." James found escape from what he called "the rude prescription of brevity at any cost"[24] in the pages of Henry Harland's *Yellow Book,* which gave him freedom as to length and thus made it possible for him happily to produce short novels for its pages.

Wolfe, somewhat like Henry James and the *Yellow Book,* was fortunate in having available to him the pages of a magazine interested in the short novel and anxious to give it an audience. That magazine was *Scribner's*, under the editorship of Alfred Dashiell from 1930 to 1936. When he became editor of the magazine, Dashiell began a series of efforts at variety and new forms of reader interest. These included two five-thousand-dollar Short Novel Contests, a Life in the United States Narrative Contest, and a series of Scribner's Biographies. The Short Novel Contest and the short novels that grew from it constitute a significant, though minor, chapter in American literary history and a major one in the career of Thomas Wolfe.

In 1930 *Scribner's Magazine* began its first Short Novel Contest, in order, the magazine said, "to provide a market for and to stimulate the writing of the long story (a neglected and highly important literary form)." [25] *Scribner's* was most inconsistent in the name it applied to the genre, using "short novel," "novelette," "long story," and even "long short story" at various times. "[T]here has not been an appropriate name given to the principal piece of fiction appearing in *Scribner's* each month," the editors declared, adding that Wolfe's *A Portrait of Bascom Hawke* "can't be labelled." [26] But they were quite explicit about the purposes of the Short Novel Contests, which were three in number: "to give an opportunity for established writers to function in the field of the long short story, which has been dormant by reason of technical barriers (too long for a short story, too short for a serial, or a novel, etc.)"; "to uncover promising new talent"; [27] and "to open the field permanently to novels of this length." [28] At another time, they said, "The chief purpose of the contest is to free writing from another commercial limitation." [29]

In their attempts to define the short novel as a genre, the editors were most specific about length—"between 15,000 and 30,000 words." [30] They reported that of the 1,672 manuscripts submitted in the first contest the average length was 25,000 words. [31] When they moved from measurable specifics to attempts to define the form in aesthetic terms, they encountered the common problems of its critics. They spoke of "the excellence of this literary form which seems to us to have so many possibilities."[32] They declared of a short novel by Grace Flandrau, *The Way of Love*: "It is impossible to conceive of this tale in any form but the one in which it now appears. It is not a short story; it is not a novel; it is the long story brought to the heights."[33] They listed as the characteristics of the short novel "adequate space for development of character and situation, combined with precision and solidity of structure" and argued that these qualities made it "intrinsically ideal for magazine publication. Since a signal virtue of this type of writing is its unity, the complete story appears in a single issue." And they were finally reduced to definition by example, citing as distinguished examples of what they meant Edith Wharton's *Ethan Frome*, Conrad's *Youth*, Willa Cather's *A Lost Lady*, De Maupassant's *Boule de Suif*, and Katherine Mansfield's *Prelude*.[34]

Twelve short novels were published in the first contest: *S.S. San Pedro* by James Gould Cozzens inaugurated the first contest in the August, 1930, issue. (The judges were to select from among short novels published the best at the end of the contest.) *Many Thousands Gone* by John Peale Bishop appeared in September. It was followed by works by Grace Flandrau, W. R. Burnett, Elizabeth Willis, James B. Wharton, and Carroll E. Robb. In March, 1931, the decision of the judges was announced; Gilbert Seldes, Malcolm Cowley, and John Hall Wheelock had adjudged John Peale Bishop's *Many Thousands Gone* the winner of the contest.[35] And a noncontest short novel, *The Weigher of Souls* by André Maurois, could be viewed by the editors as proof that the contest was "open[ing] the field permanently to novels of this length."[36] Short novels that merited publication from the first contest continued to be published, including *Jacob's Ladder* by Marjorie Kinnan Rawlings, in the April, 1931, issue. A "New $5,000 Prize Contest for Best Short Novel" was announced, to close February 1, 1932, and the editors reiterated their concern with establishing not only a market for the short novel but also with helping to lessen the "severe handicap to many writers who functioned best in works of this length."[37] The new contest got underway with *A New Break*, by Josephine Herbst (September, 1931).

When Thomas Wolfe turned over to Maxwell Perkins the manuscript of *A Portrait of Bascom Hawke* in January, 1932, he had had only one magazine publication, "An Angel on the Porch," in the August, 1929, *Scribner's Magazine*, and this work had been drawn directly out of *Look Homeward, Angel.* Perkins purchased the short novel for five hundred dollars and entered it in the contest without Wolfe's knowledge; it was published in the April, 1932, issue. Other novels in the second contest included *Mill Girls* by Sherwood Anderson, *Her Son* by Edith Wharton, *The Cracked Looking-Glass* by Katherine Anne Porter, and *The Big Short Trip* by John Hermann (August, 1932). In August the editors announced that the judges—Burton Rascoe, William Soskin, and Edmund Wilson—had selected *A Portrait of Bascom Hawke* and *The Big Short Trip* as cowinners of the second contest from the nine short novels published in the magazine and drawn from the more than fifteen hundred entries in the competition.[38] *A Portrait of Bascom Hawke* gained considerable critical praise, such as that which Laurence Stallings gave it in the NewYork *Sun*, where he wrote: "Has anyone failed to admire a story in the *Scribner's Magazine* (for April) by Thomas Wolfe? There's an eddy of energy for you; and a lyrical paean to life. ... It seems to me that Thomas Wolfe has shown in this story that his *October Fair*, announced for next fall, will be even finer than ... *Look Homeward, Angel*. ... He seems to have all the gifts, all the talents. ... 'A Portrait of Bascom Hawke' is the book of the month." [39]

Apparently Wolfe had been ignorant of the existence of the Short Novel Contest until he submitted *Bascom Hawke* to Perkins in January. Learning of the contest he resolved to write a novel to enter in it, despite the fact that less than a month remained before the contest ended. As his intended entry Wolfe set to work on a short novel fashioned on his mother's endless stories of the past. During the month of January she visited him in Brooklyn, and the immediate source of *The Web of Earth* was almost certainly her conversations. The deadline for entries in the Short Novel Contest had passed more than a month before the story was finished, but *Scribner's* promptly purchased it and published it in the July, 1932, issue.

This novella, the longest of Wolfe's short novels, comes to the reader entirely through the voice of its narrator, Delia Hawke (later changed to Eliza Gant when the novel was reprinted in *From Death to Morning*). Wolfe insisted, "It is different from anything I have ever done," and added, "that story about the old woman has got everything in it, murder and cruelty, and hate and love, and greed and enormous unconscious courage, yet the whole thing is told with the stark innocence of a child." [40] The seemingly disparate elements of the story—disjointed in temporal and logical sequence—are effectively knit together by the powerful personality of the narrator and by her obsessive search in the events of her life for the meaning of the spectral voices that spoke "Two ... Two" and "Twenty ... Twenty" in "the year that the locusts came." [41] When in 1934 Alfred Dashiell, the *Scribner's* editor, collected his favorite stories in *Editor's Choice, The Web of Earth* led the volume and Dashiell commented, "The virtue of the long story is amply demonstrated in 'The Web of Earth.' Reduced to five thousand words ... the story would have lost much of its effectiveness. Liberated from the space formula, it becomes the rich story of a life." [42]

In writing *The Web of Earth* Wolfe followed James Joyce again, as he had done in *Look Homeward, Angel.* He compared his "old woman" with Molly Bloom and seemingly felt that his short novel had a structure like that of the interior monologue at the conclusion of *Ulysses.* [43] In her resilience, her undefeatable energy, and her vitality Eliza (or Delia) approaches "the earth goddess" and is, as Louis D. Rubin, Jr., has pointed out, [44] reminiscent of the end of the "Anna Livia Plurabelle" sequence of *Finnegans Wake,* a sequence which was published in *transition* about the same time. In this short novel one understands what Wolfe meant when he referred to Eliza Gant's people as "time-devouring." Thus, *The Web of Earth* becomes a fascinating counterpiece to *A Portrait of Bascom Hawke*; for each is a character sketch of an elderly person, but where Bascom Hawke is defeated and despairingly resigned, Eliza Gant is triumphant and dominant; where Bascom is the male victim of time, Eliza is the female devourer of time; where Bascom's is the vain grasp of intellect and reason in a mad and fury-driven world, Eliza's is the groping of mystery, passion, and fear in a world where reason always falls victim to the decay of time. Never did Wolfe articulate more effectively than in these two short novels the fundamental polarities of his childhood and youth.

With two short novels successfully behind him, Wolfe next turned to organizing into short-novel form blocks of the material which he had written for the still formless "big book." In the period between March, 1933, and March, 1934, he put together four long stories or short novels from these materials, finding in the limits of the novella a means of focusing matter whose organization in larger blocks still defied him. *Scribner's Magazine* bought three of these long tales and published them in successive issues in the summer of 1934. "The Train and the City," a long short-story of twelve thousand words, appeared in the May issue. Percy MacKaye praised this story highly, saying, "From a quiet niche in your own mountains—your incomparable, tumultuous, earth-drinking, star-brooding peaks of the spirit—I write you this word of true gratitude that at last, in unspoiled words which are their counterparts, you have made them articulate with their own grandeur and fecundity,"[45] but the story lacks the unity which Wolfe had achieved in his first two short novels. *Death the Proud Brother* appeared in the June issue, and was later republished as a short novel in *From Death to Morning*. This story of twenty-two thousand words was a skillful attempt to unify a group of seemingly disparate incidents in the city through their common themes of loneliness and death, "the proud brother of loneliness." Wolfe regarded this story very highly, saying, "It is . . . one of the most important things I ever wrote,"[46] and his novelist friend Robert Raynolds praised it highly. Although it is a successful effort to impose thematic unity upon disconnected instances of death in the city, it is less effective than Wolfe's other novellas.

The third long story was *No Door*, in its original form a short novel of thirty-one thousand words, although it was published by *Scribner's* as two long stories, "No Door" in July, 1933, and "The House of the Far and the Lost" in August, 1934. In arranging the materials of this novel, Wolfe selected a group of intensely autobiographical incidents all centering on his sense of incommunicable loneliness and insularity, dislocated them in time, and bound them together by a group of recurring symbols arranged in *leitmotif* patterns, extending and enriching a method he had used in *Death the Proud Brother*. Through the recurring images and the repeated phrases of a prose poem used as a prologue, he knit together one portion of his life.

In the early months of 1933 *No Door* was completed, and by March it had been accepted by *Scribner's*. Its completion coincided with Wolfe's discovery of a plan which made work on the "big book" feasible for him again. He wrote to George Wallace: "Just after you left in January . . . I plunged into work and . . . I seemed suddenly to get what I had been trying to get for two years, the way to begin the book, and make it flow, and now it is all coming with a rush."[47] Since the structure of *No Door* is essentially that of *Of Time and the River*, since the prologue to *No Door* reappears with only minor changes as the prologue to the long novel, and since the writing of *No Door* coincides with the finding of a "way to begin the book," it is probable that the short novel was the door through which Wolfe entered *Of Time and the River*.[48] John Hall Wheelock praised *No Door* highly, and Maxwell Perkins agreed to bring out a limited edition of the short novel in its original form, but later changed his mind.[49] Its absorption into *Of Time and the River* was almost complete, and it seemingly has survived as a unit only in the form of its brief first incident, published as a short story in *From Death to Morning*, where it achieved notoriety as the basis for a libel suit brought against Wolfe and Scribner's by Marjorie Dorman and her family in 1936.

Yet *No Door* represents as sure a mastery as Wolfe ever demonstrated of the subjective, autobiographical materials for which he is
best known. Of the section published as "The House of the Far and
the Lost," Robert Penn Warren wrote in a review almost brutally
unsympathetic to *Of Time and the River*: "Only in the section dealing with the Coulson episode does Mr. Wolfe seem to have all his
resources for character presentation under control. The men who
room in the house ... with the Coulsons themselves are very precise
to the imagination, and are sketched in with an economy usually
foreign to Mr. Wolfe. ... Here Mr. Wolfe has managed to convey
an atmosphere and to convince the reader of the reality of his characters without any of his habitual exaggerations of method and style.
This section ... possesses what is rare enough in *Of Time and the
River*, a constant focus."[50] Although the Coulson episode is clearly
the most striking one in *No Door*, it is an integral part of that work,
and the entire short novel possesses the strong virtues that Warren
here assigns to the only portion of it which survived as a unified part
of the long novel.

No Door was the last of Wolfe's works of more than fifteen thousand words which Dashiell published before his editorship of *Scribner's* ended with the issue of September, 1936. Between August, 1930,
and July, 1933, Dashiell had published twenty-six short novels,
twelve in the first contest, nine in the second, and four independent
of the contests. However, between April, 1932, and July, 1933, he
published eight *nouvelles* of which four were by Wolfe. After *Scribner's* turned to other things to bolster its sagging subcription lists—
serials, "Life in the United States" narratives, biographies—Wolfe
felt the lack of a market for a form that was natural to his talents
and interests. Writing to Hamilton Basso, while he was working on
The Party at Jack's, Wolfe said: "It is all very well to talk of classic
brevity etc. but this story cannot be written that way: if it is it becomes something else. And if I do it right it is certainly worth doing.
But to get it published? I don't know. All this talk about there being
a market or a publisher nowadays for any good piece of writing is
nonsense. A writer's market, unless he chooses to live and work and

publish like James Joyce or to be one of the little magazine precious boys, is still cabin'd and confined to certain more or less conventional and restricted forms and mediums."[51] Perhaps it was his experience with *Boom Town* which Wolfe had in mind. This satiric picture of Libya Hill was originally a short novel of about twenty thousand words, written in its first form in 1932. His agent, Elizabeth Nowell, sold it in its third revision to the *American Mercury* in 1934, and it was published in the May, 1934, issue, but only after extensive editing and cutting by one of the *Mercury* editors.[52]

The discovery of an organizing principle for the "big book" brought a temporary end to Wolfe's work in the short novel form; for the next two years he devoted himself singlemindedly to *Of Time and the River.* Thus during his first period—the one of which he said, "I began to write with an intense and passionate concern with the designs and purposes of my own youth"—Thomas Wolfe produced, in addition to his two long novels, five short ones: *A Portrait of Bascom Hawke, The Web of Earth, Death the Proud Brother, Boom Town,* and *No Door.* (*The Lost Boy,* a work of almost fifteen thousand words, may be considered a short novel. It was written in 1935 and published in an abridged form in *Redbook Magazine* in November, 1937.)[53]

These short novels demonstrated Wolfe's artistry and control of his materials and perhaps instructed his sense of form. And, during the grueling years between the publication of his first novel in 1929 and *Of Time and the River* in 1935, his reputation was sustained and enriched by his short novels as much as it was by Sinclair Lewis' brief but telling praise for him as a "Gargantuan creature with great gusto for life" in his Nobel Prize address in 1930.

When he entered the second period of his career—that of which he said, "[My] preoccupation [with my own youth] has now changed to an intense and passionate concern with the designs and purposes of life"[54]—he found himself once more facing the problem of finding a new and adequate form in which to express his vision of experience. This search for an organic structure was complicated

by his growing difficulties with his publishers and his increasing un-
willingness to follow the advice of his editor, Maxwell Perkins. In
this situation, in some respects like that of 1931, Wolfe turned his
attention again to elements of his own experience that lent themselves to expression in the short novel form.

In the summer of 1936 he made his last visit to Germany, a nation
that he loved and that had heaped adulation upon him. (See Chapter
VII.) On this trip he was forced to face the frightening substratum
of Naziism, and he said, "I recognized at last, in all it frightful aspects, the spiritual disease which was poisoning unto death a noble
and mighty people." [55] That fall he used the short novel form to
dramatize this perception of the truth about Hitler's Germany, and
he elected to give his account, which he entitled *"I Have a Thing to
Tell You,"* the sharp intensity and the almost stark directness of the
action story. At this time Wolfe had great admiration for the directness and simplicity of Ernest Hemingway's style, and in this short
novel of Germany he came closest to adopting some of its characteristics. Nothing Wolfe ever wrote had greater narrative drive or
more straightforward action than this novella. The simplicity and
objectivity of *"I Have a Thing to Tell You"* were seldom sustained
for any length of time in Wolfe's work before 1936. This short
novel also displays clearly the growing concern with the issues of
the outer world which had begun to shape Wolfe's thinking. Its
serial publication in the *New Republic* issues of March 10, 17, and
24, 1937, despite his disclaimers of propaganda intent, indicates a
marked advance in the expression of political and social concerns for
Wolfe.

During much of 1937, Wolfe's energies were expended in his long
and torturous break with his publishers, Charles Scribner's Sons, certainly one of the two major emotional cataclysms of his life (the
other was his earlier break with his mistress, Aline Bernstein). He
was also deeply discouraged about his projected book, feeling that
his long planned and talked-of *October Fair*, often announced, was
somehow being dissipated in fragments. In this despairing state, he

was led by his growing sense of social injustice to attempt another experiment with a short novel as a vehicle of social criticism. He worked on this new novella, *The Party at Jack's*, during the early months of the year and spent the summer revising and rewriting it.

Wolfe felt that he was attempting in *The Party at Jack's* "one of the most curious and difficult problems that I have been faced with in a long time," the presentation of a cross-section of society through a representation of many people, ranging from policemen, servants, and entertainers to the leaders in the literary world and the rich. The characters are brought together for a single evening whose events include a party and a fire in the apartment house in which the party occurs. Wolfe used several devices, including the recurring quivering of the apartment house as the trains run in tunnels through its seemingly solid rock foundations and the conversations of the doormen and elevator operators, to underscore the contrasts among the characters and to comment on society. Wolfe feared that readers would think this short novel to be Marxist, a charge against which he defended it, saying: "There is not a word of propaganda in it. It is certainly not at all Marxian, but it is representative of the way my life has come—after deep feeling, deep thinking, and deep living and all this experience—to take its way. ... It is in concept, at any rate, the most densely woven piece of writing that I have ever attempted."[56] *The Party at Jack's* is, as Wolfe asserted, free of autobiography, except in the most incidental ways. It is also in Wolfe's late, more economical style. Its taut prose and its rapid movement, together with its effective but implicit statement of social doctrine, make it one of Wolfe's most impressive accomplishments.

Almost immediately after completing *The Party at Jack's*, Wolfe plunged into organizing his materials into another "big book" for his new publishers, Harper and Brothers, a task disrupted by his death in September, 1938. He had written—in addition to a mass of manuscript out of which three later books were assembled—two novels, a number of short stories, and seven or eight short novels. Wolfe had expended great effort upon these short novels, and in them he had given the clearest demonstrations he ever made of his craftsmanship and artistic control. Each of these novellas is marked in its unique way by a sharp focus and a controlling unity, and each represents a serious experiment with form. Yet until the publication of *The Short Novels of Thomas Wolfe* in 1961 they were virtually lost from the corpus of Wolfe's work, lost even to most of those who knew that work well.

There were two reasons for these losses. In the first place Wolfe's publishers, and particularly his editor Maxwell Perkins, were anxious that the long, introspective *Look Homeward, Angel* be followed by an equally impressive work. Perkins insisted on Wolfe's continuing the Eugene Gant story and opposed his coming before the public in a different form or manner. Had Wolfe's own inclinations prevailed *Look Homeward, Angel* would have been followed by the short novel, *K-19,* and then by *No Door,* a work of less than forty thousand words, and that small book might have been followed by a volume which Wolfe later described to his mother that would contain *A Portrait of Bascom Hawke, The Web of Earth,* and "another story which [he had] written," probably "The Train and the City."[57]

The effect which such a pattern of publication might have had on Wolfe's career is difficult to guess; possibly it would have spared him some of the agonized searching for form of his last years and frustrations which grew out of his sense of the need of having each large work followed by an equally monumental one. The career of Thomas Mann makes an interesting contrast. Mann, writing in Germany, which valued the novella highly, followed *Buddenbrooks,* a book of mammoth magnitude, with *Tonio Kröger,* a short novel of twenty-five thousand words. A quarter of a century later, Mann followed *Death in Venice,* a *"petit roman"* of thirty thousand words, with the monumental *The Magic Mountain.*

A second reason for the loss of these short novels is the nature of Wolfe's work and his attitude toward it. All the separate parts of his writing formed for him portions of a great and eternally fragmentary whole. It was all the outgrowth of the same basic desire, the

Whitmanesque attempt to put a person on record and through that person to represent America in its paradox of unity and variety, at the same time that the eternal and intolerable loneliness of the individual lost in the complex currents of time served as the essential theme for the representation of that person. As a result, Wolfe was forever reshuffling the parts of his work and assembling them in different patterns, in a way not unlike the shifting elements of the Snopes material in Faulkner's legend of Yoknapatawpha County. Thus Wolfe took the materials presented first as short novels and interwove them into the larger frames and subject matters of his "big book," fragmenting, expanding, and modifying them, and often destroying their separate integrity. Only two of his short novels escaped this process; and these two—*Death the Proud Brother* and *The Web of Earth*—were published in a collection of his shorter works, *From Death to Morning*, which has never received the critical attention that it deserves.

In his short novels Wolfe was dealing with limited aspects of experience, aspects that could be adequately developed in the limits of fifteen to forty thousand words and that could be organized into what he proudly called *The Party at Jack's*, "a single thing." When he later fragmented these short novels and distributed the fragments within the larger design of the "big books," he robbed them of their own unity in order to make them a portion of a larger, more complicated unity—"a single thing" of complex and multifarious parts. Indeed, Wolfe's treatment of his short novels when he incorporated them later into his long books (and he would probably have approved his editor's use of the longer versions of "*I Have a Thing to Tell You*" and *The Party at Jack's* in *You Can't Go Home Again*) is a key to one of Wolfe's central problems, the finding of a large form sufficient to unify his massive imaginative picture of experience. This large form that he sought would give, apparently, not the representation of a series of sharply realized dramatic moments in the life of his protagonist (and through him of America) but an actual and significant interweaving of these moments into a complex fabric of event, time, and feeling. That he struggled unceasingly for the mastery of this vast structure is obvious from his letters, from *The Story of a Novel*, and from the long books themselves. Whether he was moving toward its realization is a matter of critical debate today, as it was at the time of his death. However much one may feel that he was (and I share that belief), the fact remains that none of the published novels after *Look Homeward, Angel* succeeded in finding a clearly demonstrable unity, in being "a single thing."

The intrinsic qualities of the short novel were remarkably well adapted to Wolfe's special talents and creative methods. Although he was skilled at the revelatory vignette, in which he imprisoned a character in the instant in time, those characters and actions which were central to his effort and experience he saw in relation to the expanding pattern of life. Experience and life itself were for him, as Herbert Muller has noted, remarkably "in process." One of the distinctive aspects of Wolfe's imagination is its tendency to see life as a thing of "becoming." He saw time—"dark time," he called it—as being at the center of the mystery of experience, and its representation on three complex levels was a major concern of his work. The individual scene or person had little value to him; it had to be put back in time to assume meaning. Wolfe was very explicit about this element of his work. In *The Story of a Novel* he says:

All of this time I was being baffled by a certain time element in the book, by a time relation which could not be escaped, and for which I was now desperately seeking some structural channel. There were three time elements inherent in the material. The first and most obvious was an element of actual present time, an element which carried the narrative forward, which represented characters and events as living in the present and moving forward into an immediate future. The second time element was of past time, one which represented these same characters as acting and as being acted upon by all the accumulated impact of man's experience so that each moment of their lives was conditioned not only by what they experienced in that moment, but by all that they had experienced up to that moment. In addition to these two time elements, there was a third which I conceived as being time immutable, the time of rivers, mountains, oceans, and the earth; a kind of eternal and unchanging universe of time against which would be projected the transience of man's life, the bitter briefness of his day. It was the tremendous problem of these three time elements that almost defeated me and that cost me countless hours of anguish in the years that were to follow.[58]

Ultimately in the portrayal of an incident or individual against this complex pattern of time, that incident or individual must be seen through a perceiving and remembering self, such as David Hawke, the youth who can read the corrosion of time in the contrast between his exuberance and his uncle's resignation, in *A Portrait of Bascom Hawke*. Eliza Gant's fabric of memories in *The Web of Earth* is a record of the impact of time on her. The individual incidents of *No Door* assume their importance as portions of a personal history as they are reflected in the narrator's memory. To be fully understood such events and people must be set against the innumerable other events and people which the perceiving self has known; it is this larger context in time which Wolfe attempts to give these short novels when he incorporates them in his longer works. We can think of an event as being an objective experience which is perceived and recalled later by the self that first knew it directly; then it, as fact and as memory, becomes a part of the totality of experience that makes the web of meaning for that self. Wolfe's short novels represent that portion of the process in which the incident is remembered, isolated, organized, and understood as incident by the self. Their later fragmentation and inclusion in the long novels represent his attempt to absorb them into his total experience and to use them in all the complexity of life as elements in his search for ultimate meaning. Hence he breaks up the sequence of actions, introduces new incidents, and frequently expands the wordage of the short novels when they are incorporated into the larger structures. These incidents thereby lose some of their artistic and inherent right to achieve unity by exclusion, and they tend to become diffuse. Since Wolfe's success in achieving the larger unity for which he strove in the last three long novels is considerably less than total, the materials which he had organized into short novels have an integrity and a consummate craftsmanship which they seem to lack in the long books.

The role that *Scribner's Magazine* played in his career should not be forgotten, for the interest of *Scribner's Magazine* in the short novel was an inspiring and strong influence on Wolfe; it provided him with a market for a form of writing which he liked. It is appropriate that the final issue of *Scribner's Magazine*, that of May, 1939, should have published posthumously as part of a new—and never completed—Short Novel Contest Wolfe's last short novel, *The Party at Jack's*. Thus five of the seven or eight novellas which he published in magazines appeared in *Scribner's*. The hope of encouraging the form which Alfred Dashiell announced in 1930 was thus realized in the work of one of the most important writers whom the magazine published. *Scribner's* served for Wolfe as the *Yellow Book* did for James the vital role of giving him a welcome market for the "blest *nouvelle*."

IV   The Problem of Point of View

AMONG THE MANY strategies by which an author orders the materials of his fictional world and controls the responses of his readers, few are ultimately as important as his choices about narrative point of view. By narrative point of view, I mean the way through which the reader of a work of fiction is presented with the materials of the story, or the vantage point from which the author presents the materials of the story. There are numerous possibilities: it may be first person or third person; subjective or objective; major character, minor character, or bystander; omniscient, limitedly omniscient, or choric; scenic or panoramic; or any of several combinations of these possibilities. Looked at in another way, it may be considered what F. K. Stanzel calls "die typischen Erzählsituationen" —the kind of narrative situation—of which there are three: the first-person novel, in which the narrating self and the experiencing self are identical; the authorial novel, in which the narrator is a recognized personality but not a character in the fictional world; and the figural situation, in which the fictional world is seen through a character who is within it. *Moby-Dick* is an example of the first, *Tom Jones* of the second, and *The Ambassadors* of the third. [1]

The importance of narrative point of view—of the stance the author takes toward his material and where he places the reader in relation to it—can hardly be overestimated. It is a decision of primary importance to the realization of the writer's artistic purpose. If there

72

is irony between how a story is told and what we understand about it, as there is, for example, in Mark Twain's *Adventures of Huckleberry Finn*, that irony is a function of the author's choice of narrative point of view. Indeed, Van Wyck Brooks has argued that the happy accident of stumbling upon Huck as narrator solved so many of Mark Twain's persistent artistic problems that it made it possible for him to produce his most satisfactory work.[2] In Hawthorne's *Scarlet Letter*, the limits imposed by the device of the imaginary manuscript of Surveyor Pue contribute immeasurably both to the detachment of the narration and to the uncommitted presentation of alternatives which enriches the symbolic values of the novel. The disparate parts of *Moby-Dick* are bound together by the attitude, the personality, and the persistent voice of Ishmael. The location in time and space of the act of the telling of *David Copperfield* is fixed by the clearly designated narrator's stance. The distance that Joyce's dramatic narration established between him and Stephen Dedalus in *A Portrait of the Artist as a Young Man* redeems that book from the dangers of mawkishness and obvious autobiography, even though perhaps, as Wayne Booth insists, at the cost of a clear meaning for the novel.[3] Hemingway's early narrators, biting the bullet and keeping a stiff upper lip while they lead us to admire the courage and discipline by which they avoid mentioning the inner anguish that they everywhere reveal, become an essential part of the novels they narrate—indeed, perhaps the most direct key to their meanings. Try to imagine Conrad's *Heart of Darkness* without Marlow, or think what Jay Gatsby's story would have been without the ordering that Nick Carraway's telling of it gives in *The Great Gatsby*, or try to imagine *Daisy Miller* told by an omniscient author.

Obviously narrative point of view does many essential things for a novelist. It helps to guide the reader's responses and to establish tone; and—above all—it certifies to the reader a certain relationship of the author toward his material. The successful novelist needs to have either consciously or unconsciously a firm sense of what narrative point of view is and how it works. The evidence is clear, I believe, that Thomas Wolfe did not, and among the debilitating difficulties that plagued his work after *Look Homeward, Angel* this failure often proved to be a cardinal sin.

Look Homeward, Angel was, by Wolfe's own confession, his Joyce book. He wrote, in a letter to Norman Holmes Pearson, " 'Look Homeward, Angel' was a young man's book, a first book. . . . I was far more under the influence of writers I profoundly admired— notably, of course, Mr. James Joyce—than in the work which I was to do later."[4] The novel has obvious stylistic similarities to Joyce's *Ulysses*, but they are, on the whole, superficial. It is more deeply indebted to *A Portrait of the Artist as a Young Man*, a magnificently controlled novel about the development of a boy and young man with great artistic potential. *A Portrait of the Artist* is a triumph of technique, a classic example of the "figural situation," in which a third-person narrative point of view is used to present the world as seen by a fictional character and to maintain aesthetic distance and an aura of impersonality in an intensely autobiographical story. *A Portrait of the Artist* established an ideal, defined a goal, and demonstrated a technique for Wolfe's account of his growing up and awakening to the world around him. Thus it was inevitable that Wolfe's first extended work of fiction should be in the third person as Joyce's had been. But proof that he followed Joyce's example without fully understanding it may be found throughout *Look Homeward, Angel*. It is present in the long historical prologue— originally almost ninety thousand words before Perkins insisted that it be cut to its present thirty-five pages[5]—in the use of what Richard Kennedy has called the "choral voices"[6]—those undefined speakers, such as those in the famous prologue: "Naked and alone we came into exile. In her dark womb we did not know our mother's face; from the prison of her flesh have we come into the unspeakable and incommunicable prison of this earth."[7] And proof is present in those shifts in person and in time, such as the one at the end of the picnic scene with Laura James in Chapter 30, where some unidentified person—not Eugene Gant (unless he is telling the story in the third person), not the "chorus of the proem," but a person located in the time of writing rather than the time of action yet intimately bound up with the action in an intense emotional bondage, declares: "Come up into the hills, O my young love. Return! O lost, and by the wind grieved, ghost, come back again, as first I knew you in the timeless valley, where we shall feel ourselves anew, bedded on magic in the month of June. . . . Quick are the mouths of earth, and quick the teeth that fed upon the loveliness. You who were made for music, will hear music no more: in your dark house the winds are silent."[8] Here both reader and author have lost any certain vantage point in time or space from which the action may be viewed. Narration has given way to prophecy and lament.

Perhaps by the time he had completed writing *Look Homeward, Angel* Wolfe realized that *A Portrait of the Artist as a Young Man* was a far from ideal model for what he actually wanted to do. Clearly his several statements about turning away from Joyce seem to indicate that he had his doubts.[9] In any case, *Look Homeward, Angel* was an apprenticeship novel in the classic sense, and its treatment of the life of its protagonist from infancy to his leaving home and the environment that had nourished him in order to discover a life founded on the "philosophy" which he had gained of how to live was a treatment in keeping with such well-known examples as *Wilhelm Meister, The Way of All Flesh, Sons and Lovers,* and *Of Human Bondage.* Like these works it leaves its protagonist on the threshold of maturity, and it no more demands a sequel than those books do. Compare, for example, its concluding page with that of *A Portrait of the Artist* or Lawrence's *Sons and Lovers,* and you become aware of how much it fits the traditional form and how thoroughly, measured by the terms of the apprenticeship novel, it is completed. (Indeed, it has the most satisfactory ending of any of Wolfe's novels.)

In *A Portrait of the Artist,* Stephen Dedalus at the end is leaving his native place. His mother prays, he says, "that I may learn in my own life and away from home and friends what the heart is and what it feels." To which he echoes a heart-felt "Amen. So be it." And adds, "Welcome, O Life! I go to encounter for the millionth time the reality of experience and to forge in the smithy of my soul the uncreated conscience of my race."[10] At the conclusion of *Look Homeward, Angel* Eugene Gant is leaving Altamont and its surrounding hills and the state of Old Catawba and all that it has meant as natal place and testing ground. Wolfe writes:

"He stood naked and alone in darkness, far from the lost world of the streets and faces; he stood upon the ramparts of his soul, before the lost land of himself; heard inland murmurs of lost seas, the far interior music of the horns. The last voyage, the longest, the best... Yet, as he stood for the last time by the angels of his father's porch, it seemed as if the Square already were far and lost; or, I should say, he was like a man who stands upon a hill above the town he has left, yet does not say 'The town is near,' but turns his eyes upon the distant soaring ranges."[11]

When he turned to the next work after *Look Homeward, Angel*, Wolfe was filled with plans and projects, none of which he seemed to consider continuations of that youthful work. His new protagonist was going to be David Hawke—in other forms he was to be Joseph Doaks, George Webber, and Paul Spangler. His subject was to be, not the growing awareness of the world by an artist as a youth or a very young man, but the scope and meaning of America as it registered on the consciousness of a representative person. And what that person saw, the people he knew, the actions he witnessed, the conclusions he reached—all were to share with the protagonist the center stage. For the presentation of the world of David Hawke, Wolfe turned, apparently instinctively rather than with calculation, to the first-person point of view. Richard Kennedy says, "What narrative point of view should govern the new book ... Wolfe considered ... only briefly."[12] The manuscripts and notebooks show that he toyed with several points of view, such as the first-person observer—"I knew David. We were both born in Altamont"[13]—in a narrative device which Faulkner used with great distinction in some of his short stories, notably "That Evening Sun." But from

1930 until 1934 the material he actually completed was in the first person.

The relatively brief novel *K-19* that he had ready for the publishers in 1932 and that Scribner's actually put in production before Maxwell Perkins decided to withdraw it was a first-person narrative. (For a detailed treatment of the works discussed in this paragraph, see Chapter III.) A novel which Wolfe wished to publish in 1934, *No Door*, and which Scribner's again scheduled and then withdrew, was also in the first person. His first actual publication after *Look Homeward, Angel* was the short novel *A Portrait of Bascom Hawke*, which appeared in *Scribner's Magazine* in April, 1932; it was a first-person narration by David Hawke. The next was the short novel *The Web of Earth*, in the July, 1932, *Scribner's* a first-person narration by Delia Hawke, David's mother. The third was a long story, "The Train and the City," in the May, 1933, *Scribner's*, a first person narrative drawn from the manuscript of the abortive *K-19*. Another first-person short novel, *Death the Proud Brother*, appeared in *Scribner's* in June, 1933, and still another first-person short novel, *No Door*, was partially published in *Scribner's* in July of that year. In February, 1934, *Scribner's* published a first-person short story, "The Four Lost Men." Beginning in 1934, Wolfe wrote a number of short pieces in the third person, but he also continued to use the first person for short stories and short novels until his death. In all, seventeen of the magazine pieces that he prepared for publication himself are in the first person and seventeen in the third. There are other pieces in which it is not certain who decided what person they should be in.

At first glance that last sentence seems to state an unlikely proposition. Nevertheless, it is accurate. For example, Wolfe published "The Bell Remembered" as a first-person story,[14] but when it was republished posthumously by his editor Edward Aswell in *The Hills Beyond*, it was in the third person, and the question of who made the change is finally unanswerable. "*I Have a Thing to Tell You*" first appeared in 1936 as a first-person serial.[15] In expanded form it reappears in *You Can't Go Home Again* in the third person. "Oktoberfest" was first published as a first-person short story.[16] It reappears as an episode in *The Web and the Rock*, in the third person. "The Child by Tiger," one of Wolfe's most effective short stories, was a first-person narrative in the *Saturday Evening Post* in 1937,[17] but when it was republished as an episode in *The Web and the Rock* it had been changed to a third-person narration. "Katamoto," a third-person episode in *You Can't Go Home Again*, was originally published as a first-person story in *Harper's Bazaar* in 1937.[18]

Clearly narrative point of view was not a major and essential artistic strategy to Thomas Wolfe but rather a convenience. When, however, Wolfe's materials written in the third person in this period are examined, we find that most of them have some special nonartistic reason for having their present narrative points of view. Some, such as "The Sun and the Rain" (*Scribner's*, 1934), are lifted from the manuscript of *Of Time and the River* after Perkins had won his argument that the book should be about Eugene Gant and should be in the third person. Some, such as "The Face of the War" (*Modern Monthly*, 1935) are episodes originally written for *Look Homeward, Angel* but deleted from the book. Some, such as "The Bums at Sunset" (*Vanity Fair*, 1935) are about events removed from the direct experience of Hawke-Gant-Webber. Thus we are apparently justified in saying that, after 1930, Wolfe instinctively wrote in the first person, and that the appearance of the bulk of his work after *Look Homeward, Angel* in the third person represents editorial not authorial decision.

Indeed, in *Of Time and the River* the change to third person was insisted upon by Maxwell Perkins (Wolfe agreed and must, therefore, be held responsible) and, since Wolfe refused to go through the vast manuscript and change the substantial amounts already written in first person to third, a young editor, John Hall Wheelock, was given the job.[19] Elizabeth Nowell recounts a recurrent event that is funny, revealing, and ultimately tragic. She writes: "John Hall Wheelock, the editor at Scribner's who had changed *Of Time and the River* from the first person, in which it was originally written,

78

to the third person, would be awakened by the ringing of the phone at 2 or 3 A.M. to hear Wolfe's deep sepulchral voice say, 'Look at line 37 on page 487 of *Of Time and the River*. Do you see that "I"? You should have changed that "I" to "he." You betrayed me and I thought you were my friend! ' "[20]

Maxwell Perkins, Wolfe's editor at Scribner's, says that it was on Thanksgiving, 1933, that Wolfe brought to him "in desperation about two feet of typescript."[21] Included in this mass of manuscript were the materials that Wolfe had written and, in some cases, published since the appearance of *Look Homeward, Angel*—the David Hawke material, *K-19, No Door*—most of it material that had been written in the first person. It had a different protagonist from Eugene Gant, and was the fragments of a novel that Wolfe had not thought of as a continuation of his first book while he was writing. There is little question that Wolfe was desperate. The material he had written had fallen naturally into short units, had been successful as magazine pieces, but had failed to reach the book form that he had projected for it. (One cannot avoid wondering what Wolfe's career might have been if *K-19* and *No Door* had been published in 1932 and 1934 as books. Certainly our impression of him today as a creator of vast and formless narratives would be different.)

Perkins, with the best intentions in the world and believing that he was helping, went to work with Wolfe to bring some order and a semblance of form into this mass of manuscript material. Anyone interested in what Wolfe had in the manuscript and thought he had in mind for the book will find in the *Notebooks* (admirably edited in two volumes by Richard Kennedy and Paschal Reeves) a detailed outline for the novel, listing what had been written and what was to be written.[22] This outline shows that fragments covering action up through the concluding episode of what is now *The Web and the Rock* were included. Perkins seemingly made two decisions: that *Of Time and the River* should be a direct sequel to *Look Homeward, Angel* and that it should have its focus on Eugene Gant. "The principal I was working on," he said later, "was that this book, too, got its unity and its form through the senses of Eugene."²³ Hence a vast body of material written originally in the first person was changed to the third person, and in many cases the changes were purely mechanical. To compare the magazine versions of the material published between 1932 and 1934 with this material as it appears in *Of Time and the River* is to see that names of characters and the person of pronouns are changed—and in most cases literally nothing else.

The third person had produced confusions of voice and of stance in time in *Look Homeward, Angel*, as we have noted. But the centrality of Eugene's apprenticeship to life still had given that book a narrative force and a unity of purpose. The materials in *Of Time and the River* are far more varied. The outer world was larger and more important; the ideas that Wolfe wished to express were far less self-centered. It is probably not an overstatement to say that for him Joyce's young artist Stephen Dedalus had been replaced by Walt Whitman's generic self, that the search for the roots of artistic sensibility had given way to the search for the meaning of being an American, that the chronological structure of the first book was giving way to the ideological structure of the second one. Wolfe, who had had little to say philosophically in *Look Homeward, Angel*, had a great deal to say in *Of Time and the River*, and he was without a strong controlling narrative to give shape to how he said it. The result was that a technical difficulty in the first book—that of a narrative point of view that was sometimes fuzzy in focus and indefinite in time—became a calamity in the second book.

Of Time and the River contains some of Wolfe's finest writing. It is filled with memorable characters, scenes realized with great distinction, and episodes that exemplify Wolfe's command of language, characters, action, and scene. However, the total pattern is hazy. The ambitious project to which its individual parts are shaped does not always emerge clearly. The book follows Eugene to Harvard, recounts his experiences there, describes his father's death and its effect on Eugene, follows him then to New York City where he teaches in the School of Utility Cultures and associates for a time with the wealthy Hudson River people, then goes with him from there to Europe where he begins writing a novel and has a frustrating love affair with a girl named Ann, carries him on a poetic train trip to southern France, and concludes as he meets a woman named Esther on the boat back to America.

There is more bombast and rant in this book than in any of the others; more scenes which are not fully realized because they need to be seen and defined against the controlling thematic pattern of the book. For understandable reasons, despite the excellence of some of its parts, *Of Time and the River* has been the least popular of Wolfe's long novels. And it is long—912 closely printed pages. Distinguished critics have wrestled with its form and found it unsatisfactory. Upon its appearance, Robert Penn Warren objected that there was in it a "confusion between the sensibility that produced a [novel], as an object of art, and the sensibility of a hero in a [novel]." It was, he thought, "a novel possessing no structure in the ordinary sense of the word."[24] John Peale Bishop in 1939 accused Wolfe in *Of Time and the River* of "playing a game in which any move was possible, because none was compulsory."[25] Joseph Warren Beach asserted that "We can get further in our appreciation of Wolfe if we think of him not as a novelist but as a poet or a composer. These books yield their secret to us best if we consider them ... tone poems."[26] The most ambitious effort to come to grips with the nature of *Of Time and the River* is in a recent essay by Richard Kennedy, "Thomas Wolfe's Fiction: The Question of Genre." Kennedy finds the novel to consist of a mixture of the following materials: "Novel, essay, choral ode, descriptive travelogue, oratorical discourse, dramatic vignette, cinematographic montage."[27] He concludes that a new term is needed to define the genre in which Wolfe is working, and the term he suggests is *fictional thesaurus*. I have suggested the term *anthology*, since the effect of the work is that of a collection of related but disparate entities.

But increasingly, as I examine the book, I come to the opinion that it is an autobiographical piece of fiction, attempting to deal with its protagonist as both a person and a representative American, and that the issue at stake is not genre but technique, and, in regard to technique, primarily narrative point of view. If *Of Time and the River* were a first-person narrative, the meditations, the invocations, the essays, the philosophic digressions, and the travelogues would have a clearly defined source, and that source would be the protagonist, whom I would prefer to think of as David Hawke rather than Eugene Gant. Many years ago I pointed out certain parallels between *Look Homeward, Angel* and Laurence Sterne's *Tristram Shandy*.²⁸ If *Of Time and the River* were in the first person, the parallels between it and Sterne's novel would be equally apparent. The several parts would have a common and defined source, and the place and time of their writing would be clear. When, for example, Eugene's brother Ben is mentioned in the train sequence that constitutes the first part of the novel, and the mention triggers a passage of reminiscence and apostrophe, there would be no confusion about who is speaking and at what time. As it stands now, the confusion between the thoughts of Eugene and the voice of Wolfe is great, and when he writes: "For now October has come back again, the strange and lonely month comes back again, and you will not return. Up on the mountain, down in the valley, deep, deep, in the hill, Ben—cold, cold, cold," it seems to be Wolfe speaking in the present rather than Eugene meditating in the past. When later that year he uses the same words to dedicate *From Death to Morning* to the memory of his brother, our worst suspicions are confirmed. There is inherent confusion when a third-person narrative about a provincial boy entering New York City is interrupted without warning by the author who asks, "For what is it that we Americans are seeking always on this earth? Why is it we have crossed the stormy seas so many times alone, in a thousand alien rooms at night hearing the sounds of time, dark time . . . " It is the simple confusion of who is speaking and when. But put those broodings into Eugene's mind and locate him later in time than the time of action of the story, so that he is looking back upon himself, and it all becomes clear. I submit that it also really becomes what Wolfe intended when he originally wrote it. At the beginning of Book VII is a passage on time, which opens, "Play us a tune on an unbroken spinet, and let the bells ring, let the bells ring!" It continues this way—very beautifully, I might add—for four pages, and concludes with an address to figures from the past: "Shall your voices unlock the gates of my brain? Shall I know you, though I have never seen your face? Will you know me, and will you call me 'son'?"[29] Lifted out as a prose poem, this section is magnificent. As an episode in a third-person novel it is confusing. As a retrospective account by a first-person narrator it would have authority and dramatic propriety.

In *You Can't Go Home Again* this difficulty is accentuated, at least as an editorial problem, by the fact that the book was being assembled by an editor from manuscript and notes left by Wolfe at the time of his death. When we come upon the grand and inspiring passage called "The Promise of America," which begins "Go, seeker, if you will, throughout the land and you will find us burning in the night," and which concludes "So, then, to every man his chance—to every man, regardless of his birth, his shining, golden opportunity— to every man the right to live, to work, to be himself, and to become whatever thing his manhood and his vision can combine to make him—this, seeker, is the promise of America,"[30] a question that, considering the grandiloquence of the long passage, seems almost to be a quibble raises itself. Since George Webber, the third-person protagonist, certainly can't be speaking these words, and since not he but Wolfe is writing the novel, whom does Wolfe intend us to see as the speaker? Or to express it in terms dear to the New Critics, what speaker and situation are intended which, being recognized, give the passage dramatic propriety?

This problem finally became too much for Edward Aswell to wrestle with, and he abandoned the effort to fit Wolfe's first-person writing into the third-person frame of *You Can't Go Home Again*, and left the last Book as a letter written by George Webber to

Foxhall Edwards. This section, actually drawn in large part from Wolfe's speech at Purdue, contains splendid passages, such as the ones beginning "I believe that we are lost here in America, but I believe we shall be found," and "Mankind was fashioned for eternity, but Man-Alive was fashioned for a day." [31] As a part of a letter from the protagonist, they achieve a certain dramatic justification. But they differ in fact very little if at all from numerous such passages that have been liberally sprinkled through *Of Time and the River*, *The Web and the Rock*, and earlier sections of *You Can't Go Home Again*.

We often talk knowingly about the difficulties of the first-person narrator in *Moby-Dick* and the sometimes ludicrous strategies to which he puts Melville in getting the story told. But imagine, if you can, what *Moby-Dick* would have been as a third-person narrative, without the cetological lore, the philosophical disquisitions, the witty play with language and idea, and the narrative events coming to us through the medium of Ishmael's recollection, meditation, and voice. Or try to imagine *Tristram Shandy* as a third-person narrative. It is something like this that Wolfe attempted, at Perkins' behest, in *Of Time and the River*.

To be what Wolfe told Fitzgerald in a famous letter that he aspired to be, "a putter-inner" rather than a "taker-outer," [32] he needed the most inclusive possible narrative point of view, and he knew it. As late as September, 1936, he was making in his *Notebooks* a list of "Great 'I' Books of the World: Moby-Dick, Huck Finn, Sorrows of Werther, David Copperfield, Gulliver, Rousseau's Confessions, Remembrance of Things Past, Leaves of Grass, The Confessions of a Fool, Robinson Crusoe." [33] These were fine models for what he wanted. All his life he sought a mode that would allow him to write dramatic scenes, to brood over their meanings, to discuss their emotional value, and to exhort his readers, and still to maintain dramatic propriety. In a letter making what proved to be a successful application for a Guggenheim fellowship, Wolfe in 1929 wrote of his abandoning of the theater as his medium: "I had to find a medium where

I could satisfy my desire for fullness, intensity and completeness. I could never do this in the theatre."[34] When he wrote instinctively, he seems most often to have chosen the first person and it was well suited to his needs. But he either did not fully understand what he had done or, understanding it, lacked the courage of his artistic convictions. In the shift to third person he helped to defeat the artistic purposes to which he gave his life with a touchingly single-minded devotion.

V Rhetorical Hope
and Dramatic Despair

THOMAS WOLFE was the master of two distinct modes of writing—although there are unkind critics, such as Bernard De Voto, who would say that he was mastered by them. One of these modes is that of rhetoric; the other is that of dramatic rendering. By rhetoric I mean the direct statement of ideas and emotions in language designed to persuade the reader. In fiction it is the substitution of the description of emotion for the evocation of emotion. On the other hand, dramatic rendering presents characters and actions and makes its appeal through the feelings they evoke. This distinction was in Henry James's mind when he defined the "sign of the born novelist" as being "a respect unconditioned for the freedom and vitality, the absoluteness when summoned, of the creatures he invokes," and contrasted it to "the strange and second-rate policy of explaining or presenting them by reprobation or apology—of taking the short cuts and anticipating the emotions and judgments about them that should be left, at the best, to the perhaps not most intelligent reader."[1]

The two are often fundamentally incompatible, but when they are used to reinforce each other they can function with great strength. Contrast, for example, these two selections from *Of Time and the River*. In the first the dying W. O. Gant is talking with his wife:

"Eliza,"—he said—and at the sound of that unaccustomed word, a name he had spoken only twice in forty years—her white face and her worn brown eyes turned toward him with the quick and startled look of an animal—"Eliza," he said quietly, "you have had a hard life with me, a hard time. I want to tell you that I'm sorry."

And before she could move from her white stillness of shocked surprise, he lifted his great right hand and put it gently down across her own.[2]

The second selection is a meditation on Gant's death as it affects his son Eugene. Although it runs on for several pages, the opening is typical:

October had come again, and that year it was sharp and soon: frost was early, burning the thick green on the mountain sides to massed brilliant hues of blazing colors, painting the air with sharpness, sorrow and delight—and with October. Sometimes, and often, there was warmth by day, an ancient drowsy light, a golden warmth and pollenated [*sic*] haze in afternoon, but over all the earth there was the premonitory breath of frost, an exultancy for all the men who were returning, a haunting sorrow for the buried men, and for all those who were gone and would not come again.

His father was dead, and now it seemed to him that he had never found him. His father was dead, and yet he sought him everywhere, and could not believe that he was dead, and was sure that he would find him. It was October and that year, after years of absence and of wandering, he had come home again.[3]

In these passages Wolfe writes of the same fundamental situation— and one of his major themes—death. In the first he writes as a novelist and in the second as a prose poet. But this mixed style bothers us relatively little, for the rhetorical passage extends and universalizes the particular incident that is presented with objective force in the first selection. The notebooks contain ample evidence that such prose poems—and this one in particular—were sketched out independent of their later use.[4] But this fact is ultimately of little significance, for however he came to write them first, in his early books Wolfe usually wedded these rhetorical passages effectively to their final dramatic context.

At the opening of Book VII of *Of Time and the River*, there is a much less certain union of scene and rhapsody. This is the section that begins: "Play us a tune on an unbroken spinet. . . . Waken the turmoil of forgotten streets, let us hear their sounds again unmuted, and unchanged by time, throw the light of Wednesday morning on the Third Crusade, and let us see Athens on an average day."[5] This famous passage is an attempt to impose the themes of time and the quest for the father on material in which they are not necessarily apparent. In other words, here rhetoric is not reinforcing dramatic scene but is being used as a substitute for it. And the problem is further complicated by the fact that in the passage on October and death, the brooding rhetoric is Eugene's and thus has a kind of dramatic propriety, while in the passage on the unbroken spinet the rhetoric seems to be the expression of some undefined auctorial persona who differs from Eugene, and who is, in fact, commenting on the protagonist's experience. The temptation is strong to say that Wolfe as recorder of the conversation of Gant and Eliza is working as a novelist, and that Wolfe evoking music from the unbroken spinet is indulging in direct self-expression.

That Wolfe should have felt no compulsion to synthesize these elements is not surprising, for he seems to define reality in terms of negations, to deal in oppositions, to be unable to bring forth any idea without setting against it a contradiction. And he seems, too, to have a confident faith that the synthesis of these opposites is a consistent function of reality itself, that it inevitably happens and does not need his guiding hand. Thus he can shift from scene to exhortation, from action to explanation, from immediacy to nostalgic perspective without sensing that he is doing primary violence to his view of the world.[6] The result is that his books consist of segments written in different styles and contrasting modes. Thus he produces works which, if judged in the terms of Northrop Frye's definitions of genres,[7] are mixtures of two or three fictional modes, or, in Mr. Kennedy's term, are fictional thesauruses.[8]

The tendency for these modes to be separate rather than reinforcing increases very much in the posthumous novels, despite the fact that Edward Aswell assembled them from manuscript material and in so doing exercised great freedom in excision, rearrangement, and even rewriting on occasion. Of course, acting against Aswell's attempt to achieve unity through editing was the circumstance of his having to work with a vast and very fragmentary and incomplete manuscript.

You Can't Go Home Again, the book in which I wish to examine Wolfe's use of these two modes, is a fictional record of the conflict of the American dream with a capitalistic society and the descent of that dream into nightmare. Early in the book, its protagonist, George Webber, says that "we are all savage, foolish, violent, and mistaken; that, full of our fear and confusion, we walk in ignorance upon the living and beautiful earth, breathing young, vital air and bathing in the light of morning, seeing it not because of the murder in our hearts."[9] Wolfe has expressed here in miniature a controlling theme and a shaping opposition that governs the book. For almost as clearly as John Steinbeck did, he contrasts the dream and promise represented by the natural world with the nightmare that man makes for himself within it. The dream is basically simple and rural; its betrayal is the achievement of complex urban and industrial forces.

You Can't Go Home Again cannot accurately be called a novel. It lacks a formal plot; it is a collection of incidents that happened to or are observed by the protagonist but in which that protagonist frequently plays only a minor part. It was left in a fragmentary form at Wolfe's death and was assembled by his new editor Aswell, working from an outline and having to choose among versions, write links, change names, and give the appearance of a unified work of fiction to a mass of manuscript of an incomplete novel. Yet the work has special merits that none of Wolfe's other works possess, and although it is an anthology of parts, the parts themselves are often magnificently realized. It stands at the opposite end of the spectrum from Wolfe's first novel, *Look Homeward, Angel*. That book was the lyric cry of a self-centered and introspective boy, a record of the adventures of his spirit in "the meadows of sensation." *You Can't Go Home Again* is the social testament of a maturing—if not fully mature—man.

In *Look Homeward, Angel*, the self-discovery of the artist was the focus, but by the time of *You Can't Go Home Again* Wolfe had come to believe that such a focus was wrong. He has George Webber say of his first novel—which was transparently also Wolfe's—"The young genius business . . . the wounded faun business . . . twists the vision. The vision may be shrewd, subtle, piercing, within a thousand special frames accurate and Joycean—but within the larger one, false, mannered, and untrue."[10] In the later book the focus has shifted to the outer world, and he attempts to make the central personality function in a manner he described once in a letter: "The protagonist becomes significant not as the tragic victim of circumstances, the romantic hero in conflict and revolt against his environment, but as a kind of polar instrument round which the events of life are grouped, by means of which they are touched, explained, and apprehended, by means of which they are seen and ordered."[11]

In this respect *You Can't Go Home Again* is markedly similar to the work of Herman Melville—a writer to whom Wolfe's debts have not been fully acknowledged. In fact, structurally there are remarkable parallels between the works of the two men. Melville's protagonists are usually minor actors in his works, and the dramatic action is centered on other characters whom the protagonist observes. The weight of interpretation rests upon this almost passive but observing narrator and is more a function of style and metaphysical conceit than of action. This characteristic is obvious in *Moby-Dick*, where from time to time Ishmael almost becomes Emerson's "transparent eyeball," through whom we view Captain Ahab and his quest. Yet Ishmael comes from the voyage of the *Pequod* having learned not Ahab's course but the error of it. A similar role is played by Redburn, by White-Jacket, and by Taji in *Mardi* (although Melville apparently gives the final answer to Babbalanja in that work). When Melville, in *Pierre*, shifts from the first-person discursive narrator to the third person many of the difficulties which we also encounter in Wolfe appear, including the great problem of distinguishing between the attitudes held by Pierre Glendenning and those held by the author. The result is that *Pierre* is often called autobiographical in a derogatory sense. Wolfe's effort to use a first-person narrator in *Of Time and the River*—an effort defeated by his publishers—would have resolved the similar problem in this work to a substantial extent. *You Can't Go Home Again* would also have benefited very much from first-person narration; indeed, the last section shifts to the first person, but so late that the reader has the mistaken impression that it is Wolfe speaking directly rather than George Webber.

The essential vision of this personality is that of the provincial, middle-class American. Wolfe had grown up in a small southern mountain town, close to the towering hills and responding intensely to the natural forms of beauty around him. He had absorbed from the sociopolitical Populism which was still strong in North Carolina during his childhood and youth a democratic liberalism, and he brought to bear upon his people a criticism—very much like that of Sinclair Lewis—both mocking and loving. This attitude is shown in the satire of *Look Homeward, Angel*, where the young artist simply rejects the ugliness and materialism of the environment in which he lives, dreaming of shining cities, distant people, and inevitable triumphs.

The structure of *Look Homeward, Angel* and the maturing of the protagonist are consonant; between the outer view of society and the inner seeking of the soul there is a shared and constant dream, the aspiring dream of every middle-class provincial American boy who has turned his back upon home to seek triumphs in the citadels of culture and power. *Look Homeward, Angel* is structurally the most satisfying of Wolfe's novels not only because the *Bildungsroman* has a built-in pattern and wholeness but also because the American boy's dream is at its center—a dream not yet torn by fundamental doubts; its realization is not only possible, it seems almost within the outstretched, grasping fingers.

But Gant-Webber moves from the hill-encircled world of his childhood into a series of persistent disillusionments. He greets the enfabled rock of Manhattan with a joyous cry, only to discover that

91

it harbors cruelty, falseness, and betrayal. He seeks friendship with a limber-wristed aesthete, Francis Starwick, and only when the fact is driven home with a force so great that it can no longer be resisted does he acknowledge that Starwick is a homosexual. He visits Europe, but everywhere the promised order is denied him. He goes to Hitler's Germany and finds himself the darling of a great capital city; it takes him a while to recognize beneath the orderliness, the beauty, the symmetry, the green faerie world of the Tiergarten and the efficiency of the city trams, that there is the calamity of man's injustice and hatred, the bitter desire to emasculate and to destroy, and so he must bid farewell to "the other part of his heart's home." But it is America caught in the bitter struggle of the Depression that put his dream to its most severe test and converted it into a nightmare of poverty and suffering.

Like Whitman, whom he resembles more than he does any other American writer, Wolfe celebrates the beauty and glory of his native land, the wonder and grandeur of its towering mountains and its rolling plains. Like Whitman he makes music from the names of places and people, streams and towns. Like Whitman he sees himself as a representative American. But like the Whitman of *Democratic Vistas*, Wolfe, too, sees the cancerous growth that gnaws away at the body politic. Wherever he turns he finds hungry men, mistreated men, men weighed down by injustice. How to reconcile the two—the glorious promise of America and the injustice, cruelty, and oppression of America—becomes for him both a personal problem and an artistic dilemma.

You Can't Go Home Again is the record of the ultimate failure of that effort at reconciliation. When Wolfe moves from the focus on the individual to a focus on society, he needs something other than the coexistence of these attitudes. Either they must be reconciled or one must triumph over the other. Or if they are to be held in balance, they must be treated with equal force and dramatic conviction. It is not enough to have one dramatized and the other rhetorically expressed.

Wolfe's view of the American nightmare, pretty clearly grounded in his attitude toward the economic system, is the middle-class Agrarian view opposed to industrial capitalism. George Webber says at one place in *You Can't Go Home Again*: "Sometimes it seems to me ... that America went off the track somewhere—back around the time of the Civil War, or pretty soon afterwards. Instead of going ahead and developing along the line in which the country started out, it got shunted off in another direction—and now we look around and see we've gone places we didn't mean to go. Suddenly we realize that America has turned into something ugly—and vicious—and corroded at the heart of its power with easy wealth and graft and special privilege."[12] *You Can't Go Home Again* is a record of that wrong track, told in the form of almost disjointed episodes of disillusionment and failure.

You Can't Go Home Again consists in large part of materials originally written as self-contained units—"Boom Town," "The World That Jack Built," and " 'I Have a Thing to Tell You.' " As a result sections like Books III and IV and the conclusion, where the hortatory and rhetorical voice of the author, either thinly disguised as George Webber or in several cases not disguised at all, are more different in mode from the dramatic than such passages had been in the earlier novels. One is inclined to say that in fact in their present form such passages are not representative of their author's intentions—as indeed Hamilton Basso declared upon the publication of the book[13] and many others, including Richard S. Kennedy,[14] have noted since. But I fear they are letting Wolfe off a little more easily than they are justified in doing. There are, in fact, two thematic elements in the novel—thematic elements that are not truly congenial—and each is expressed in a distinctly different stylistic mode, so that we can with some justice say that *You Can't Go Home Again* is a mixture of rhetorical hope and dramatic despair. The rhetorical passages and the dramatic scenes in *You Can't Go Home Again* differ from the earlier books also in subject matter. In this novel what Webber does and thinks matters less than what he sees: hence there is a much stronger social content in the action of the book. And the rhetorical sections, which in the earlier books had elaborated upon the emotions surrounding events as the "timeless valley" section at the end of Chapter 30 does in *Look Homeward, Angel*, tend here to express more abstract attitudes about the social world, as the famous "Credo" that closes the novel does.

The increasing presence of these disparate elements largely resulted, I think, from Wolfe's growing concern with the outer world and its problems, a concern that led him frequently to use a kind of incident that appears only occasionally in the earlier works. The life which had impressed itself hauntingly upon his mind during the years of his maturity, it must be remembered, was the life of Depression-stricken America. He knew it through the suffering of his own family in Asheville, a suffering which he portrayed in the last five chapters of the first book and in Chapters 25 and 26 of *You Can't Go Home Again*; and he knew it through direct observation in Brooklyn and Manhattan. In *The Story of a Novel* he is very explicit about what he saw in New York during the Depression:

> Everywhere around me . . . I saw the evidence of an incalculable ruin and suffering. My own people, the members of my own family had been ruined, had lost all the material wealth and accumulation of a lifetime. . . . And that universal calamity had somehow struck the life of almost everyone I knew. Moreover, in this endless quest and prowling of the night through the great web and jungle of the city, I saw, lived, felt, and experienced the full weight of that horrible human calamity.
>
> I saw a man whose life had subsided into a mass of shapeless and filthy rags, devoured by vermin; wretches huddled together for a little warmth in freezing cold squatting in doorless closets upon the foul seat of a public latrine within the very shadow, the cold shelter of palatial and stupendous monuments of wealth. I saw acts of sickening violence and cruelty, the menace of brute privilege, a cruel and corrupt authority trampling ruthlessly below its feet the lives of the poor, the weak, the wretched, and the defenseless of the earth.[15]

You Can't Go Home Again tells of George Webber's life in Brooklyn; of the real-estate boom and collapse in his hometown, Libya

Hill; in a complex and carefully wrought short novel, of the world of the very rich in contrast to that of the laboring classes that serve it; of the disillusionment that follows Webber's success as a novelist; of his journey to England and of a meeting with a famous novelist, Lloyd McHarg—Sinclair Lewis under very thin disguise—who shows him the emptiness of fame; in a tightly constructed short novel, of his love for Germany and his sense of its evil, and finally— in a letter to his editor—a statement of what he feels his credo to be. It is loaded with dramatic pictures of the nightmare world which Wolfe believes America in the Depression to be. And, as he usually does, Wolfe makes his statements through representative characters, through typical actions, through descriptive passages that become vignettes that express his meaning, and most emphatically through direct rhetorical assertion. To a startling degree the dream in *You Can't Go Home Again* is expressed through rhetorical assertion, and the nightmare through dramatic presentation. The nightmare makes the more powerful impact, although the dream may be more quotable.

Wolfe seems to see a common—and simplistic—basis for the darkness that engulfs the American dream, and an examination of a few of the dramatic modes in the novel points to it. Four characters, each indicative of the failure of the promise, show a distorted way of life. Judge Rumford Bland, the syphilitic blind man, who embodies much of the best tradition of the South of his boyhood and yet is totally corrupt, appears only briefly in the novel, when Webber meets him on the train to Libya Hill. His background has to be dragged in as remembrance, yet he is certainly a powerful representative of his culture. He makes his living through the most cruel and usurious lending to Negroes. He has an office as an attorney in a disreputable building within thirty yards of the city hall, and he is a creature of the night. Though he was an able man, there was, Wolfe wrote, "something genuinely old and corrupt at the sources of his life and spirit." But he added, "At the very moment that [people] met him, and felt the force of death and evil working in him, they also felt—

oh, call it the phantom, the radiance, the lost soul, of an enormous virtue. And with the recognition of that quality came the sudden stab of overwhelming regret."[16]

Another figure of this nightmare evil is Adolf Hitler, "the dark messiah." Webber—and Wolfe—had felt at first in Germany that "it was no foreign land to him," and there he had tasted the intoxication of great acclaim. It was not easy for him finally to see in *Der Führer*, who had brought such great material order to Germany, the "shipwreck of a great spirit." He wrote of Webber's experience: "The poisonous emanations of suppression, persecution, and fear permeated the air like miasmic and pestilential vapors, tainting, sickening, and blighting the lives of everyone he met. It was a plague of the spirit—invisible, but as unmistakable as death."[17]

Another is Mr. Merrit, the representative of the Federal Weight, Scales, and Computing Company, who was all Rotarian smiles and good fellowship but who, when overheard tongue-lashing Webber's friend Randy Shepperton, gave George the feeling that he was "in some awful nightmare when he visions someone he knows doing some perverse and abominable act." When later Randy tries to explain that Merrit has to do these things because "he—he's with the Company," Webber remembers a picture he had seen

... portraying a long line of men stretching from the Great Pyramid to the very portals of great Pharaoh's house, and great Pharaoh stood with a thonged whip in his hand and applied it unmercifully to the bare back and shoulders of the man in front of him, who was great Pharaoh's chief overseer, and in the hand of the overseer was a whip of many tails which he unstintedly applied to the quivering back of the wretch before him, who was the chief overseer's chief lieutenant, and in the lieutenant's hand a whip of rawhide which he laid vigorously on the quailing body of his head sergeant, and in the sergeant's hand a wicked flail with which he belabored a whole company of groaning corporals, and in the hands of every corporal a knotted lash with which to whack a whole regiment of slaves.[18]

Still another is Mr. Frederick Jack, Wall Street financier, living in great luxury and playing with stocks and dollars in a vast and amusing gamble. Speaking of such speculators, Wolfe said, "They bought, sold, and traded in an atmosphere fraught with frantic madness. . . . it was one of the qualities of this time that men should see and feel the madness all around them and never mention it—never admit it even to themselves." At the other end of this mad gamble of speculation is a figure absurd enough to be in a contemporary black comedy, Libya Hill's town sot, old Tim Wagner—"diseased and broken . . . his wits were always addled now with alcohol," but the word had gotten around among real-estate speculators that he had a mysterious power of financial intuition, so the men of the town "used him as men once used divining rods," and he rode in a magnificent car with a liveried chauffeur, and moved with "princely indolence."[19]

All these men are exploiters, but Wolfe has too a large gallery of the exploited. They include Randy Shepperton, a kind and generous man; the anonymous citizens of Libya Hill who are swept under in the collapse; the servants at Jack's upon whom the success of his personal life depends; Mr. C. Green, who commits suicide by leaping from the Admiral Drake Hotel and only in that violent moment elicits attention to the gray cipher which his life has been; Lloyd McHarg, Nobel Prize novelist for whom world fame is not enough and who constantly tastes bitter ashes on his tongue.

The two finest sections of the book were originally written as short novels—"The World That Jack Built" and " 'I Have a Thing to Tell You.' " "The World That Jack Built"—the title is a pun—is a 175-page account of a great party given by Mr. and Mrs. Frederick Jack just a week before the stock market collapse which precipitated the Depression. This novella is Wolfe's best and most objective piece of sustained narrative. It is rich in social satire, in portraits of people from all classes, and in interlinked symbols that carry a heavy freight of meaning. The party ends in a fire which drives the guests and apartment house residents into a courtyard where for a moment they feel a sense of community; the fire also takes the lives of two gentle, kindly elevator operators, one old and one young, but both of whom believe in the economic system. Wolfe was here attempting to imprison a view of a society in a single complex social act, modeling his effort on Proust's *Sodom et Gomorrah*.[20] At the conclusion he comes to a direct judgment of the people of this world. He sees them as gifted and personally honorable, but he condemns "their complaisance about themselves and about their life, their loss of faith in anything better." Webber is at what he realizes to be the apex of one aspect of his dream—the highest point of success and acceptance by the world's great—yet he is dismayed rather than delighted: "Now to have the selfless grandeur turn to dust, and to see great night itself a reptile coiled and waiting at the heart of life! . . . To find man's faith betrayed and his betrayers throned in honor, themselves the idols of his bartered faith!" [21]

But there is another aspect of Wolfe's work which can best be understood if we contrast him with John Dos Passos, a writer with whom social historians often link him, as a novelist of the 1930s deeply concerned with the quality of experience in that anguished decade. Such a comparison is apt, for both writers attempted to imprison a record of American life in long, ambitious works with many formal oddities, works that can be called novels only if the term is loosely used. Henry Steele Commager has said that "Dos Passos was the most social minded of the major novelists" between the two world wars and that "Thomas Wolfe's quarrel with his society remained . . . personal and . . . artistic." [22] But the differences go deeper than this. Dos Passos belonged, as Alfred Kazin has noted, to "those American writers from the upper class, born on the eve of our century . . . [who] were brought up in . . . the last stable period in American history" [23] and whose dreams of an admirable order were betrayed by the First World War, so that they left its battlefields, where they had been ambulance drivers and Red Cross workers, with a profound sense of disillusionment. Wolfe, on the other hand, was born into a middle-middle-class family in which his personal security seemed threatened by intense domestic schisms, with the result that, despite an overly possessive mother, he appeared always to have seen himself as alone and defenseless.[24] Furthermore, he grew up in a small southern provincial city, imbibed from his closest companions—the books he read—most of the ideals of a standard middle-class world, was educated in a state university which he regarded as a wilderness outpost of "great Rome," and was too young to participate in the war, which—like many young middle-class sixteen- and seventeen-year-olds of the time—he romanticized as the last chivalric crusade.[25]

Furthermore, the long years of introspection which culminated in the lyrical *Look Homeward, Angel* pretty effectively shut him off—except for the fairly superficial satire of the Sinclair Lewis type—from a critical examination of the postulates of middle-class America. He vigorously declared himself not to be of the "Lost Generation," and could, on occasion, in letters and elsewhere, attack the critics of American life with all the pride of a Rotarian and the unquestioning energy of the provincial.[26] When, in the loneliness of Europe, he discovered that America was his subject, the America he discovered was still tied for him in powerful ways to the nineteenth-century dream which had gone up in the holocaust of the world war for writers like John Dos Passos, Ernest Hemingway, E. E. Cummings, and Edmund Wilson.

Hence, to the end, Wolfe held firmly to a belief in America that was of a different dimension and quality from that of his contemporaries, while he portrayed in telling detail in his pictures of the life around him many of the assumptions and despairs of the Depression world he inhabited. Expressed another way, Wolfe moved physically and artistically out into the great world of Boston, New York, and Europe, but he remained a sojourner rather than a native, a spectator rather than a participant, an observer rather than a true believer in the postulates of this larger world he inhabited for most of his adult life. Hence he brought the childlike vision of experience continuingly to bear on a steadily widening world, and therein lay one of his greatest powers; but he also brought to bear on the complexities of commitment in that larger world the simpler and uninstructed faith of the Populist democracy in which his social and political being had been nurtured. What he saw and what he believed came into increasingly tormented conflict, and he neither felt the need nor had the time in which to reconcile them. But he did have two methods of writing which allowed him in the late years to do a kind of justice to both vision and belief. That they rent the ideological fabric of his work would, I think, have bothered him relatively little.

Again the contrast with John Dos Passos is illuminating. In *U.S.A.* Dos Passos attempted to make the dynamics of history in his time the fundamental structure of his work, and he brought to it fresh and complex techniques—the Newsreels, the case histories of fictional representative Americans, and the biographical sketches of real persons who embodied common beliefs or attitudes. Along with these objective treatments Dos Passos included another mode of statement, "the Camera Eye," which gives us a lyrical and intense expression of the author's attitudes and emotions at the time of the action of the story. The Camera Eye sections are not fixed in some later time; they record the growing disillusionment of the author, as he encounters a world of widening experience. He moves from the child's view in "The Camera Eye (7)" which ends: "we clean young American Rover Boys handy with tools Deerslayers played hockey Boy Scouts and cut figure eights on the ice Achilles Ajax Agamemnon I couldn't learn to skate and kept falling down"[27] to the despair of "The Camera Eye (50)" which begins "they have clubbed us off the streets   they are stronger   they are rich" and reaches the ultimate expression of rejection in:

all right we are two nations
America our nation has been beaten by strangers who have bought the laws and fenced off the meadows and cut down the woods for pulp and turned our pleasant cities into slums and sweated the wealth out of our people.[28]

Wolfe presented dramatic pictures of that same world, pictures which portrayed it in terms not significantly different from those of Dos Passos. But Wolfe's are drawn not objectively by experimental methods but directly as the experience of his increasingly faceless protagonist. When the author Wolfe wishes to speak, he does so directly, and from time to time we are confused as to whether he intends his remarks to be comments on the protagonist's experience or comments by the protagonist. These rhetorical comments reflect Wolfe's relatively static view and are seemingly fixed in the present rather than the time of action of the book. In Dos Passos' metaphor, the lens setting of Wolfe's camera eye undergoes surprisingly little adjustment as the book progresses.

I suppose this is what Robert Penn Warren was talking about when he made his famous wisecrack about Wolfe: "It may be well to recollect that Shakespeare merely wrote *Hamlet*; he was *not* Hamlet." [29] But that remark is actually more scintillating than sensible; for the genres in which the two writers worked are radically dissimilar. Wolfe *did* choose both to play Hamlet and to write it, for his great subject was the impact of the world on a protagonist frankly quite like himself. In Shakespeare's play there is action and there is rhetoric; the action is Shakespeare's presentation of Hamlet's world; the rhetoric is Hamlet's (and others') interpretation of that world. I suppose what bothers us about *You Can't Go Home Again* is that what George Webber sees and what happens to him is very much like Hamlet's description of the world as

> an unweeded garden,
> That grows to seed; things rank and gross in nature
> Possess it merely. [30]

Yet many of his remarks about it, his rhetorical flourishes, smack a little too much of Polonius—or, to be fairer, of Walt Whitman evoking the spirit of America and its promise.

It is significant, I think, that when Wolfe, in *The Story of a Novel*, describes the growth of the impulse that led him to see America as his proper subject, that launched him on an artistic effort that has marked similarities to that of the epic poet, he assigns the motive force to loneliness and a haunting sense of loss. This occurred in Europe, and Wolfe says, "I discovered America during these years abroad out of my very need of her. The huge gain of this discovery seemed to come directly from my sense of loss." And he adds a little later, "Now my memory was at work night and day, in a way that I could at first neither check nor control and that swarmed unbidden in a stream of blazing pageantry across my mind, with the million forms and substances of the life that I had left, which was my own, America."[31] In a sense, then, the substance of Wolfe's work was America recollected in nostalgia. Even *You Can't Go Home Again* primarily describes events that occurred in 1929 and 1930 (the German episode is later but it is unique in this respect), but he views them from the vantage point of a later time. Indeed, Wolfe's whole concept of time in the novel required that a sense of the past and the present commingle against an awareness of eternity: thus he shares with Dos Passos a great interest in time and history, but in his case it is history viewed more philosophically than socially.

In *You Can't Go Home Again* Wolfe skillfully uses the novelist's basic tool, character, to portray his world and its corruption. Judge Rumford Bland, whom everyone instinctively knew to be evil, is a microcosmic representation of the town of Libya Hill. Randy Shepperton is the average American caught in the Depression, and Wolfe is very explicit about it. He says, "Behind Randy's tragedy George thought he could see a personal devil in the form of a very bright and plausible young man, oozing confidence and crying 'Faith!' when there was no faith. . . . And it seemed to George that Randy's tragedy was the essential tragedy of America." Mr. Jack epitomizes the capitalistic system, and again Wolfe is explicit: Mr. Jack enjoyed, he says, "the privilege of men selected from the common run because of some mysterious intuition they were supposed to have." And he adds, "It seemed to Mr. Jack . . . not only entirely reasonable but even natural that the whole structure of society from top to bottom should be honeycombed with privilege and dishonesty." Amy Carleton, rich millionairess of many marriages and of total moral collapse, symbolizes the decay of high society. Wolfe writes, "It seemed, therefore, that her wealth and power and feverish energy could get her anything she wanted . . . [But] The end could only be destruction, and the mark of destruction was already apparent upon her." And C. Green is a type of all the nameless, faceless people who are the victims of an inhuman system in an unseeing city. Of him Wolfe declares: "He was life's little man, life's nameless cipher, life's manswarm atom, life's American—and now he lies disjected and exploded on a street in Brooklyn! He was a dweller in mean streets . . . a man-mote in the jungle of the city, a resident of grimy steel and stone, a mole who burrowed in rusty brick." And the indictment does not stop with people, but extends to descriptions of scenes and actions. Of a hill in Libya Hill he writes: "It had been one of the pleasantest places in the town, but now it was gone. An army of men and shovels had advanced upon this beautiful green hill and had leveled it down to an ugly flat of clay, and had paved it with a desolate horror of white concrete, and had built stores and office buildings and parking spaces—all raw and new." [32]

In a vignette that defines his position well he writes of Libya Hill, effectively embodying in a series of images what seems to have been a fundamental position for him:

The air brooded with a lazy, drowsy warmth. There was the last evening cry of robins, and the thrumming bullet noises in undergrowth and leaf, and broken sounds from far away—a voice in the wind, a boy's shout, the barking of a dog, the tinkle of a cow bell. There was the fragrance of intoxicating odors—the resinous smell of pine, and the smells of grass and warm sweet clover. All this was just as it had always been. But the town of his childhood, with its quiet streets and old houses which had been almost obscured below the leafy spread of trees, was changed past recognition, scarred now with hard patches of bright concrete and raw clumps of new construction. It looked like a battlefield, cratered and shell-torn with savage explosions of brick, cement, and harsh new stucco. And in the interspaces only the embowered remnants of the old and pleasant town remained—timid, retreating, overwhelmed —to remind one of the liquid leather shuffle in the quiet streets at noon when the men came home to lunch, and of laughter and low voices in the leafy rustle of the night. For this was lost![33]

Nazi Germany, with its old dark evil, comes finally to symbolize for him the end of the path on which America also is traveling. "It was," he says, "a picture of the Dark Ages come again—shocking beyond belief, but true as the hell that man forever creates for himself." And he adds, "I realized fully, for the first time, how sick America was, and saw, too, that the ailment was akin to Germany's— a dread world-sickness of the soul." This condition of sickness strikes George Webber with a sense of profound disillusionment. Wolfe declares: "To find man's faith betrayed and his betrayers throned in honor, themselves the idols of his bartered faith! To find truth false and falsehood truth, good evil, evil good, and the whole web of life so changing, so mercurial! It was so different from the way he had once thought it would be—and suddenly, convulsively, forgetful of his surroundings, he threw out his arms in an instinctive gesture of agony and loss." This despair comes to one who, Wolfe says, knew "that if he was ever to succeed in writing the books he felt were in him, he must turn about and lift his face up to some nobler height." For Wolfe the writers of his time were people each of whom "had accepted part of life for the whole ... some little personal interest for the large and all-embracing interest of mankind." And Webber asked himself, "If that happened to him, how, then, could he sing America?"[34]

Yet sing America Wolfe did. In spite of all he saw about him, he remained more totally committed to the nineteenth-century American dream of an egalitarian society than any other major American novelist of this century, and at place after place in his novels he employed his great gift for poetic language to create ringing assertions of hope for the success of that democracy. A part of that faith was a still unshaken belief in man himself. In a long section, "The Locusts Have No King," he writes:

This is man: for the most part a foul, wretched, abominable . . . hater of his kind, a cheater, a scorner, a mocker, a reviler, a thing that kills and murders in a mob or in the dark. . . .
[But] Behold his works:
He needed speech to ask for bread—and he had Christ! He needed songs to sing in battle—and he had Homer! . . . He needed walls and a roof to shelter him—so he made Blois! . . . It is impossible to scorn this creature. For out of his strong belief in life, this puny man made love. At his best, he *is* love. Without him there can be no love, no hunger, no desire.[35]

And he extends this faith to America in one of his two or three best known passages, one that is written in a very Whitmanesque context, that of being seated at night on the hackles of the Rocky Mountains and looking to East and West and thus gaining a vast continental vision. He concludes: "So, then, to every man his chance—to every man, regardless of his birth, his shining, golden opportunity—to every man the right to live, to work, to be himself and to become whatever thing his manhood and his vision can combine to make him—this, seeker, is the promise of America." Even in these ecstatic moments, he is not blind or forgetful of the dark canker at the heart of his native land, but this evil is an enemy whose triumph is unthinkable to Wolfe: "I think," he says, "the enemy is here before us, too. But I think we know the forms and faces of the enemy, and in the knowledge that we know him, and shall meet him, and eventually must conquer him is also our living hope."[36] His final judgment of America is one that Whitman would have applauded:

I believe that we are lost here in America, but I believe we shall be found. And this belief, which mounts now to the catharsis of knowledge and conviction, is for me—and I think for all of us—not only our own hope but America's everlasting, living dream. . . . America and the people in it are deathless, undiscovered, and immortal, and must live.
I think the true discovery of America is before us. . . . I think the true discovery of our own democracy is still before us. And I think that all these things are certain as the morning, as inevitable as noon.[37]

These are magnificent words and they express a confidence in man, a faith in democracy, and an allegiance to America and its old dream which it is heartening to hear. Who else of all our writers since Whitman has celebrated man and America with a nobler rhetoric and a more inspiriting assurance? But, as I have already suggested, these sentiments—and I think that Wolfe meant them from the bottom of his heart—are asserted in rhetorical passages rather than exemplified in the episodes of the novel. They come in sections of hortatory prose and are appropriately poetic rather than dramatic in rhythm and in content. The separation between action and idea, which we observed beginning in passages such as the "Unbroken Spinet" rhapsody, is here almost complete. The novelist portrays a dispiriting and despairing world, but the poet-seer lifts his voice to chant the ideal and the promise of America.

Few of us would want to dispense with the dramatic scenes that make *You Can't Go Home Again* a book of truly splendid fragments. And few of us would want to give up the firm assertion of the American dream and possibility which this provincial man kept somehow unsullied through all his contacts with the Depression world. I also suspect that few of us would seriously question that *You Can't Go Home Again* would have been a different and a far better work had Thomas Wolfe lived to find a way of putting the visionary dream and the disillusioning view of man into some harmonious relationship to each other.

Max Lerner has declared that Wolfe's prevailing mood is "the sense of being ravaged and lost, yet finding some ... assertion of life's meaning."[38] And J. B. Priestley, writing admiringly of Wolfe's position in the great tradition of western literature, declared, "No matter how piercing and appalling his insights, the desolation creeping over his outer world, the lurid lights and shadows of his inner world, the writer must live with hope, work in faith."[39] Though imperfectly, Wolfe shored up hope against the ultimate despair, and fixed our eyes for the moment on distant goals and noble aspirations.

VI   The Web of the South

WHEN THOMAS WOLFE went north after his graduation from the University of North Carolina, he went as a southerner, to write of southern subjects in George Pierce Baker's "47 Workshop" at Harvard, and to compose his first novel out of the southern scenes of his childhood with an autobiographical candor and an accuracy shocking to the residents of his native city. Yet Thomas Wolfe never returned for long to the South, once he had left it—indeed, he declared that "you can't go home again"—and some critics have believed, as Maxwell Geismar suggested, that Wolfe "was born in the South, but he shared with it little except the accident of his birth."[1]

In his sprawling, loosely constructed tales and novels, he heaped a gargantuan scorn upon his native region, condemning what in *Look Homeward, Angel* he called the southerners' "hostile and murderous intrenchment against all new life . . . their cheap mythology, their legend of the charm of their manner, the aristocratic culture of their lives, the quaint sweetness of their drawl."[2] In *The Web and the Rock*, betraying his mingled disgust and sense of shame, he expresses his anger at "the old, stricken, wounded 'Southness' of cruelty and lust," at men who "have a starved, stricken leanness in the loins," and at the lynchings that end with castrations. The southern intellectual fared little better in Wolfe's novels. He had contempt for the Agrarians whom he called in *The Web and the Rock* "the refined young gentlemen of the New Confederacy . . . [who]

retired haughtily into the South, to the academic security of a teaching appointment at one of the universities, from which they could
issue in quarterly installments very small and very precious magazines which celebrated the advantages of an agrarian society." And
he wrote with feeling in the same novel of "the familiar rationalizing
and self-defense of Southern fear and Southern failure: its fear of
conflict and of competition in the greater world; its inability to meet
or to adjust itself to the conditions, strifes, and ardors of a modern
life; its old, sick, Appomattox-like retreat into the shades of folly
and delusion, of prejudice and bigotry, of florid legend and defen-
sive casuistry . . ." [3]

This South was feminine to him—what he called once *"the female
principle*—the *earth* again . . . a home, fixity"[4]—and in his thinking
he opposed it to the father principle, which, in *The Story of a Novel*,
he called "the image of a strength and wisdom external to his need
and superior to his hunger, to which the belief and power of his own
life could be united."[5] From the maternal and subjective South, "the
dark Helen of his blood," he turned to storm the male citadels of the
North and to find in the "enfabled rock" of the northern city a defense against the web of the South. Yet this South beat in his brain and
pounded in his veins. "Every young man from the South," he said
in *The Web and the Rock*, "has felt this precise and formal geog-
raphy of the spirit," in which South and North are sharply dichoto-
mized autonomies; and the qualities in young southerners brought
to the North "a warmth you lacked, a passion that God knows you
needed, a belief and a devotion that was wanting in your life, an integrity of purpose that was rare in your own swarming hordes. They
brought . . . some of the warmth, the depth and mystery. . . . They
brought a warmth of earth, an exultant joy of youth, a burst of living
laughter, a fullbodied warmth and living energy of humor."[6] Wolfe
could proudly boast in a letter to James Boyd, "I'm a Long Hunter
from Bear Creek, and a rootin', tootin', shootin' son-of-a-gun from
North Carolina"; and he could write Maxwell Perkins that "The
people in North Carolina . . . are rich, juicy, deliberate, full of pun-

gent and sardonic humor and honesty, conservative and cautious on top, but at bottom wild, savage, and full of the murderous innocence of the earth and the wilderness."[7] What he said of his character George Webber is true of Wolfe himself: "He was a Southerner, and he knew that there was something wounded in the South. He knew that there was something twisted, dark, and full of pain which Southerners have known all their lives—something rooted in their souls beyond all contradiction."[8] But all his knowledge of her darkness and damnation could not completely stifle his love for the lost and ruined and burning Helen in his blood.

That his vision of his native region was both obsessive and ambiguous was not surprising. Wolfe was born to a northern father and a southern mother, and the division of life into male and female, North and South, wanderer and homebound, was a simple extension of what he saw daily as a boy. He grew up in a southern mountain town, but at a time when it was changing into a resort city, flourishing in the shadow of the baronial estate of the Vanderbilts, the pseudo-French chateau "Biltmore," and literally mad for money. He went to college at Chapel Hill, a southern state university, but at the time when that school was beginning the pattern of liberalism that made it the symbol of New South progressivism, completely opposite to the agrarianism of Vanderbilt University. Ambiguous and contradictory though his views of his native region were, the South was a theme and a subject for much of Wolfe's work, and it existed for him in a sensuous, irrational, emotional state of mutual attraction and repulsion. And this contradiction and ambiguity, this coexisting intense love and passionate hatred are characteristic not only of Wolfe's attitudes toward the South but also of his total work.

Few American novelists have projected more ambitious programs or had more demanding plans for their novels. The motive force of his works seems to have been his desire to express the elements of a universal experience, and this universal experience was for him closely tied up with the national, the American experience. That the elements which made up his all-encompassing effort were woven from the filaments of his self and that that self was both woven and torn by his southern heritage should be beyond dispute; but in the interest of illuminating a little of both Wolfe and the literature of his region it may be worth while to point to some of the southern qualities in his work.

The urge to represent America, to embody it in a work of art, although by no means unique to the region, has been persistent in southern literature. The southerners of the antebellum period often raised their voices in support of a native literature and stood with the "Young America" group of critics in their intensely nationalistic demands for art in the 1840s and 1850s, despite the serious political differences between them and the New York critics. They distrusted the "internationalism" of New Englanders like Longfellow and of New Yorkers like the editors of the *Knickerbocker Magazine*. Yet these southerners were aware that the nation could better be represented by drawing its particularities than by picturing the whole. In 1856, for example, William Gilmore Simms, of South Carolina, had written: "To be *national* in literature, one must needs be *sectional*. No one mind can fully or fairly illustrate the characteristics of any great country; and he who shall depict *one section* faithfully, has made his proper and sufficient contribution to the great work of national literature."[9] This view is not far from Wolfe's own, when he insists upon the representation of his unique self as the proper subject for a national art. Wolfe was like Thoreau, who said, "I should not talk so much about myself if there were any body else whom I knew as well. Unfortunately, I am confined to this theme by the narrowness of my experience."[10] However, for Wolfe, the observation of his fellow men was a basic part of that experience, as it was not for Thoreau.

It is also typical of the southern writer that this epic portrayal of America should constitute a project of great magnitude and tremendous complexity. Wolfe's letters, *Notebooks*, and *The Story of a Novel* carry the evidence of the vastness of scope and the complexity of design of the "work in progress" on which he expended his days and hours and which he left incomplete. It is startling to one who has accepted the standard view of Wolfe's work as the spontaneous and unpremeditated overflow of the author's powerful feeling, recollected in abnormal intensity, to find him writing to Maxwell Perkins, "I think you may be a little inclined to underestimate the importance of arrangement and presentation, and may feel that the stories can go in any way, and that the order doesn't matter much." In the light of his efforts to get on paper the theme, the argument, the structure of the large work as he labored on its parts, such a statement—although it does not redeem his novels from formlessness—makes poignant and telling Wolfe's protests against the publication of *Of Time and the River* in the form in which Perkins sent it to press.[11]

This large design would have traced the history of the Pentlands (or, later, the Joyners) from the Civil War to the present, emphasizing the southern roots of the generic hero. It would have included thousands of characters and episodes—the whole, Wolfe said, to be "seen *not by a definite personality*, but haunted throughout by a consciousness of *personality*,"[12] and that personality was to be the perceptive "self" through whom the writer could know and express his America. Before a work of such magnitude as he projected, time became the great enemy. The scope of his ambitious plan—which was to be no less than the record of his nation and his people told through one representative man—merits in its magnitude comparison with the master projects of literary history, with those of Balzac, Zola, and Tolstoy. To embark upon such vast projects has also been typically, although by no means exclusively, southern, perhaps because the southerner tends to distrust abstraction and to doubt that one can see a "World in a Grain of Sand/And a Heaven in a Wild Flower." Whatever the reason, southern writers have tended to plan work of enormous scope, such as Simms's seven linked volumes of historical fiction on the Revolution; James Branch Cabell's many-volumed and incomplete record of Poictesme; Ellen Glasgow's fictional record in thirteen volumes of Virginia's social history from the Civil War to the 1940s (whether or not such a structure was her original intention or a design she imposed after a good portion of the fact); and William Faulkner's vast record of Yoknapatawpha County. Wolfe, like these other southerners, set himself a task that staggers the imagination and defies the reality of time. Little wonder that Faulkner considered him among the greatest of American writers because he dared the most.

Near the beginning of his first novel Wolfe wrote, "Subtract us into nakedness and night again, and you shall see begin in Crete four thousand years ago the love that ended yesterday in Texas. . . . Each moment is the fruit of forty thousand years."[13] This concern with time grew more intense as his career developed. The artist's problem, he believed, is the resolution of a three-fold consciousness of time into a single moment so that scenes can represent "characters as acting and as being acted upon by all the accumulated impact of man's experience so that each moment of their lives was conditioned not only by what they experienced in that moment, but by all that they had experienced up to that moment."[14] Whether or not Wolfe is indebted to Proust and Bergson for these ideas, he certainly envisions his characters as set in a complex fabric of time, and their actions as having remote roots and immeasurable forward extensions. Louis D. Rubin, Jr., has noted that "The interplay of past and present, of the historical and the contemporaneous, causes all the modern Southern writers to be unusually sensitive to the nature and workings of time."[15] This interplay is one of the basic materials of Wolfe's fiction.

Wolfe shares with many southern writers his concerns with the reality of the past in the present and with the nature of time. One can find examples of the southern writer's concern with time and his belief that it is not only fact or sequence, but, more important, a key to the nature of human experience, in Robert Penn Warren, particularly in *The Ballad of Billie Potts* and *World Enough and Time*; in Ellen Glasgow; in the elaborate dislocations of time sequence in many of Faulkner's narratives; in Allen Tate's "Ode to the Confederate Dead;" in the inverted structure of William Styron's *Lie Down in Darkness*; in Eudora Welty's *Losing Battles*; and in many other places. It is not surprising that one of Wolfe's best-known short stories should be "Chickamauga" and that the novel fragment on which he was working at the time of his death, *The Hills Beyond*, deals with his southern ancestors in the nineteenth century. Among twentieth-century American novelists only the southerners have with any frequency treated the past outside the pattern of romance and adventure. Faulkner, Warren, Glasgow, and Cabell have written extensively with a historical orientation.

The mixture of styles in which Wolfe wrote is also not uncommon in southern writing. On one level Wolfe illustrates with great effectiveness the concrete, the immediate, the sensuous. It is this quality in his work that gives many of his pages an intensity which almost approximates direct experience. This lyric aspect of his writing, in which the object is evoked with such power that it seems to be rubbed against the reader's exposed nerve ends, this ability to make "the world's body" vividly real, succeeds again and again in giving the reader new insights; in Wolfe's terms, in making "the utterly familiar, common thing ... suddenly be revealed ... with all the wonder with which we discover a thing which we have seen all our life and yet have never known before." A passage from *Of Time and the River* will illustrate the centrality of the concrete in Wolfe's writing. Eugene Gant is daydreaming and not worrying about where the money to fulfill his dreams is to come from.

If he thought about it, it seemed to have no importance or reality whatever—he just dismissed it impatiently, or with a conviction that some old man would die and leave him a fortune, that he was going to pick up a purse containing hundreds of thousands of dollars while walking in the Fenway, and that the reward would be enough to keep him going, or that a beautiful and rich young widow, true-hearted, tender, loving, and

113

voluptuous, who had carrot-colored hair, little freckles on her face, a snub nose and luminous gray-green eyes with something wicked yet loving and faithful in them, and one gold filling in her solid little teeth, was going to fall in love with him.[16]

Here, where he is mocking Eugene's stereotyped dreams, the rich young widow is made concrete and detailed, the lucky purse is found in a particular place. This use of the particular, this tendency to distrust the conceptual and abstract, is one of the most widely recognized characteristics of southern writing. As Robert Penn Warren has pointed out, the southerner lives in "the instinctive fear ... that the massiveness of experience, the concreteness of life, will be violated ... [in] the fear of abstraction."[17] Virginia Rock has noted that the southern poet feels "not only a rage for order but also a rage for the concrete, a rage against the abstract."[18] Even in criticism, southerners have concentrated their attention on particular works of art and have not formulated abstract systems. As Allen Tate put it, "There was no Southern criticism; merely a few Southern critics."[19]

Closely associated with this concern for the concrete is Wolfe's delight in folk speech, dialect, and speech mannerisms. His works are full of accurate transcriptions of vivid speech. His characters seem sometimes to talk endlessly, but they always talk with vigor and with great distinctiveness of diction, syntax, and idiom. Yet the same writer who displays these startlingly effective qualities of lyric concreteness and accuracy of speech is also guilty of excesses in both quantity and quality of rhetoric perhaps unequaled by any other American novelist. With the power to evoke a particular object, scene, or character with remarkable clarity, he is unwilling to let these creations speak for themselves, but must try by sheer force of rhetoric to give expression to the peculiar meanings that they suggest, to define ineffable feelings, to formulate the inchoate longings and uncertain stirrings of spirit he feels all men share. These qualities are manifest in the following passage from *Of Time and the River*, where Wolfe is trying to define the "fury" that drives Gant toward the North and away from the South.

It is to have the old unquiet mind, the famished heart, the restless soul; it is to lose hope, heart, and all joy utterly, and then to have them wake again, to have the old feeling return with overwhelming force that he is about to find the thing for which his life obscurely and desperately is groping—for which all men on this earth have sought—one face out of the million faces, a wall, a door, a place of certitude and peace and wandering no more. For what is it that we Americans are seeking always on this earth? Why is it we have crossed the stormy seas so many times alone, lain in a thousand alien rooms at night hearing the sounds of time, dark time, and thought until heart, brain, flesh, and spirit are sick and weary with the thought of it: "Where shall I go now? What shall I do?" [20]

Set beside some of the apostrophes from *Look Homeward, Angel*, like the one to Laura James at the end of Chapter 30, this passage seems restrained, yet it represents pretty clearly that rhetorical groping toward understanding and expression which is a large element in Wolfe's work. He is fascinated by language, enchanted by words, carried away by rhetorical devices. A kind of primitive logomania is in him: if the word can be found and uttered, vast forces are unleashed and great truths miraculously uncovered.

The drift toward rhetoric is the aspect of Wolfe's work most frequently called southern. Alfred Kazin observed of Wolfe and Faulkner: "It is their rhetoric, a mountainous verbal splendor, that holds these writers together . . . the extravagant and ornamental tradition of Southern rhetoric." Wilbur J. Cash believed that it was their use of the rhetorical tradition that tied Faulkner and Wolfe to earlier southern literary traditions, and Joseph Warren Beach felt that "Wolfe's inclination to extravagant and ornamental writing" should be associated with "something in the tradition of Southern culture." [21] Certainly the passion for the sound of the word, the primitive desire to give the name, the sense of the power present in the magic of incantation, show up with alarming frequency in southern writing. The particular linguistic combination that Wolfe used— the combination of concrete detail, accurate speech, and incantatory rhetorical extravagance—is also present to a marked degree in the works of Faulkner, particularly since 1936, and in the novels of Robert Penn Warren.

Wolfe likewise shares the southerner's willingness to accept and find delight in paradox. At the heart of the riddle of the South is a union of opposites, a condition of instability, a paradox: a love of individualism combined with a defense of slavery and segregation, a delight in polished manners and at the same time a ready recourse to violence, the liberalism of Thomas Jefferson coexisting with the conservatism of John C. Calhoun. Such paradoxes bother southerners less than they would bother their northern neighbors, for while they hunger for order and are moved by a rage for tradition, they can at the same time accept instability as a permanent aspect of human existence and the unresolved contradiction as a part of man's condition. Southern writers often value paradox as a primary element in art. Cleanth Brooks, for example, finds the meaning in poetry in the paradoxes that are to be found in word, image, and structure. The Fugitive poets, notably John Crowe Ransom, find the full meaning of an incident in the comprehension of its persistent ironies. Allen Tate sees the meaning of a poem in the "tension" created by the conflict between its intension and extension.

Wolfe saw his world and himself through an only semilogical application to life of the Hegelian dialectic. He seemed to need to define a thing's opposite before he could comprehend the thing, and to have a naïve faith that somehow the meaning was manifest if the opposites were stated. Hence, there is in his work on practically every level—sentence, paragraph, scene, theme, large project—a structure of paradox.

But all these attributes of Wolfe's work individually are essentially superficial qualities of his "southernness." So strong a combination of these attributes as he displays does not often occur in America outside the South; yet these qualities suggest rather than define a distinctively southern quality. In certain other respects, however, Wolfe seems definitively southern. One of these is his attitude toward capitalistic industrialism; another is his sense of the tragic implications of experience; and a third is his deep-seated sense of human guilt.

That Wolfe had little patience with the group of southern writers known as the Agrarians is obvious from what has already been quoted. He regarded their intellectualism as false, their devotion to the life of the soil as pretentious and unreal, and he heaped scorn on them more than once, calling them by the opprobrious name "New Confederates." Yet one has the feeling that much of his contempt rested on ignorance of what the Agrarians were advocating, and that he would have been pretty much of their party if he had known what that party really was. However, he belonged loosely to the New South school, which saw in industrial progress the key to a new and better life and believed that the South must emerge from its retreat to the past into the reality of the modern world. In *The Web and the Rock* he wrote:

There was an image in George Webber's mind that came to him in childhood and that resumed for him the whole dark picture of those decades of defeat and darkness. He saw an old house, set far back from the traveled highway, and many passed along that road, and the troops went by, the dust rose, and the war was over. And no one passed along that road again. He saw an old man go along the path, away from the road, into the house; and the path was overgrown with grass and weeds, with thorny tangle, and with underbrush until the path was lost. And no one ever used that path again. And the man who went into that house never came out of it again. And the house stayed on. It shone faintly through that tangled growth like its own ruined spectre, its doors and windows black as eyeless sockets. That was the South. That was the South for thirty years or more.

That was the South, not of George Webber's life, nor the lives of his contemporaries—that was the South they did not know but that all of them somehow remembered. It came to them from God knows where, upon the rustling of a leaf at night, in quiet voices on a Southern porch, in a screen door slam and sudden silence, a whistle wailing down the midnight valleys to the East and the enchanted cities of the North, and Aunt Maw's droning voice and the memory of unheard voices, in the memory of the dark, ruined Helen in their blood, in something stricken,

117

lost, and far, and long ago. They did not see it, the people of George's age and time, but they remembered it.

They had come out—another image now—into a kind of sunlight of another century. They had come out upon the road again. The road was being paved. More people came now. They cut a pathway to the door again. Some of the weeds were clear. Another house was built. They heard wheels coming and the world was *in*, yet they were not yet wholly of that world.[22]

Yet Wolfe was also keenly aware that industrial progress and the things associated with it could have damaging effects on American and southern culture. Writing to his mother, in May, 1923, he condemned "progress" and commerce in scathing terms: "What I shall try to get into their dusty little pint-measure minds is that a full belly, a good automobile, paved streets, and so on, do not make them one whit better or finer,—that there is beauty in this world,—beauty even in this wilderness of ugliness and provincialism that is at present our country, beauty and spirit which will make us men instead of cheap Board of Trade Boosters, and blatant pamphleteers." [23] He defined the "essential tragedy of America" as "the magnificent, unrivaled, unequaled, unbeatable, unshrinkable, supercolossal, 99-and-44-one-hundredths-per-cent-pure, schoolgirl-complexion, covers-the-earth, I'd-walk-a-mile-for-it, four-out-of-five-have-it, his-master's voice, ask-the-man-who-owns-one, blueplate-special home of advertising, salesmanship, and special pleading in all its many catchy and beguiling forms." [24] Certainly for him, capitalistic industrial progress had as little appeal as it did for the Agrarians; for him, as for the Twelve Southerners who wrote *I'll Take My Stand*, the modern industrial world had become a perversion of the American dream. The Twelve Southerners declared, "If a community, or a section, or a race, or an age, is groaning under industrialism, and well aware that it is an evil dispensation, it must find the way to throw it off. To think that this cannot be done is pusillanimous. And if the whole community, section, race, or age thinks it cannot be done, then it has simply lost its political genius and doomed itself to impotence."[25] George Webber shared these sentiments when he said, in *You Can't Go Home Again:*

And the worst of it is the intellectual dishonesty which all this corruption has bred. People are *afraid* to think straight—*afraid* to face themselves—*afraid* to look at things and see them as they are. We've become like a nation of advertising men, all hiding behind catch phrases like "prosperity" and "rugged individualism" and "the American way." And the real things like freedom, and equal opportunity, and the integrity and worth of the individual—things that have belonged to the American dream since the beginning—they have become just words too. The substance has gone out of them—they're not real any more.[26]

Admittedly, this sounds more like Sidney Lanier's condemnation of "Trade" than Donald Davidson's advocacy of the Agrarian way, yet the enemy that all three faced was an enemy well known to the South and commonly confronted by southerners.

Wolfe looked upon himself as a radical, even, as he once called himself, a "Revolutionary," and he angrily expressed his hatred of the gross injustice and inhumanity that the Depression produced. But to him the solution was never material; indeed, the substitution of the material for the spiritual was the cause for his belief "that we are lost here in America," and only his confidence that ultimately America would put aside the material for the spiritual made it possible for him to add, "but I believe we shall be found."[27]

Wolfe is peculiarly southern, too, in the degree to which he sees the darkness, pain, and evil in life, and yet does not succumb to the naturalistic answer of despair. "The enemy," he tells us in *You Can't Go Home Again*, "is old as Time, and evil as Hell, and he has been here with us from the beginning. I think he stole our earth from us, destroyed our wealth, and ravaged and despoiled our land. I think he took our people and enslaved them, that he polluted the fountains of our life, took unto himself the rarest treasures of our own possession, took our bread and left us with a crust."[28]

Wolfe seemed to feel, as George Webber did, "the huge and nameless death that waits around the corner for all men, to break their backs and shatter instantly the blind and pitiful illusions of their hope." He was supremely the novelist of death in American literature, for the ending of life was an obsessive theme with him. All his characters come to face the fact of death; as he expressed it, "They knew that they would die and that the earth would last forever. And with that feeling of joy, wonder, and sorrow in their hearts, they knew that another day had gone, another day had come, and they knew how brief and lonely are man's days." And the end, at least in its physical sense, was ugly. In *Of Time and the River* he described it this way: "This was the sickening and abominable end of flesh, which infected time and all man's living memory of morning, youth, and magic with the death-putrescence of its cancerous taint, and made us doubt that we had ever lived, or had a father, known joy: this was the end, and the end was horrible in ugliness. At the end it was not well." [29] In *The Story of a Novel* Wolfe is explicit about this darkness and evil in life. "Everywhere around me . . . I saw the evidence of an incalculable ruin and suffering," he said, and enumerated the "suffering, violence, oppression, hunger, cold, and filth and poverty" he saw, so that through "the suffering and labor of [his] own life" he shared the experiences of people around him. [30]

This sense of evil and suffering is more typical of southern writers than of other Americans, for a variety of reasons: the South's distrust of progress, its refusal to believe in perfectibility, its experience of compromise and paradox—all culminated in the defeat in the Civil War and its long and bitter aftermath. As C. Vann Woodward has cogently argued, the South is the only American region where the principles of progress and the concept of perfectibility are demonstrably false. "Nothing," he asserts, "about [its] history is conducive to the theory that the South was the darling of divine providence." [31] This sense of defeat led Ellen Glasgow to say that she could never recall a time when "the pattern of society as well as the scheme of things in general, had not seemed to me false and even malignant," [32] and the same feeling found expression in the dark damnation of Faulkner's world and the ambiguous calamities of Robert Penn Warren's.

When, however, the nation as a whole began to experience the cataclysms of the twentieth century and to react to scientific and philosophic views of man that were less optimistic, the American artist outside the South tended to turn to programs of Utopian reform or satiric correction or naturalistic despair. The southern writer on the other hand, older in the experience of calamity and defeat, saw the tragic grandeur of man, the magnificence of his will in the face of disaster, and the glory with which he maintained the integrity of his spirit in a world of material defeat. Southern writers have often used their history to make a tragic fable of man's lot in a hostile world, and to celebrate the triumph of the human spirit when challenged by an idea or a responsibility. As Ellen Glasgow asserts, "One may learn to live, one may even learn to live gallantly, without delight."[33] And as Ike McCaslin says in Faulkner's "Delta Autumn," "There are good men everywhere, at all times. Most men are. Some are just unlucky, because most men are a little better than their circumstances give them a chance to be."[34] This view of man changes defeat into tragic grandeur and touches the spectacle of suffering with the transforming sense of human dignity.

Thomas Wolfe's view of man and life had this tragic sense. In *The Story of a Novel* he expressed it very directly. "And from it all, there has come as the final deposit, a burning memory, a certain evidence of the fortitude of man, his ability to suffer and somehow to survive."[35] At the conclusion of Chapter 27 of *You Can't Go Home Again*, Wolfe states that man to him is "a foul, wretched, abominable creature . . . and it is impossible to say the worst of him . . . this moth of time, this dupe of brevity and numbered hours, this travesty of waste and sterile breath." Yet Wolfe stands in awe of man's accomplishments. "For there is one belief, one faith, that is man's glory, his triumph, his immortality—and that is his belief in life. . . . So this is man—the worst and best of him—this frail and petty thing who lives his days and dies like all the other animals and is forgotten. And yet, he is immortal, too, for both the good and evil that he does live after him."[36]

The southern writer is often obsessed with a sense of guilt and the need for expiation. Robert Penn Warren calls this feeling by its theological name in his poem "Original Sin," and sees it as the inevitable result of our lost innocence; in Allen Tate's "The Wolves" it is a threatening evil to be faced always in the next room; in William Faulkner it may be symbolized by the vicariously shared guilt which Quentin Compson must assume and die to pay for in *The Sound and the Fury*, or the inheritance of the father's which Ike McCaslin vainly tries to repudiate in "The Bear." This sense of guilt may be the product of the pervasive Calvinism of the region; it may be the product of the poverty and suffering that the region has known; it is certainly in part the result of the guilt associated with slavery in the nineteenth century and the Negro's second-class citizenship in the twentieth—a guilt most thoughtful southerners have felt. In any case, it appears to be a hallmark of the serious twentieth-century southern writer. And it is a hallmark that Thomas Wolfe's work certainly bears. He states his sense of his own guilt explicitly in *The Story of a Novel*.

And through the traffic of those thronging crowds—whose faces, whose whole united and divided life was now instantly and without an effort of the will, my *own*—there rose forever the sad unceasing murmurs of the body of this life, the vast recessive fadings of the shadow of man's death that breathes forever with its dirgelike sigh around the huge shores of the world.

And *beyond*—forever *above, around, behind* the vast and tranquil consciousness of my spirit that now held the earth and all her elements in the huge clasp of its effortless subjection—there dwelt forever the fatal knowledge of my own inexpiable *guilt*.[37]

In *You Can't Go Home Again* he explicitly links this sense of guilt with the South and in turn sees the South as a symbol and in a sense a scapegoat for the national hurt.

Perhaps it came from their old war, and from the ruin of their great defeat and its degraded aftermath. Perhaps it came from causes yet more ancient—from the evil of man's slavery, and the hurt and shame of human conscience in its struggle with the fierce desire to own. It came, too, perhaps, from the lusts of the hot South, tormented and repressed below the harsh and outward patterns of a bigot and intolerant theology.... And most of all, perhaps, it came out of the very weather of their lives. ...

But it was not only in the South that America was hurt. There was another deeper, darker, and more nameless wound throughout the land....

We must look at the heart of guilt that beats in each of us, for there the cause lies. We must look, and with our own eyes see, the central core of defeat and shame and failure.[38]

Thomas Wolfe did not live to complete his representation of his America through the portrait of himself as generic man, and out of the novels, short stories, and letters we piece out the pattern he was trying to follow and we guess at the meanings and intentions. One thing seems clear: Wolfe was a southerner, torn by the tensions and issues that thoughtful southerners feel, oppressed as they tend to be with the tragic nature of life, and feeling as they often do a sense of guilt that demands some kind of expiating action. The work he completed had demonstrable southern qualities; the total work, had he lived to complete it, would probably have had these qualities too. The South did, indeed, burn in his blood and on his pages like a "ruined Helen"—beautiful, passionate, and dark with violence and guilt.

But although Thomas Wolfe shared many of that combination of qualities of mind and spirit that in some arrangement or other we call "southern," he differed in significant ways from many of his fellow southerners, who had different geographical and spiritual roots. For despite the fact that the southern region has had a unique identity, the term "South" is too broad an abstraction to be handled with very much precision by its historians or critics. There are not one but many Souths; and these may fall, at the next level of abstraction, into a three-part grouping made by geographical differences, major variations in social patterns, and various strains of race and culture resulting from different kinds and times of migration, so that "the South" is comprised of at least three distinct subregions with radical differences among themselves—differences almost as great as those between the total region and the rest of the nation. These subregions certainly overlap at many points, and they share many common characteristics, so that, except for the extreme forms of each of these subregions, they seem to shade into each other almost imperceptibly, despite the fact that each maintains a geographical distinctiveness.

Geographically the southeastern United States consists of a broad coastal plain rich in rivers and readily accessible to those who boarded frighteningly frail crafts and sailed them over unknown seas to Roanoke Island, into the James River, and into the Cooper and Ashley rivers at Charleston. At the edge of the Atlantic coastal plain is the "fall line," a geological formation which separates the plain from the rolling hills. This fall line passes through Richmond, Virginia; Raleigh, North Carolina; Columbia, South Carolina; and Milledgeville, Georgia. Behind it the gentle rise of the Piedmont stretches westward until it suddenly flings itself skyward to form the Southern Appalachian and Blue Ridge mountains. Westward from the first ranges of the Blue Ridge and the Appalachian mountains is the Great Valley. The entire southeastern region is bounded on the east and south by the Atlantic and Gulf coastal plains and is marked latitudinally by climate variations. Virginia, the Carolinas, Tennessee, and much of Georgia are in a humid, warm, temperate zone. Florida, Alabama, Mississippi, and Louisiana are in a humid, semitropical zone. Hence we can, with some accuracy, talk of a temperate coastal South—variously called the Tidewater and the Low Country—of a Piedmont South which extends into and includes the Appalachian and Blue Ridge mountains, and of a Deep South which is largely a semitropical Gulf Coast plain.

Both the southern seaboard and the Deep South were haunted by the dream of baronial splendor. As a powerful dream, it realized itself in a mannered but intense code of violence in the Gulf plain states. Whatever limited reality it had came from the seaboard planter world. But behind the Tidewater and the Low Country was a world of sturdy, egalitarian men who settled and dominated the westward sweep of continent beyond the "fall line." The Piedmont hills, the mountain ranges, and the mountain valleys were first colonized primarily not by the British with Cavalier pretensions, who entered through the southern Atlantic ports and then moved inward, but by those of Scotch-Irish, Scottish, and German origin who came through the middle Atlantic ports of Philadelphia, Chester, and New Castle, and moved westward through the Great Valley for about a hundred miles until the tall mountains raised barriers that deflected them south. They came down the broad cattle trails into the Piedmont South, settling in Virginia, the backcountry of the Carolinas, Tennessee, and Georgia. There they created a social world marked by the grim Calvinistic attitudes of the dour Scottish Presbyterians and took unto themselves the Piedmont and mountain regions stretching from what is now West Virginia to a point in central and south Georgia.

When the Great Migration of the Scotch-Irish began in 1717, few of the migrants questioned the propriety of social classes or the value of a society with stability based on a concept of upper, "middling," and "lower" orders. But in America, particularly in mountainous Virginia and the backcountry of the Carolinas, class lines were soon blurred almost beyond recognition, and traditional distinctions underwent massive erosion. These people of the Piedmont created a special and frequently grim way of life so radically different from the Tidewater culture, which was only a few hundred miles away, that they might almost have lived on different continents. In this grim social world of the frontier Piedmont, the Scotch-Irish were quick-tempered, impetuous, inclined to work by fits and starts, reckless, and given to too much drinking. Their pietistic, puritanic Calvinism was yoked to an intense acquisitiveness, so that they earned the claim that a "Scotch-Irishman is one who keeps the commandments of God and every other thing he can get his hands on." Thus they formed a harsh society marked by widespread crudity and high animal spirits. It was an egalitarian, individualistic, religiously dissenting world. To those who visited it from the coastal plain area, it appeared to be lawless and frightening. The Anglican itinerant minister Charles Woodmason, who tried to serve the South Carolina backcountry from 1766 to 1768, left in his journal a record of the dismay with which he viewed the region. He declared that these people's chief characteristics were lawlessness, vile manners, ignorance, slovenliness, and primitive emotionalism in religion.[39]

Their pragmatic view of life, their folk-version Calvinism, and their anti-intellectual individualism created a special world favorable to egalitarian democracy and having little patience with and no respect for aristocratic pretensions. This cotton country and hill country, made up of small farms, small towns, and small cities spaced very far apart, maintains to this day many of its early characteristics.

It is very far removed from the melancholy great oaks and broad plantations of the Tidewater which is Thomas Nelson Page's and Ellen Glasgow's world and almost equally removed from the tropical lushness and richness of the Deep South, best represented by William Faulkner. Here in the decades immediately before the Revolution was the sharp cutting edge of the frontier. Although by 1790 the Scotch-Irish represented no more than a quarter of a million Americans, their strength of character shaped the conventions of the world in which they lived and made them the controlling force for awhile in the westward movement. It was and is a country at the mercy of the capriciousness of weather and the vicissitudes of the cotton market. In this century it has been a land racked by diseases peculiar to poverty, a harsh sharecropper system, and by low income and little education. It is no accident that this area has been a central target for a war on poverty and economic and social distress by a socially minded federal government from the early days of Franklin Roosevelt's presidency to the Appalachian programs of Lyndon Johnson.

There has not been a time since the eighteenth century when this Piedmont and mountain South has not had its chroniclers, and its recorders have had a remarkable unanimity of opinion and attitude toward its inhabitants. The most obvious characteristic of this body of writers, aside from their exaggerated tendency toward the grotesque, is an emphasis upon a disordered society, a sense that there is neither in social custom nor in religious belief an ordering principle which is acceptable to the writer. As early as 1728, William Byrd in his *A History of the Dividing Line* portrayed backcountry North Carolinians, whom he called the inhabitants of "lubberland," with an amused awareness that at least by his standards they were grotesques. Augustus Baldwin Longstreet described the people of the Georgia Piedmont in a series of sketches written in the 1830s and collected in book form in 1835 as *Georgia Scenes*. His is the detached view of a cultivated lawyer and judge seeing these people as cruel and unlearned denizens of a world remote from the social order which Judge Longstreet revered.

The early novels about the southern frontier described the same kinds of people and judged them against a concept of an aristocratic social order, notably in the case of William Gilmore Simms's "Border Romances" and most obviously in his *Guy Rivers* (1834), which is laid in frontier Georgia. In midcentury, George Washington Harris in his comic character Sut Lovingood created a kind of American *Til Eulenspiegel* in this region. During the local color movement writers like "Charles Egbert Craddock" (Mary N. Murfree) presented, with a summer visitor's condescension, a whimsical picture of the eccentricities of the mountain people of this region.

In the twentieth century the region has called forth notable novelistic efforts, among them the works of T. S. Stribling, particularly in *Teeftallow* and in his trilogy *The Forge*, *The Store*, and *Unfinished Cathedral*; Erskine Caldwell, in his earlier and more serious period when his Rabelaisian exaggeration was redeemed from vulgarity by his social concerns; Lillian Smith, in her tractarian novels and essays; and most recently Flannery O'Connor, whose two novels and two volumes of short stories may very well represent the best writing done by a southerner during the past quarter of a century.

The writers of this tradition used many different literary forms. They have, however, all sought in differing ways for some outside, some external control by which they can judge the value of the society which they discuss. This society is in many ways more nearly American and less distinctively southern, except for its grotesquerie, than the societies of the Deep South or of the Tidewater and the Low Country; and the standard by which it is judged, whether it be that of social justice, of religious order, or of moral indignation, has always been an outer and different standard from that embraced by the local inhabitants. Ellen Glasgow, of the Tidewater, and William Faulkner, of the Deep South, on the other hand, have found the standards by which to judge their societies in the ideals of their citizens, however little these ideals found firm expression in either of the cultures.

Many of the writers who deal with the Piedmont South, including Thomas Wolfe, launch attacks upon its impoverished culture much like those made by the middle-western writers who participated in "the Revolt from the Village"—writers like E. W. Howe, Joseph Kirkland, Hamlin Garland, and Sinclair Lewis, who was a major influence on Thomas Wolfe's work. Where Ellen Glasgow used the novel of manners and William Faulkner the symbolic romance to give their fictional representations of the South, Thomas Wolfe turned to a kind of fiction which was lyric rather than dramatic, which was characterized by autobiographical plots rather than by tight structures, and which dealt with the problem of the definition of the self in relation first to a middle-class Piedmont South and later to the great world outside the region. The South which Wolfe knew was consciously Roundhead in its political allegiance, strongly egalitarian and individualistic in its view of man, characterized by rough, coarse, crude, and graceless manners and conventions, and grimly Calvinistic in its religious orientation.

In this respect, Thomas Wolfe takes his place very clearly and plainly as a writer about a South that is significantly different from that which occupies the popular, romantic imagination. That Wolfe knew that his world was a different one from that of many other southerners he made very clear. In *The Web and the Rock*, he contrasts two sections of the South in terms of "Old Catawba" and South Carolina. In making this distinction, he echoes that old, old remark that North Carolina is a vale of humility between two mountains of conceit. He says:

Old Catawba has the slants of evening and the mountain cool. You feel lonely in Old Catawba, but it is not the loneliness of South Carolina. In Old Catawba, the hill boy helps his father building fences and hears a soft Spring howling in the wind, and sees the wind snake through the bending waves of the coarse grasses of the mountain pastures. And far away he hears the whistle's cry wailed back, far-flung and faint along some mountain valley, as a great train rushes towards the cities of the East. And the heart of the hill boy will know joy because he knows, all world-remote, lonely as he is, that some day he will meet the world and know those cities too.[40]

Against that sense of difference and of outward movement, Wolfe poses a view of South Carolina that is far from complimentary:

These people are really lost. They cannot get away from South Carolina, and if they get away they are no good. They drawl beautifully. There is the most wonderful warmth, affection, heartiness in their approach and greeting, but the people are afraid. Their eyes are desperately afraid, filled with a kind of tortured and envenomed terror of the old, stricken, wounded 'Southness' of cruelty and lust. Sometimes their women have the honey skins, they are like gold and longing. They are filled with the most luscious and seductive sweetness, tenderness, and gentle mercy. But the men are stricken. They get fat about the bellies, or they have a starved, stricken leanness in the loins.[41]

Such a distinction Wolfe pushes beyond the limits of reality. The difference between South Carolina and North Carolina is far less than he indicates it as being; but he sees all of North Carolina in terms of his own mountain and Piedmont region and all of South Carolina in terms of the Low Country society. He declares, "Old Catawba is a place inhabited by humble people. There is no Charleston in Old Catawba, and not so many people pretending to be what they are not. . . . Now their pretense is reduced to pretending that they amounted to so much formerly. And they really amounted to very little." Yet Wolfe knows, too, that "Old Catawba" is not of a piece. In *The Web and the Rock* he says:

Down in the East, in Old Catawba, they have some smack of ancientry. The East got settled first and there are a few old towns down there, the remnants of plantations, a few fine old houses, a lot of niggers, tobacco, turpentine, pine woods, and the mournful flat-lands of the coastal plain. The people in the East used to think they were better than the people in the West because they had been there a little longer. But they were not really better. In the West, where the mountains sweep around them, the people have utterly common, familiar, plain, Scotch-Irish faces, and names like Weaver, Wilson, Gudger, Joyner, Alexander, and Patton. The West is really better than the East. . . . The West is really a region of good small people, a Scotch-Irish place, and that, too, is undefined, save that it doesn't drawl so much, works harder, doesn't loaf so much, and shoots a little straighter when it has to. It is really just one of the common places of the earth, a million or two people with nothing very extraordinary about them.[42]

Thus Wolfe's attitude toward his immediate region is also ambiguous; for, while he is highly critical of the crass materialism of the Piedmont, he also loves it and finds it better than the Tidewater.

Certainly Wolfe does not embrace the concept of the nobility of the Old South. Even in his early plays, such as *The Mountains* and *Mannerhouse*, Wolfe dealt in unfriendly and destructive ways with the legend of the aristocratic South. His second long play, *Welcome to Our City*, is an attack on the social conventions and beliefs of his own region. This quality in Wolfe's work led his Chapel Hill classmate, Jonathan Daniels, in reviewing *Look Homeward, Angel* in the Raleigh, North Carolina, *News and Observer*, to declare that in that book "North Carolina and the South are spat upon."[43] Such critical attitudes are not surprising about a writer in the tradition within which Wolfe grew up. Freed from the deep emotional commitment typical of the Tidewater and the Deep South, Wolfe could look calmly and critically at his region, deplore its weaknesses, and love its strengths, without indulging in the emotional upheaval over this ambivalent attitude which Quentin Compson suffers in Faulkner's

Absalom, Absalom! The tendency of Faulkner and writers like Ellen Glasgow is, in their different ways, to have as a subject a social order which serves as a frame within which they may describe their characters, so that the region and its history, the people and their customs, ultimately work upon the individual characters in their books at the same time that they are created by these characters. Thus a complex and subtle interrelationship between character and region emerges from their novels. On the other hand, for Wolfe no such firm structure of society existed; and he turned, as Whitman had earlier turned, and as Tocqueville had suggested that the American democratic artist must always turn, from the egalitarian social world to the inner self for the true subject of his work.

The South which Wolfe lived in as a boy and young man he saw as an entangling web to be broken through in the effort toward self-realization. The past makes few compulsive demands upon him, for Thomas Wolfe is fleeing the hills relatively unencumbered by history, looking back at the past not in love or pain but in anger, and finally turning, like Eugene Gant at the end of *Look Homeward, Angel,* "like a man who stands upon a hill above the town he has left, yet does not say, 'The town is near,' but turns his eyes upon the distant soaring ranges." [44] These ranges were not only geographically but spiritually to the north and west. Thus Wolfe becomes relatively free of his past—the first twentieth-century southern American writer of major stature who deserts his region to embrace a national and then an international identity. Though he has a firm sense of the social world he is leaving, the center of his books is not that social world but himself.

Look Homeward, Angel, Wolfe's first book, is the record of the growth of a child from his birth until his college education is completed. It places a very great premium upon the impact on its protagonist, Eugene Gant, of the physical world, the social structure, and the actions of individual friends and acquaintances. Wolfe traces here the experiences of a delicate boy struggling to know himself in "the limitless meadows of sensation." But this boy, by Wolfe's own

131

definition, is unique only in the degree of his sensitivity, not in his basic nature. "Each of us," he declares in the opening of the book, "is all the sums he has not counted." [45] It is in the spirit of this generic man that Wolfe defines the lonely search of his characters, the search for communion, the search for meaning, the search for the deepest nature of the self, the old Wordsworthian search backward into the individual's origins in order to find the nature and meaning of the self.

When Eugene Gant moves from Altamont, he moves outward into the great world; and though he takes with him many of the qualities which he sees as the virtues of the South, he consciously leaves his native region for what he believes to be a better world. In *The Web and the Rock* Wolfe's protagonist remembers "all the times when he had come out of the South and into the North, and always the feeling was the same—an exact, pointed, physical feeling marking the frontiers of his consciousness with a geographic precision. ... It was a geographic division of the spirit that was sharply, physically exact, as if it had been cleanly severed by a sword. ... He ducked his head a little as if he were passing through a web. He knew that he was leaving the South." [46] Certainly Wolfe is not right in attributing to all southerners that sense of expansion and release which crossing the Potomac gives him. Indeed, that kind of release is something which neither Ellen Glasgow nor William Faulkner would have wanted or expressed.

Of Time and the River carries his protagonist from Altamont to Harvard, then to New York City, and finally to Europe. Eugene Gant experiences in this steadily outward movement an increasing necessity to describe and to define himself, not as a southerner but as an American, and to begin a roll call of names and places which includes the South as simply a part of the larger world but does not isolate it as a unique subject. Typically in his catalogues—close in content and cadence to those of Walt Whitman—are lists of names such as he gives in one place in *Of Time and the River* where he names "The Wilderness; and the names of Antietam, Chancellorsville, Shiloh, Bull Run, Fredericksburg, Cold Harbor ... Cowpens, Brandywine, and Saratoga; of Death Valley, Chickamauga, and the Cumberland Gap. The names of the Nantahalahs, the Bad Lands, the Painted Desert, the Yosemite, and the Little Big Horn; the names of Yancey and Cabarrus counties; and the terrible name of Hatteras." The significance of such a catalogue is its indiscriminate inclusiveness, just as his "continental thunder of the states" begins with "Montana, Texas, Arizona, Colorado, Michigan, Maryland, Virginia, and the two Dakotas."[47] Such catalogues are recurrent in Wolfe—he lists the names of Indian tribes, of railways, of hoboes, of great rivers, and his listing does not end in America but goes on to the Tiber and the Thames. Wolfe's characters, through their absorption of great ranges of experience and their merging of myriad persons with themselves, become archetypes of the American.

In *The Web and the Rock* Wolfe repeats many of the incidents of the earlier work in recounting the experience of George Webber, whose record begins when he is a child in Libya Hill, another thin disguise for Asheville, and who moves on out into the larger world of the North and of Europe. In *You Can't Go Home Again*, George Webber returns briefly to the South, writes a novel, travels in England and on the continent, and experiences both directly and vicariously the "complex fate" of being an American. At the conclusion of the novel, Webber gives an emphatic expression to a nationally oriented sense of democracy and its promise.

In *You Can't Go Home Again*, Webber sees people and actions more frequently than he participates in events, and the forms in which he sees them are often virtually self-contained units of the length of tales and novellas. Indeed, as it did for Faulkner, experience very often came to Wolfe in actions which were friendly to representation in short stories and short novels. After *Look Homeward, Angel*, which is itself an uneven book, Wolfe did not again produce a work in which the individual episodes are not more impressive than the whole of which they are a part. Both Faulkner and Wolfe attempted to formulate large structures which adequately controlled and shaped the individual dramatic scenes and in which their works appear naturally to fall. Faulkner chose the historical and social history of his region and used it to reflect universal experience. Wolfe, on the other hand, had as his focus the realization of one generic American; thus his form was autobiographical. In his firmly democratic insistence on himself as representative of the equality of man, he, like Walt Whitman, attempted to sing America by celebrating himself and in the process of so doing created a new self who was that of representational America. The central search which Wolfe's characters are embarked upon is a search for what he once called "surety" and that he symbolically represented as "the search for the father"[48]—that is, a search for a home in a homeless land, a search for communion in a lonely world, the endless and always unfruitful quest for the lost leaf, the stone, the unfound door which leads out of the self into the surrounding brotherhood of man.

Wolfe and Faulkner share the quality of intensity, as they also share the verbal pyrotechnics of which each is capable. Both writers can wrap language into special forms and out of these special forms create new, fresh, and original meanings. Yet there is a fundamental difference in the ways they use language. In Faulkner's case the syntax of the sentence often proves an inadequate container for the intensity of the words, and his great sprawling sentences run on and on and on. The tone of Faulkner's voice becomes loud, even, on many occasions, strident, and his complexity is one of symbol, of *leitmotif*, of image, and above all of cadence and rhythm. We encounter its difficulties immediately and must wrestle with them with some success before we get to the inner core of his work. Though Wolfe has many of these qualities, he also has them under a kind of control quite different from that of Faulkner, for Wolfe's sentences are seldom—very seldom indeed—difficult; and when they present us with special words or special constructions, it is usually in those few passages where the influence of James Joyce is most plainly before us. Wolfe can write with so great a crystal clarity and directness that it becomes simply the transmission of a palpable world.

Wolfe's difficulties are not on the surface but are in the interrelationships, frequently difficult to see, which he is attempting to establish through the record of an individual experience. George Webber said in *You Can't Go Home Again*, "I'm looking for a way ... I think it may be something like what people vaguely mean when they speak of fiction. A kind of legend, perhaps. Something—a story—composed of all the knowledge I have, of all the living I've seen. Not the facts, you understand—not just the record of my life—but something truer than the facts—something distilled out of my experience and transmitted into a form of universal application."[49]

So there is only one real subject of Wolfe's work, and that subject is the American self, whether it is called Eugene Gant or George Webber; and this personality is the product in very direct ways of the experiences which Wolfe has had. Many of these illuminating and instructive experiences are ones in which George Webber, or Eugene Gant, does not directly participate except as spectator and commentator. This pattern of development for Eugene Gant and George Webber is grounded in the South, but it is grounded in a South which is steadily expanding outward, as that South is known through the protagonist of the novels.

The attitude which Wolfe took toward his own region was certainly not a very friendly one despite the real affection that in many ways he had for it. In leaving the South he felt that he was taking leave of a group of people who were part of his blood and birth but of whom he could say:

The Joyners were a race as lawless as the earth, as criminal as nature. They hurled their prodigal seed into the raw earth of a mountain woman's body, bringing to life a swarming progeny which lived or died, was extinguished in its infancy or fought its way triumphantly to maturity against the savage enemies of poverty, ignorance, and squalor which menaced it at every step. They bloomed or perished as things live or die in nature—but the triumphant Joyners, superior to all loss or waste, lived forever as a river lives. Other tribes of men came up out of the earth, flourished for a space, and then, engulfed and falling, went back into the earth from which they came. Only the Joyners—those horror-hungry, time-devouring Joyners—lived, and would not die.[50]

Wolfe summarized George Webber's life and the pull between South and North by the web of earth and the rock of the city in these words:

Thus, day by day, in the taut and tangled web of this boy's life, the two hemispheres that touched but never joined, contended, separated, re-combined, and wove again. First came the old dark memory of time-haunted man and the lost voices in the hills a hundred years ago, the world-lost and hill-haunted sorrow of the time-triumphant Joyners. Then his spirit flamed beyond the hills, beyond lost time and sorrow, to his father and his father's earth; and when he thought of him his heart grew warm, the hot blood thudded in his veins, he lept all barriers of the here and now, and northward, gleaming brightly there beyond the hills, he saw a vision of the golden future in new lands.[51]

In *The Web and the Rock* this outward extension of the self is most nearly comprehended in the action of a single novel. The story of Monk Webber begins with his childhood of dreaming percep-tions of beauty, a beauty which was suddenly interrupted by the inherent violence which underlay his world and which is symbolized by the explosive, mad, and murderous eruption of the Negro Dick Prosser in the chapter "The Child by Tiger." He moves on to Pine Rock College, where his most significant actions were his choosing Dostoevski over Dickens and attending a football victory over Vir-ginia. Then he goes to New York City, and there, as he tries to write, he comes to believe "that every man on earth held in the little tene-ment of his flesh and spirit the whole ocean of human life and time, and that he must drown in this ocean unless, somehow, he 'got it out of him'—unless he mapped and charted it, fenced and defined it, plumbed it to its uttermost depths, and knew it to its smallest pock-ets upon the remotest shores of the everlasting earth." He goes to Europe and meets and falls in love with Mrs. Esther Jack and con-tinues the affair back in America. He goes back to Europe, engages in a fight in Munich at the Oktoberfest, and, while recovering in a hospital, comes to his moment of self-knowledge—the knowledge that limitations must be accepted, that "we who are men are more than men, and less than spirit." He knows that the "web" of the Southland home has been broken. His thoughts turn back to the re-collection of the childhood dream—"and morning, morning in the thickets of the memory, and so many lives-and-deaths of life so long ago, together with the thought of Winter howling in the oak, so many sunlights that had come and gone since morning, morning, and all the lost voices—'Son, where are you?'—of lost kinsmen in the mountains long ago. . . . That was a good time then."[52] But he knows, too, that "you can't go home again." Now his liberated, Whitmanesque imagination can stretch over the whole continent and seek out, as he does in *You Can't Go Home Again*, the represen-tative American.

Faulkner and Wolfe shared many things—being "southern," ver-bal power, intensity, probing introspection—but they differed in sig-nificant ways. For Faulkner was the novelist of the rural South and its traditions of social order, and Wolfe was the spokesman of the New South, the South which was embracing the future of indus-trialism and capitalism and whose sons dream of great cities and the vast nation. Thus, where Faulkner used a rural county and the ma-terial around it to write a cosmic tragedy, Wolfe sought in his pages to show through the experience of one southerner what it meant to be American. Faulkner's characters are embedded in history; Wolfe's are dramatizations of attitudes that are national and epic rather than sectional and mythic. Wolfe's fiction was determined by the Pied-mont middle-class southern world which he knew. When he moved from it, he moved outward to embrace the nation and to attempt to realize the promise of America, but the "dark Helen" of the South never ceased to beat in his pulse and in his blood. Although he could not go home again, neither could he ever totally leave home.

VII   Europe as His Catalyst

IT IS CUSTOMARY to see in an American writer who spent a substantial amount of his artistically formative period in Europe the impact upon him of his membership in two national cultures forming either a cosmopolitanism or an expatriated culture. Thus in the nineteenth century many writers seeing Europe in contrast to America found in it an aesthetic and moral challenge and emerged from their experience of the two cultures broadened, deepened, and enriched. This was particularly true of American writers in Italy.[1] In more recent times, most American writers seem to have sought in Europe a milieu more congenial to their aspirations and their inner selves than America and have embraced Europe as a truer spiritual—and often physical—home than they could find in the Western Hemisphere. This was true of England in the case of Henry James and T. S. Eliot and of France in the case of the group we commonly call the "Lost Generation."

Neither of these responses describes with any completeness the role that Europe played in the career of Thomas Wolfe, although most of the writers who have attempted to deal in any interpretive way with Wolfe's European experiences have treated him as being basically one of the expatriates. George M. Reeves, Jr., in *Thomas Wolfe et l'Europe*, a detailed examination of Wolfe in Europe, says: "Wolfe appartient au groupe d'écrivains qu'on a appelé La Génération Perdue. . . . Sa vie suit donc le cycle commun à tout un groupe d'écrivains américains de l'entre-deux guerres: révolte contre les

États-Unis, fuite en Europe, et retour en Amérique."[2] And Europe certainly played as great a role in Wolfe's artistic development as it played in the careers of the "Paris Expatriates," whose "recording secretary" and best historian, Malcolm Cowley, included Wolfe as a member of the group and saw his differences as being primarily that he did not serve in World War I as most of the expatriates did and that he preferred Germany to France. Cowley even sees Wolfe's hunger for a lost and unattainable home as typical.[3]

This is a classification with which Wolfe would have been unsympathetic. In a speech at Purdue University in 1938, he said:

> I mention all this . . . because of its reference also to a charge that has sometimes been made by some of my friends. One of them, for example, not more than three or four years my senior, is very fixed in his assertion of what he calls "the lost generation"—a generation of which he has been quite vociferously a member, and in which he has tried enthusiastically to include me. "You belong to it, too," he used to say. "You came along at the same time. You can't get away from it. You're a part of it whether you want to be or not"—to which my vulgar response would be: "Don't you you-hoo me!"
>
> If my friend *wants* to belong to the Lost Generation—and it really is astonishing with what fond eagerness those people hug the ghost of desolation to their breast—that's *his* affair. But he can't have me. If I have been elected, it has been against my will; and I hereby resign. I don't feel that I belong to a lost generation, and I have never felt so.[4]

Yet, unmistakably, Europe played a significant and perhaps a central role in Wolfe's life and literary career. From his twenty-fourth year, in which he made the first of seven trips to Europe, until his death just before his thirty-eighth birthday, Wolfe spent over one quarter of his time across the Atlantic.[5] In the critical formative period between 1924 and 1931—a period during which he was finding that extended prose fiction was his métier and, after writing *Look Homeward, Angel*, was seeking a theme and a subject matter for the rest of his work—he made five trips to Europe, totaling thirty-four months and representing 45 percent of his time. A mere listing of the places which he visited or in which he lived for brief periods is impressive. It includes England, France, Switzerland, Italy, Germany, Austria, Czechoslovakia, and Denmark; and it touches almost every famous city which a visitor would normally have seen.[6] The two countries in which he spent the longest periods of time were England and France, although the country to which he felt the warmest spiritual affinity clearly was Germany.

Wolfe's career as a writer of prose fiction began and flourished during his European travels. His first extended prose narrative, the semifictional account of his first voyage abroad, "Passage to England," he began on shipboard in the form of notes which he continued to compile in England. He began the formal writing of this narrative in Tours. Typically, it never appeared in its original form but its subject matter was used in portions of several of his books.[7] He says of Eugene Gant, in language remarkably close to that which he used many times about himself:

He had come to Tours, telling himself that now at last, at last, he was going "to settle down and write," that he was going to justify his voyage by the high purpose of creation . . . with desperate resolve he sat down grimly now to shape these great designs into the stern and toilsome masonry of words. . . . And yet, write he did. Useless, fragmentary, and inchoate as were these first abortive efforts, he began to write now like a madman—as only a madman could write. . . . And in those words was packed the whole image of his bitter homelessness, his intolerable desire, his maddened longing for return. In those wild and broken phrases was packed the whole bitter burden of his famished, driven, over-laden spirit—all the longing of the wanderer, all the impossible and unutterable homesickness that the American, or any man on earth, can know. They were all there . . . and in them was the huge chronicle of the billion forms, the million names, the huge, single, and incomparable substance of America.[8]

On his second European trip, while in Paris, he began writing the rough outline of the book which became *Look Homeward, Angel.* In London during that trip the actual final form of the book began to be shaped in the summer of 1926, and much of the first third of the first draft was completed before he returned to New York in December of that year. His third European trip was also given over to intense work on his novel. Thus this first hauntingly evocative record of the autobiographical protagonist Eugene Gant was conceived from the vantage point of England and France and composed out of Wolfe's deep loneliness and hunger for America. It came into being, as he said in *The Story of a Novel*, because he "had felt the bitter ache of homelessness, a desperate longing for America, an overwhelming desire to return."[9]

Shortly after the draft of *Look Homeward, Angel* was completed and submitted to the publishers, Wolfe made his fourth European trip. During this journey, he spent a great deal of time in Germany and Austria. He was in Munich during the *Oktoberfest*, a festival celebrating the October beer. During the festival he became embroiled in a fist fight which became a brawl and he received injuries that placed him for a time in a hospital. While he was hospitalized, he took stock of himself in a foreign land and he came, he says, to a reconciliation with the nature of the world. This reconciliation is the subject matter for the concluding chapters of *The Web and the Rock*, where he and his battered body conclude that "They had discovered the earth together . . . they had discovered it alone, in secrecy, in exile, and in wandering . . . He knew that we who are men are more than men, and less than spirit."[10] Before he returned home from this fourth trip, he had learned of the interest of Charles Scribner's Sons in publishing *Look Homeward, Angel*; and thus the following year was spent in America putting the book which he had written in Europe into publishable form. It appeared in October, 1929.

In May, 1930, Wolfe returned to Europe, this time on a John Simon Guggenheim Memorial Fellowship, to begin work on his second novel. He was there for ten months, during which he frantically sought a subject and a theme, an organizing principle for his new book. In *The Story of a Novel*, he says of this period:

I think I may say that I discovered America during these years abroad out of my very need of her. The huge gain of this discovery seemed to come directly from my sense of loss. I had been to Europe five times now; each time I had come with delight, with maddening eagerness to return, and each time how, where, and in what way I did not know, I had felt the bitter ache of homelessness, a desperate longing for America, an overwhelming desire to return.

During that summer in Paris, I think I felt this great homesickness more than ever before, and I really believe that from this emotion, this constant and almost intolerable effort of memory and desire, the material and the structure of the books I now began to write were derived. . . . It was as if I had discovered a whole new universe of chemical elements and had begun to see certain relations between some of them but had by no means begun to organize the whole series into a harmonious and coherent union. . . . There was nothing at first which could be called a novel. I wrote about night and darkness in America, and the faces of the sleepers in ten thousand little towns; and of the tides of sleep and how the rivers flowed forever in the darkness. I wrote about the hissing glut of tides upon ten thousand miles of coast; of how the moonlight blazed down on the wilderness and filled the cat's cold eye with blazing yellow. I wrote about death and sleep, and of that enfabled rock of life we call the city. I wrote about October, of great trains that thundered through the night, of ships and stations in the morning; of men in harbors and the traffic of the ships.[11]

Thus he was writing down in notebooks and in great ledgers fragments which later were to find their way into his books and which were records in almost poetic form of his love and hunger for his native land. It was here, for example, that he first wrote down what finally became the famous passage on October in *Of Time and the River*. In its notebook form, it begins, "And in America the chinquapins are falling. The corn sticks out in hard and yellow rows upon dried ears, fit for a winter's barn and the big yellowed teeth of crunching horses; and the leaves are turning, turning up in Maine," [12] an obvious foreshadowing of Chapter XXXIX in *Of Time and the River* where these lines are transmuted into this passage, where the sense of contrast, of October remembered in a strange land, is present as a hardly distinguishable but still echoing resonance: "Now October has come again which in our land is different from October in the other lands. The ripe, the golden month has come again, and in Virginia the chinkapins are falling. Frost sharps the middle music of the seasons, and all things living on the earth turn home again. The country is so big you cannot say the country has the same October. In Maine, the frost comes sharp and quick as driven nails, just for a week or so the woods, all of the bright and bitter leaves, flare up." [13] That year in Switzerland, in Montreux, he found what was to be the theme for much of his work, the theme, as he expressed it, "of wandering forever and the earth again," a very appropriate theme for one possessed as he was with a desperate need for home and an endless urge to wander.[14] He returned in 1931 to America, where he continued to struggle—with the frantic energy that he describes in *The Story of a Novel*—to merge these experiences into a book. At last, over his protests, the vast manuscript was sent to the printer in 1934, and the book appeared in 1935 as *Of Time and the River*.

He did not return to Europe until 1935, and then for only two brief periods; but these were periods that seemed to have been profoundly constructive in shaping his final view of the world. In 1935 he was in Paris, London, and Berlin from March until July 4. From his experiences in Berlin, Wolfe learned much that shaped the course of his brief remaining career. His love affair with Berlin was intense on both sides: Byronic in its extravagance, like a *blitzkrieg* in its brevity, and a little ludicrous. "Byron, they say, awoke one morning at the age of twenty-four, and found himself a famous man," Wolfe said. "Well, I had to wait some ten years longer, but the day came when I walked at morning through the Brandenburger Gate, and into the enchanted avenues of the faery green Tiergarten, and found that fame . . . had come to me."[15]

Wolfe was first in Berlin in May and June, 1935, and was back in August and September the next year for the Olympic games. His affair with Berlin ran its course from initial enchantment to sorrowful farewell in these two summers. Before 1935, Wolfe had known only the southern part of Germany, of which he said, "I had gone back to it in ten thousand dreams and memories of time and of desire—the sunken bell, the Gothic town, the plash of waters in the midnight fountain, the Old Place, the broken chime, and the blond flesh of secret, lavish women." Wolfe came to Berlin in this extravagant mood, but more than Wagnerian romanticism was working for Hitler's Berlin with him. He went to Berlin weary from a five-year struggle with *Of Time and the River* and was, he said, "fed up to the roots of my soul with . . . being *alone*."[16] Thus it is not surprising that he found in Berlin a mistress suited to his romantic adoration.

His first novel, *Look Homeward, Angel*, published in Berlin in a fine translation by Hans Schiebelhuth, was greeted with praise by German critics, who called it, in Herman Hesse's words, "the most impressive poetical work from present-day America." Its poetic qualities and its freedom from political commitment made Wolfe a writer about whom both the repressed German intellectual and the Nazi party member could agree. Hence, he satisfied a cultural hunger in the Berliners, and his visits were what Martha Dodd, the daughter of the American ambassador, called "the most vital experience literary Berlin had in the Hitler years."[17]

Wolfe's was the Berlin of the Tiergarten and Charlottenburg. Its eastward extension from the Brandenburger Gate was almost exclusively along the Unter den Linden. To the west it extended to Westend and to the beaches and restaurants of the Wannsee and the Grunewaldsee. This was, in 1935 as it is now, the visitor's Berlin, the city of gay nightlife, of restaurants, cafés, and fine stores, of twinkling lights, great trees, and parks.

His first view of the city came as his train from Hannover moved to the Bahnhof Am Zoo. From there he went three blocks to his hotel, and then on to a reception at the American ambassador's house on Tiergarten Strasse. He said, "Along the streets in the Tiergarten, in all the great gardens, and along the Spree Canal the horse chestnut trees were in full bloom. The crowds sauntered underneath the trees on the Kurfürstendamm, the terraces of the cafés were jammed with people, and always, through the golden sparkle of the days, there was a sound of music in the air."[18] It was plainly love at first sight.

Wolfe lived both summers at the Hotel Am Zoo on the Kurfürstendamm—well established, in that day and in this, as a leading Berlin hotel and a headquarters for journalists and writers, and the home now of the International Film Festival. But he spent so much time with the Dodds that he could say that he was almost a resident of the American Embassy. Martha Dodd introduced Wolfe to important places, political figures, and celebrities, among them Charles A. Lindbergh and William L. Shirer, who included a complimentary vignette of Wolfe in his *Berlin Diary*. She took him to Weimar, where he shouted rhapsodies to "the demented wind" in the great trees at Goethe's garden house, much as he had shouted them to the winds and trees in his native North Carolina Mountains. Wolfe was delighted by the flaming blood beech, the pines, the limes, and the great flowering horse chestnuts of northern Germany. He visited Schiller's tomb at Weimar, thought he found Luther's spirit at Eisenach, relived the Venusburg drama at the Wartburg, and returned through the dark beauty of the Harz Mountains. His mind was haunted by the spirit of Germany's past, and he declared that "there was not a man or woman alive in the world who was not, in one way or another, the richer for . . . this German spirit in art, literature, music, science, and philosophy."[19]

Wolfe was the center of what seemed a revival of that spirit. The Romanisches Café on Budapester Strasse, in the shadow of the Kaiser Wilhelm Gedächtniskirche, a center of literary life in pre-Hitler Berlin, came back to life during his visit. There, both inside and on its famed terrace, he held court among literary and intellectual figures who had seldom been seen abroad since Hitler came to power.

Wolfe joined in the life of artists and writers in cafés and wine restaurants near the Zoological Garden and the Tiergarten. He and Heinz Ledig-Rowohlt, the son of his publisher, Ernst Rowohlt, roamed the Kurfürstendamm, Berlin's equivalent of Fifth Avenue. They frequented the garden of the Alte Klause; the Café of Anne Menz on the Augsburger Strasse, where they ate chicken soup at three in the morning; and the Café Bristol on the Kurfürstendamm, a place famed for its nougat cakes. Wolfe attended notoriously exuberant parties at Ernst Rowohlt's flat on the Rankestrasse and shopped on the Tauentzienstrasse, a street of fine stores. Thus he stayed most of the time within the sound of the striking clock in "the great, bleak masses" of the Gedächtniskirche.

What he saw was a vast city, then the largest in area in the world, with buildings intermingled among lakes, gardens, and trees. He wrote of "the chains of endlessly lovely lakes" and the "beautiful bronze upon the tall poles of the *kiefern* trees." He praised the "broad sweep" of Unter den Linden, "the vast avenues of the faery Tiergarten," and the trees in the center of the Kurfürstendamm that had "that deep and dark intensity of German green which . . . has a kind of forest darkness." He addressed rhapsodies to "the glittering trains of the Stadtbahn" and their "beautiful, shining cars—deep maroon, red, and golden yellow." He praised the trams, declaring that "like everything the Germans built, the tram and its roadbed were perfect in their function."[20] A well-known photograph shows Wolfe standing at the door of a tram, almost dwarfing it by his enormous height.

Sometimes he wandered further. Once, after an all-night session in the Kurfürstendamm cafés, he went to the Grunewaldsee, whose dark surface so mirrored the ancient fir trees around the lake that Wolfe gave an animal cry of delight. There, at the Schloss Marquardt, he had breakfast and entertained his friends with imitations of American Indians. He frequented Schlichter's on the Martin-Luther Strasse, a special epicure's delight, and sometimes ate lunch at Habel's on Unter den Linden. He also explored Potsdam briefly. The Funkturm in Charlottenburg, a radio tower with its steel lattice rising to 450 feet and a restaurant at 165 feet which had a magnificent view of the city, delighted him.

Wolfe called the Olympia Stadium in Charlottenburg "the most beautiful and most perfect in its design that had ever been built." The pageantry surrounding the Olympic games in 1936 was, he believed, "breathtaking in its beauty and magnificence," a "massed splendor of banners"—the whole a tribute to organization which he called "superb." He even thrilled to the marching soldiers. He wrote of the Brownshirts as "young men laughing and talking with each other—the Leader's bodyguards, the Schutz Staffel units, the Storm Troopers, all the ranks and divisions in their different uniforms—[as] they stretched into unbroken lines from the Wilhelm-Strasse up to the arches of the Brandenburger Tor." And he described with seeming approval "the solid smack of 10,000 leather boots as they came together with the sound of war."[21] Here, certainly, was a young man responding with an almost Germanic fervor to the sights and sounds of Hitler's Germany.

The physical city he knew no longer exists, for it lay in the center of the path of the Allied bombers. Its landmarks were destroyed or they suffered major damage—the Brandenburger Tor, the Kurfürstendamm, the Zoological Gardens. The trees of the Tiergarten were used as fuel by the Berliners in the late years of the war. The Romanisches Café, where Wolfe was lionized, exists today in an ultramodern building in the Europa Center, where it survives primarily as a collection of relics of its own past. The Kaiser Wilhelm Gedächtniskirche stands now with its ruined tower incongruously linked to a very modern structure. If Wolfe could visit Berlin now, not only the Wall but almost everything would be different.

But the Berlin that Wolfe loved, in fact, no longer truly existed when he was enchanted with it, for it had already fallen victim to Hitler's Third Reich. Although the restrictive Nazi monetary policies forced Wolfe to go to Berlin to spend the royalties that he could not otherwise receive, it took him a long time to see that the Germany he loved had fallen before the march of the Brownshirts. But he came at last to see these soldiers not as the heroes which he first described them as but as "young barbarians dressed like soldiers," and he came at last to know that all the greenness, efficiency, color, and organization of Berlin was "a picture of the Dark Ages come again—shocking beyond belief, but true as the hell that man forever creates for himself." When this knowledge came, he recognized that he must say farewell to his mistress-city, and he said it in sorrow, and with a tremendous sense of loss, but still in Wagnerian terms:

147

"Old master, wizard Faust, old father of the ancient and swarm-haunted mind of man, old earth, old German land with all the measure of your truth, your glory, beauty, magic and your ruin; and dark Helen burning in our blood, great queen and mistress, sorceress—dark land, dark land, old ancient earth I love—farewell!" [22]

The love affair thus ended, and the Germany that had given him the greatest measure of recognition and of joy that he had ever known was forever closed to him after he published his picture of the Nazis' inhumanity to man in the short novel, *"I Have a Thing to Tell You."* [23] For, with the novelist's sense of people and emotions, Wolfe finally saw, beneath the world of green trees and lakes, beneath the breadth of clean streets and the ponderous grace of Gothic buildings, the darkness of the Nazi world.

Wolfe's love affair with Berlin was brief, ecstatic, tempestuous, overblown, and adolescent, and it ended in the sorrow of parting; but, like many adolescent love affairs, it was for him a major initiation into maturity.

Though he had only two years remaining in which to realize the vision which he caught on that occasion and which he expressed most plainly in his short novel *"I Have a Thing to Tell You,"* these brief journeys brought him face to face with a rampant evil that was loose in his world and forced him to a major and soul-searching re-evaluation of his easy acceptance of life and the life principle as unqualifiedly good. As Bella Kussy says, "In Germany under the Nazis he had seen the ultimate political and social effects of that vitalism which has been the supreme impetus and characteristic of his own life and work. Still susceptible to its fascination and power, still conscious of it as basic and essential and all-pervasive in his own life, he sees that he must either accept its social consequences or reject it completely; and he has enough humanity and resolution in him to do the latter." [24] Out of this rejection comes what Miss Kussy calls "Wolfe's new democratic 'social consciousness.' " Unquestionably the greater maturity, social awareness, and objectivity of *You Can't Go Home Again* result in large part from this instruction in the human capacity for evil.

Wolfe's European experiences clearly did serve to broaden and enrich him, to instruct him in the nature of his world, and to give him detachment and distance from which to view his subject matter. Europe in this sense was in a major way a catalyst for an intensely American talent. Between Wolfe and America a reaction occurred that might be called "catalysis"—"an action or reaction between two or more persons or forces provoked or precipitated by a separate agent or force, especially by one that is essentially unaltered by the reaction." Europe served as this separate agent for Wolfe.

His European experiences were by no means unique, nor was his response to them. His was essentially the response of the self-conscious provincial who elects analysis over adulation and looks upon Europe from the vantage point of an openly American bias. In several respects, Wolfe's reaction to Europe was similar to some of Mark Twain's reactions, notably in *The Innocents Abroad*.[25] It is necessary to recognize that, as it did for travelers like Mark Twain, Europe was for Wolfe another frontier of experience but still an essentially American frontier. It was in this respect that he differed most significantly from those members of the "Lost Generation" who turned their backs upon the America of the middle class, the *Saturday Evening Post*, the Saturday night movie, the small town, and the Sunday band concert, and sought in a religion of art practiced in an environment of beauty a substitute for a way of life which they did not admire and in which they could not comfortably live.[26] They clustered around salons and in the offices of little magazines and were a powerful force in the maturing of American literary art. It is difficult to overestimate their value in the development of a sense of form and a formalist critical doctrine in American writing. But Wolfe was never happy or comfortable with them. He always tended to mock the aesthetes. In his long satiric description of Professor Hatcher's celebrated drama course at Harvard, he had laughed at those who found pretentious art a religious exercise. He was especially contemptuous of their "arty talk," of which he said:

It gave to people without talent and without sincerity of soul or integrity of purpose, with nothing, in fact, except a feeble incapacity for the shock and agony of life, and a desire to escape into a glamorous and unreal world of make believe—a justification for their pitiable and base existence. It gave to people who had no power in themselves to create anything of merit or of beauty—people who were the true Philistines and enemies of art and of the artist's living spirit—the language to talk with glib know-ingness of things they knew nothing of—to prate of "settings," "tempo," "pace," and "rhythm," of "boldly stylized conventions," and the wonder-ful way some actress "used her hands." And in the end, it led to nothing but falseness and triviality, to the ghosts of passion, and the spectres of sincerity.[27]

Wolfe's Francis Starwick in *Of Time and the River* was a de-vastating portrait of a midwesterner who has come East and then to Europe and who embraces all the shibboleths of the young art group. One episode that is revelatory of Wolfe's strong preference for America has to do with Starwick's enthusiasm for French names: "But their genius for names is quite astonishing!—I mean, even in the names of their towns you get the whole thing," he says, and then mocks the *"horrible"* appropriateness of some of the names in Eu-gene's region: "Beaverdam and Balsam, and Chimney Rock and Craggy and Pisgah and The Rat ... Old Fort, Hickory, and Bryson City ... Clingman's Dome and Little Switzerland ... Paint Rock and Saluda Mountain and the Frying Pan Gap."[28] Here the guise of fiction has, for the moment, been dropped; these are quite literal names from the North Carolina mountains.

Wolfe himself was never a part of an artistic group. He was al-ways separate from his fellows, and he lived in a solitary world. He declared in an autobiographical fragment which exists in many ver-sions, one of which Edward Aswell published as "God's Lonely Man": "My life, more than that of anyone I know, has been spent in solitude and wandering. ... From my fifteenth year—save for a single interval—I have lived about as solitary a life as a modern man can have. I mean by this that the number of hours, days, months, and years that I have spent alone has been immense and extraordi-nary."[29] He was a lonely and solitary traveler both at home and in Europe. Furthermore, he was offended by those with whom he came in contact who were even on the edges of the expatriate movements, the most startling example being F. Scott Fitzgerald whom he seems to have disliked intensely.[30]

He went to Europe initially with all the romantic expectations of a small-town or country boy who loved books. England was for him the enchanted isle, rich in story, rich in all the range of literary associations. He considered England "Heaven."[31] In London he declared himself to be "now lost in the beauty and mystery and fascination of this ancient and magnificent city." In Paris, on the first journey, he felt himself "entering a new world of art and letters."[32] He made the standard pilgrimages and visited the literary shrines, and was, in general, a wide-eyed and romantic tourist. He was much like George Webber, of whom he wrote: "He was single, twenty-four years old, American. And . . . like certain tens of thousands of [young Americans], he had gone forth to seek the continental Golden Fleece."[33] But he came to see his romantic quest as a little ridiculous and mocked himself in ballad parody: "The night was long, the way was cold: the minstrel young was overbold: he carried in his great valise, two pairs of socks and one chemise, and in his hand, to stay the curse, the Oxford Book of English Verse. Under a sky of leaden grey, he went from Chartres unto Potay, and from that point he journeyed on, until he came to Orleans."[34]

Wolfe continued to like England throughout his life, but he cared for France hardly at all. He distrusted and disliked the French people, and seemingly only among the peasant class could he find Frenchmen with whom he felt at home. He wrote: "The Frenchman is lacking in true wisdom: he is tragically poisoned in his art, his life, his education."[35] The Germans, on the other hand, were his father's people; and somehow Germany was for him the fatherland. It was for him, as he described it as being for George Webber, "the other part of his heart's home, a haunted part of dark desire, a magic domain of fulfillment. It was the dark, lost Helen that had been forever burning in his blood—the dark, lost Helen he had found . . . old

151

German land with all the measure of your truth, your glory, beauty, magic." [36]

What has been pointed out by many people about Wolfe in relation to New York is also true of his relation to Europe, that he was the perennial provincial, the country boy, fascinated by the city, fascinated by the world; and it was with an open-eyed and provincial astonishment that he looked out upon the Europe which he toured. He once wrote a friend: "What mistakes I failed to make in Paris, I managed to make in other parts of the continent before I was through. I seem to have been born a Freshman—and in many ways I'm afraid I'll continue to be one." [37]

Not only was he rapidly plunged into the depths of loneliness and his masses of mistakes on these solitary pilgrimages, he also was angered by attacks upon America of the sort that was common among the expatriate groups; and he rose vigorously to the defense of his native land in terms that would have been appropriate in Asheville's Rotary Club. He said, for example, in a letter to his mother:

American vulgarity and American Philistinism is a source of much satire and jest; also the American tourist who spends his money here. I suppose, like all nations, we have our vulgarities; but I have seen no group of people more vulgar in its manners, its speech, and the tone of its voices than the French middle class and no matter how materially-minded our own people have been, or are now, there is a certain satisfaction in knowing that, at least, they wash themselves with some regularity.

I shall never go about waving my country's flag—I believe I recognize a great many of our faults, but the faults I recognize are not the faults Europeans accuse us of. That is what sometimes annoys me. They may curse us all they please if they only curse us for sins we have committed; but they are forever cursing us for things we are not guilty of. [38]

These European experiences would hardly have been the raw materials for a writer aiming at a well-made novel of the School of Flaubert or Henry James; and to appreciate fully what Europe contributed to Wolfe, it is necessary to recognize that his true subject and his consistent one, binding together into a unity the diffuse parts of his sprawling books, is his own deep immersion in experience and, in particular, the experience of being an American. He is not a novelist in the true sense of the word; he is a maker of epics; and, like Whitman, he recognized that the American epic was ultimately the song of the democratic man sung by himself. In his common experiences of the length and breadth, the light and darkness, the beauty and ugliness of his land and his people, Wolfe found the subject for his work. In attempting to realize it, he created self-contained, dramatic, lyric, and rhapsodic passages which become, like the segments of *Leaves of Grass*, short but total records of parts of his experience. What Europe gave him more than anything else was not its storied history or the beauty of its landscape or the grace of its culture or the ability to associate with great men but simply a sense of difference, an awareness that somehow these differences defined what it is to be American. He went to Europe not to escape but to seek the dream of a paradise. He found not paradise but loneliness. Out of that loneliness came his subject. Out of that subject there came a desperate awareness that the American artist must seek and find new traditions and new methods.

What emerges finally from his experience with Europe is not his expatriation or necessarily any internationalism in his cultural view but rather an awareness of an artistic task that the American writer must undertake in difficulty and with fear but in which he must succeed if, as Wolfe sees it, he is to be both artist and American. Without Europe, his relationship to his own land and his own past might never have been clear to him. Hence Europe was a catalyst, not an actor in the reaction; and out of that catalysis came the declaration with which he closed *The Story of a Novel*, perhaps as profound a judgment about the complex fate of being an American as he was ever to make:

It is not merely that in the culture of Europe and of the Orient the American artist can find no antecedent scheme, no structural plan, no body of tradition that can give his own work the validity and truth that it must have. It is not merely that he must make somehow a new tradition for himself, derived from his own life and from the enormous space and energy of American life, the structure of his own design; it is not merely that he is confronted by these problems; it is even more than this, that the labor of a complete and whole articulation, the discovery of an entire universe and of a complete language, is the task that lies before him.

... Out of the billion forms of America, out of the savage violence and the dense complexity of all its swarming life; from the unique and single substance of this land and life of ours, must we draw the power and energy of our own life, the articulation of our speech, the substance of our art.

For here it seems to me in hard and honest ways like these we may find the tongue, the language, and the conscience that as men and artists we have got to have. Here, too, perhaps, must we who have no more than what we have, who know no more than what we know, who are no more than what we are, find our America.[39]

Thus did the catalytic Europe bring the artist Wolfe to an aware-ness of his subject America. As Kathleen Hoagland said of Wolfe, "I know why he writes like he does. He's in love with America."[40] Europe made him achingly aware of that love.

VIII   The Epic Impulse

THE TERM *epic*, like *novel*, describes a loosely defined group of narratives that defy precise or wholly satisfactory
definition. But in the common—and often in the sophisticated—sense,
it refers to a long account, usually poetic, of the mighty deeds of a
hero of great importance, consists of numerous episodes, is vast in its
scope and elevated in its style. Robert Scholes and Robert Kellogg
see it as a primitive amalgam of "actual historical persons, places, or
events" with "characters derived from myth," so that it is "poised
between the world of ritual and legend . . . and the world of history
and fiction," and becomes "a kind of anthology of heroic deeds in
chronological order."[1] Although few words are used more loosely,
epic is almost always a term indicative of worthily ambitious intent
and courageous inclusiveness, and it usually is considered to embody
the ideals of a nation or a race through the use of an archetype of the
nation's dreams as its protagonist. The supreme example of this aspect of the epic is Virgil's *Aeneid*, which, as Seymour M. Pitcher
has observed, was "deliberately conceived . . . to give meaning to the
destiny of a people, asserting the implications of their history and
recognizing the significance of contemporary events in relation to
the past."[2] The epic, thus, has been the customary way in which
peoples and nations have comprehended their history, recorded their
dreams, and defined their ideals; and in the epic hero they have given
dramatic expression to their national aspirations. As John Crowe
Ransom has said, "The epic arises as the expression of a nation which

has gone through strife. And it's the representation of the struggle to maintain its ideals and to express its religion and its culture and its heroism." [3]

This hunger to define the essence of a way of life and to find in one heroic figure the epitomization of the national ideal has been present in America from its earliest awareness of its distinctive differences from Europe. The older art forms had been definitions of a concept of a hierarchical society, based upon caste, class, and birth. The American experiment was a new expression of man's imagination of himself, a fresh view of man's potential as political entity, as social atom, and as creative experiment. To look back upon the early years of the American experiment from the last third of the twentieth century is to see as old what was startlingly new a hundred and fifty years ago; to accept as obvious what was once shockingly strange; to see man in a context that now seems inevitable but which then was apparently an attack upon the historically accepted context for human beings. The American experiment had its most obvious manifestations in a political revolution, but that political revolution was but one portion of a radical change in the concept of man. Behind the democratic American hovered the long shadows of man's Utopian dreams, and in his hands rested the destiny of human hopes. The human imagination had been given a new image, and that image cried aloud for literary expression.

It is, accordingly, not surprising that Americans from the Revolution onward should have "fixed their literary ambitions on the Great American epic." [4] And the effort to pour the new wine of America into the old wineskins of the traditional epic was widespread and usually disastrous. Among the attempts to sing America and define its soul, Joel Barlow's *The Vision of Columbus* and *The Columbiad* and Richard Emmons' *The Fredoniad*—ambitious, earnest, and unsuccessful—are early types of an effort that later took such diverse forms as Longfellow's *Hiawatha*, Stephen Vincent Benét's *John Brown's Body* and his fragmentary *Western Star*, and Robert Penn Warren's *Brother to Dragons*. All these poets set themselves in their different ways the task of creating what Roy Harvey Pearce has called "that strange, amorphous, anomalous, self-contradictory thing, the American epic."[5] But even Barlow had understood that his task was a new one, freed from the falsities of other societies and ages. "This is the moment in America," he declared, "to give such a direction to poetry . . . that true and useful ideas of glory may be implanted in the minds of men . . . [to replace] the false and destructive ones that have degraded the species in other countries," by which he specifically meant the "pernicious doctrine of the divine rights of kings" which Homer and Virgil had taught.[6]

However far from realization he may have been, Hector St. John de Crèvecoeur's "American" was the national ideal: "*He* is an American who, leaving behind him all his ancient prejudices and manners, receives new ones from the new mode of life he has embraced, the new government he obeys, and the new rank he holds. . . . The American is a new man, who acts upon new principles; he must therefore entertain new ideas, and form new opinions. From involuntary idleness, servile dependence, penury, and useless labor, he has passed to toils of a very different nature, rewarded by ample subsistence."[7] Virgil's *Aeneid* begins, "*Arma virumque cano*," and the "man" is a mighty warrior-hero. But the "man" whom the American maker of epics had to sing was Crèvecoeur's "new man." As Roy Harvey Pearce says, "The history of the American epic is the history of attempts to realize that possibility."[8]

Alexis de Tocqueville, an aristocratic Frenchman who toured America in 1831, was fascinated by the impact that this new vision of man would inevitably have on literature, and finally concluded that the only effective subject for the democratic poet is himself: "Among a democratic people poetry will not be fed with legends or the memorials of old traditions. . . . All these resources fail him; but Man remains, and the poet needs no more. The destinies of mankind, man himself taken aloof from his country and his age and standing in the presence of Nature and of God, with his passions, his doubts, his rare prosperities and inconceivable wretchedness, will become the chief, if not the sole, theme of poetry among these nations." He also asserts that it is not the past but the future in which the democratic man is interested. "As all the citizens who compose a democratic community are nearly equal and alike, the poet cannot dwell upon any one of them; but the nation itself invites the exercise of his powers."[9] Thus the national hero tends to be lost.

But the nation itself as subject also presents problems. For artistic treatment it asks for emphasis on history, which has little reality to the democratic writer whose eyes are fixed on the future, or emphasis on the picturing of its social and political structure. And here the paucity of native materials makes itself felt. James Fenimore Cooper, in 1828, could despairingly write of America: "There are no annals for the historian; no follies (beyond the most vulgar and commonplace) for the satirist; no manners for the dramatist; no obscure fictions for the writer of romance."[10] And Nathaniel Hawthorne, in 1859, could complain of "the difficulty of writing a romance about a country where there is no shadow, no antiquity, no mystery, no picturesque and gloomy wrong."[11] The American literary artist early understood that, as John Morton Blum has expressed it, "The United States was born in history, too late to symbolize its aspirations in the exploits of an Apollo or an Arthur. . . . In the beginning the Olympus of Americans was a place inhabited by men, not gods."[12] One way around such a problem appears to be to write of those whom Benét celebrated in *Western Star*:

> . . . all these, the nameless, numberless
> Seed of the field, the mortal wood and earth
> Hewn for the clearing, trampled for the floor,
> Uprooted and cast out upon the stone
> From Jamestown to Benicia.
> This is their song, this is their testament.[13]

But such attempts seem not to succeed, perhaps because they show the epic urge but lack adequate dramatic centers.

Once more it is Tocqueville who gives us a clue. "I am persuaded," he said, "that in the end democracy diverts the imagination from all that is external to man and fixes it on man alone."[14] What

Tocqueville is describing here is not a process limited to America, of course. But in Europe and England its artistic expression had to overcome the inertia of literary conventions resting on a real social order. For example, the Byronic hero—remote, powerful, brooding, beyond good and evil—was for a time an effective spokesman for Europe's hunger for freedom before his society reached a stage when the hero was not a tenable image. In England, as Jacques Barzun has noted, "the Byronic hero comes to an end when he joins the Fabian Society."[15] In America no such delay occurred; for however fascinating the brooding Byronic hero might be to the individual Romantic, as a symbol of freedom in an egalitarian society he was not only practically without value but even a little absurd.

The American celebrator of his nation had ultimately to turn to himself as the only adequate material for the epic hero, and to wrestle from the resistant substance of his experience those common qualities which he shared with all his brother Americans. When Walt Whitman opens his epic with the customary annunciation of his subject, he says, in what seems to be conscious imitation of Virgil:

> I celebrate myself, and sing myself,
> And what I assume you shall assume,
> For every atom belonging to me as good belongs to you.[16]

He was taking an inevitable course; Virgil's *virum* has become those aspects of Walt Whitman which he shares with all men. As Roy Harvey Pearce has observed: "The author of the American epic must be his own hero, as his epic is the record of his struggle to make something of himself and of the world which constitutes his central subject. Thus in some way or another he must tell all; he wills himself to be incapable of dissembling or repression, lest something of the creative self be left out."[17] In these terms Pearce finds, not the traditional imitations of the epic, but rather Whitman's *Song of Myself*, Ezra Pound's *Cantos*, Hart Crane's *The Bridge*, and William Carlos Williams' *Paterson* to be the most nearly successful approaches to an American epic poem.

This tendency to make the American epic autobiographical[18] is not limited to poetry. American novelists have also and often aspired to the creation of a fictional epic of their land, and, particularly after the Civil War, America sought to produce the "Great American Novel" instead of the American epic poem.[19] They were, perhaps, encouraged by Henry Fielding's definition of the novel as the "comic epic poem in prose." William Gilmore Simms, in 1835, said, "The modern Romance is the substitute which the people of today offer for the ancient epic. The form is changed; the matter is very much the same."[20] When Herman Melville produced in *Moby-Dick* the most original of American romances, one of the problems which he felt that he faced was that of writing of heroic deeds in a world of "commoners." He wishes to give his mariners an "august dignity" that he declares to be "not the dignity of kings and robes, but that abounding dignity which has no investiture. . . . If, then, to meanest mariners, and renegades and castaways, I shall hereafter ascribe high qualities . . . Bear me out in it, thou great democratic God!"[21]

Many others have labored to make the Muse at home in a new land or to fashion from the "kingly commoners" a national hero for a democratic nation. Writing of John Dos Passos' trilogy *U.S.A.*, John Braine said:

To take the U.S.A. as a subject for a novel one needs to have not only an enormous talent but a clarity of vision amounting to simple-mindedness. . . . the more the novelist thinks about it the more impossibly complex the theme becomes, and at the same time the more naive he considers himself for even considering it. He will write about the part of the country he knows the best, and if he tells the truth about this, he hopes he will tell the truth about the whole. . . . One doesn't produce a novel about a country and a period but about human beings, and their environment must be rooted in the author's own experience.[22]

Whether doomed ultimately to such frustrating conclusions or not, American novelists—like American poets—have often attempted to meet the challenge. Cooper attempted it with *The Leatherstocking Tales*; Simms in seven loosely connected romances of the American Revolution with General Francis Marion as their epic hero; Melville attempted it in *Moby-Dick*, Ross Lockridge in *Raintree County*, Carl Sandburg in *Remembrance Rock*.

But in many respects the most massive and impressive of the efforts to fashion an American epic was that of Thomas Wolfe. The vast, incomplete, and imperfect work on which he labored and which he persisted in calling simply "the book," was an effort at the "Great American Novel" that surpasses even Dos Passos' *U.S.A.* in scope, ambition, and intensity, although it is badly flawed in parts. At the time of his death in 1938, just before his thirty-eighth birthday, Wolfe had published two long novels, a collection of short stories and short novels, and an essay on literary method. He left behind an enormous mass of manuscript out of which his editor quarried two more novels and another collection of short pieces. All these works have a common subject and one almost universally recognized as Wolfe's own experience in his world presented under the transparent disguises of two protagonists, Eugene Gant and George Webber. Although this subject is treated in a variety of literary modes, forming a potpourri of dramatic scenes, narrative passages, lyrical descriptions, tone-poems, rhetorical incantations, and satirical social sketches, the works are all portions of one vast effort much like Whitman's attempt, as he expressed it, "to put a *Person*, a human being (myself, in the latter half of the Nineteenth Century, in America,) freely, fully, and truly on record."[23]

To look at Wolfe's "book" as an attempt at an American epic helps us see what he is about and appreciate at least some of the causes for his successes and his failures. He felt a compulsive need to "sing America." As he expressed it in 1936: "I have at last discovered my own America. . . . And I shall wreak out my vision of this life, this way, this world and this America, to the top of my bent, to the height of my ability, but with an unswerving devotion, integrity and purity of purpose that shall not be menaced, altered or weakened by any one."[24] In addition to this epic urge, the nature and content of his work was shaped by the quality of his personal experience, by the influence of John Livingston Lowes's theory of the imagination, and by the special way in which he wrote. Out of the interactions of these things with his powerful rhetoric and his dramatic talent came a body of writing which corresponds with remarkable accuracy to the special shapes and tensions of the American epic.

His brief life was successively pastoral, provincial, urban, national, and international; and it embraced a great range of experience. It was in Europe that he discovered his true subject, America (or perhaps more accurately the American experience). He said: "I discovered America during these years abroad out of my very need of her. The huge gain of this discovery seemed to come directly from my sense of loss."[25] Out of the memories induced by this "bitter ache of homelessness," this "desperate longing for America," Wolfe began the writing which was to give him what appears to be a permanent place in American letters. The first of the volumes of his "book," *Look Homeward, Angel*, appeared in 1929, just nine years before his untimely death. In those nine years he read, wrote, traveled, and "lived," with great energy and obsessive intensity. He traveled over much of Europe and America, wrote millions of words, consumed books—all in a gargantuan effort to encompass the contradictory and complex experience of being a democratic man, a son of America and its dream, a twentieth-century prophet-seer. As much, perhaps, as anyone else has ever done, Wolfe did live out the common American experience: he was the small-town, middle-class provincial who moved to great centers of learning, to New York—"the enfabled rock"—and then to Europe, which served as an intellectual and emotional vantage point from which to look homeward and evaluate the American experience.

As he moved through these stages, Wolfe was formatively influenced in his concept of art and the artist by John Livingston Lowes's theories of the functioning of the creative imagination. He studied under Lowes while Lowes was writing his justly famous study of Coleridge, *The Road to Xanadu*, and heard Lowes read chapters of this new book to his classes. Indeed, Wolfe's name appears—misspelled—in footnotes to the volume, where he is credited with having identified the source of Coleridge's "Like April hoar-frost spread," an image which, Lowes says, had slipped "into the 'thousand-celled darkness' of Coleridge's unconscious mind."[26] And Wolfe wrote a term paper for Lowes on "The Supernatural in the Poetry and Philosophy of Coleridge."[27] Lowes's theory greatly encouraged Wolfe's innate epic impulse, for he believed that an artist stored experiences of all kinds—physical, emotional, intellectual, and vicarious—in his "deep well of unconscious cerebration," and that there, in the fullness of time, "the shaping power of the imagination" worked upon it to create an ordered cosmos out of this teeming and fecund chaos.[28] Lowes said: "The imagination never operates in a vacuum. Its stuff is always fact of some order, somehow experienced; its product is that fact transmuted. I am not forgetting that facts may swamp imagination, and remain unassimilated and untransformed." At another place he said: "For the Road to Xanadu, as we have traced it, is the road of the human spirit, and the imagination voyaging through chaos and reducing it to clarity and order is the symbol of all the quests which lend glory to our dust. . . . For the work of the creators is the mastery and transmutation and reordering into shapes of beauty of the given universe within us and without us."[29] Wolfe added to these ideas a conviction that "*conscious* interests and efforts at all times" are working in the making of art from the matter in the "deep well of unconscious cerebration."[30] Thus Lowes's ideas, together with certain of his cadences and phrases, encouraged Wolfe's frantic attempt to "stockpile" experience of all kinds, with the intention of later drawing consciously upon it for the materials of his art.

Out of his commitment to this view of the imagination probably came at least the sanction if not the full impulse for Wolfe's effort to engulf all experience. He seems plainly to be writing autobiographically when he says of Eugene Gant:

He was driven by a hunger so literal, cruel and physical that it wanted to devour the earth and all the things and people in it . . . He read insanely, by the hundreds, the thousands, the ten thousands . . . It would now seem to him that . . . at this moment something precious, irrecoverable was happening in the streets, and that if he could only get to it in time and see it, he would somehow get the knowledge of the whole thing in him —the source, the well, the spring from which all men and words and actions, and every design upon this earth proceeds.[31]

In *The Story of a Novel,* speaking directly of his experiences as a writer, Wolfe says: "Three years of work and perhaps a million and a half words went into these . . . great ledgers. . . . It included everything from gigantic and staggering lists of the towns, cities, counties, states, and countries I had been in, to minutely thorough, desperately evocative descriptions . . . of an American railway train. There were lists of the rooms and houses in which I had lived or in which I had slept for at least a night. . . . There were countless charts, catalogues, descriptions that I can only classify here under the general heading of Amount and Number."[32] Few writers have ever immersed themselves in the turbulent stream of experience more thoroughly than Wolfe; few writers have tried to touch more segments of America and know them with greater sensory surety.

In addition to this passion for experience, Wolfe had too a sensibility and a memory unusual in their power to recall odors, sounds, colors, shapes, and the feel of things with great precision. When these qualities were combined with his hunger for experience, Wolfe possessed a subject matter appropriate to the ambition of an epic poet, and he could, with some justification, feel that his experience approached that of everyman-in-America's and was thus a subject adequate to describe the democratic protagonist.

Wolfe's method of working, too, yielded itself quite easily to the attempt at a modern epic. With a remarkable ear for speech and eye for physical detail and with an equally keen sense of character and of dramatic action, Wolfe as person encountered experiences which seem to have come to him in relatively short and self-contained units. Many of these units are self-sufficient short stories and short novels— both forms in which he did excellent work. It is when these short stories and short novels become the materials of the long narratives that they begin to lose much of their objectivity and dramatic intensity. Even in *Look Homeward, Angel*, frequently and accurately called his most unified work, the individual episodes exist so independently that many can be extracted and published as self-contained units—short stories—without doing violence to their fundamental meaning.[33] The satiric portrait of Professor Hatcher's playwriting course in *Of Time and the River* is a unified piece that is broken into four separate parts.[34] The picture of Abraham Jones, a detailed character study in the same novel, is also fragmented into three parts.[35] The posthumously published novels were assembled by Edward Aswell and, therefore, the unity or the fragmentary character of their episodes cannot be directly attributed to Wolfe. However, some of their finest parts originally appeared as self-contained units in magazines; for example, "The Child by Tiger" in *The Web and the Rock*, "Boom Town," "The Party at Jack's," and " 'I Have a Thing to Tell You' " in *You Can't Go Home Again*.[36]

Wolfe's method seemingly was to write these episodes with much of the objectivity of an observer, and then later to fit them into the experience of the observer. Hence they play a part not unlike the long and varied vicarious experiences of Walt Whitman in *Song of Myself*. Such a method is not a very fruitful one for the novel, but for the epic it is reasonably workable. If we can consider the novel, at least in its "well-made" examples, to be not unlike Aristotle's tragedy, we may use Aristotle to gain for the epic a liberty from these binding restrictions of plot, consistency, and causation to which the tragedy—and some forms of the novel—is subject. Indeed, although it is highly questionable that Wolfe ever sought or relied upon authority for his artistic methods, Aristotle's discussion of the structure of the epic is almost a discussion of Wolfe's method in his "book." Aristotle says: "Epic poetry has, however, a great—a special—capacity for enlarging its dimensions." Distinguishing between a controlling action and episodes, he says: "Thus the story of the *Odyssey* can be stated briefly. A certain man is absent from home for many years; he is jealously watched by Poseidon and left desolate. Meanwhile his home is in a wretched plight—suitors are wasting his substance and plotting against his son. At length, tempest-tossed, he himself arrives; he makes certain persons acquainted with him; he attacks the suitors with his own hand and is himself preserved while he destroys them. This is the essence of the plot; the rest is episode." Indeed, Aristotle asserts, "The epic imitation has less unity [than tragedy has] . . . the poem is composed out of several actions." [37] Such a definition applied to Wolfe's "book" would find in its controlling action—that is, "the essence of its plot"—the experiences of Wolfe (under the guises of Eugene Gant and George Webber) as he moved from childhood and "the meadows of sensation" through adolescence to maturity in his search for identity as an American. The rest are "episodes," events which, however real to those who participate in them, are significant in the making of this American primarily in what they teach him about the difficulty of being a democratic man on this continent. The search aims at bringing him self-knowledge, but as he matures it aims increasingly at bringing him a definition of the representative aspects of his national being. As his life was an outward movement, so are his books outward movements. From the absorption in the self, he moves to an absorption in society. The road from *Look Homeward, Angel* to *You Can't Go Home Again* is the trail of the epic impulse. From the baby's contemplation of its own toe, Wolfe moves to the serious portrayal of the social world, but always in terms of how that world registers on his own consciousness and becomes a part of his experience as a representative American.

Eugene Gant was a person of whom Wolfe could say that, as a boy, "He did not want to reform the world, or to make it a better place to live in." [38] He came finally to see, even in those he loved "his vision of the grand America . . . the structure of that enchanted life of which every American has dreamed . . . a world distilled of our own blood and earth, and qualified by all our million lights and weathers, and we know that it will be noble, intolerably strange and lovely, when we find it." [39] And before his career was to reach its untimely end, he was to be able to take his reader to the place "where the hackles of the Rocky Mountains blaze in the blank and naked radiance of the moon" and bid him "make your resting stool upon the highest peak" and from that vantage point survey the vast and lonely sweep of continent to east and west. And to find in a Negro boy in the Chicago slums, in a young baseball player in "the clay-baked outfields down in Georgia," and in an intense and studious Jewish boy in "the East-Side Ghetto of Manhattan" the essence of his native land and the symbols of its grand design and promise.[40] Thus he can declare: "So, then, to every man his chance—to every man, regardless of his birth, his shining, golden opportunity—to every man the right to live, to work, to be himself, and to become whatever thing his manhood and his vision can combine to make him—this, seeker, is the promise of America."[41]

However flawed as novels and imperfect as art his books may be, Thomas Wolfe's works constitute a major and remarkably successful effort to write his autobiography as that of a representative American and to embody in the record of his time and deeds on this earth a vision of the nature and the hope of his democratic land.

Notes

CHAPTER I

1 *The Web and the Rock* (New York, 1939), 683.
2 Elizabeth Nowell (ed.), *The Letters of Thomas Wolfe* (New York, 1956), 587, 656.
3 *The Story of a Novel* (New York, 1936), 31.
4 *The Hills Beyond* (New York, 1941), 218.
5 Nowell (ed.), *Letters*, 279.
6 Floyd C. Watkins, *Thomas Wolfe's Characters: Portraits from Life* (Norman, Okla., 1957), 9.
7 *Look Homeward, Angel* (New York, 1929), vii.
8 *Ibid.*, 3, 192–93.
9 Nowell (ed.), *Letters*, 370.
10 *The Story of a Novel*, 8–9.
11 John Hall Wheelock (ed.), *Editor to Author: The Letters of Maxwell E. Perkins* (New York, 1950), 61.
12 Nowell (ed.), *Letters*, 487.
13 Robert Penn Warren, "The Hamlet of Thomas Wolfe," in Richard Walser (ed.), *The Enigma of Thomas Wolfe* (Cambridge, Mass., 1953), 132. Originally published in the *American Review*, May, 1935.
14 Bernard De Voto, "Genius Is Not Enough," in *Forays and Rebuttals* (Boston, 1936), 324–33. Originally published in the *Saturday Review of Literature*, April 25, 1936, pp. 3–4, 14–15.
15 Nowell (ed.), *Letters*, 714.
16 *The Web and the Rock*, 693.
17 Nowell (ed.), *Letters*, 714.
18 Walser (ed.), *The Enigma of Thomas Wolfe*, Preface.
19 Nowell (ed.), *Letters*, 212.
20 *Ibid.*, 241, 234, 489.
21 *Ibid.*, 445.
22 Louis D. Rubin, Jr., *Thomas Wolfe: The Weather of His Youth* (Baton Rouge, La., 1955).
23 "Interview with William Faulkner," in Malcolm Cowley (ed.), *Writers at Work: The Paris Review Interviews* (New York, 1958), 124.
24 *The Web and the Rock*, vi.
25 *Of Time and the River* (New York, 1935), 231.
26 *The Story of a Novel*, 39.
27 *Look Homeward, Angel*, 2.

28 Margaret Church, "Thomas Wolfe: Dark Time," in *Time and Reality: Studies in Contemporary Fiction* (Chapel Hill, N.C., 1963), 207–26.
29 *The Story of a Novel*, 52.
30 *The Hills Beyond*, 14, 22, 29–30, 42.
31 *Of Time and the River*, 155.
32 Karin Pfister, *Zeit und Wirklichkeit bei Thomas Wolfe* (Heidelberg, 1954).
33 *The Web and the Rock*, 626.
34 C. Hugh Holman and Sue F. Ross (eds.), *The Letters of Thomas Wolfe to His Mother* (Chapel Hill, N.C., 1968), 42.
35 *The Story of a Novel*, 59.
36 Pamela Hansford Johnson, *Hungry Gulliver: An English Critical Appraisal of Thomas Wolfe* (New York, 1948), 151.
37 E. B. Burgum, "Thomas Wolfe's Discovery of America," in *The Novel and the World's Dilemma* (New York, 1947), 320.
38 C. Vann Woodward, *The Burden of Southern History* (Baton Rouge, La., 1960), 171.
39 *The Story of a Novel*, 60.
40 *You Can't Go Home Again* (New York, 1940), 434–36.
41 Walt Whitman, "Song of the Exposition," 11. 55–60.
42 Andrew Turnbull (ed.), *The Letters of F. Scott Fitzgerald* (New York, 1963), 251.
43 *You Can't Go Home Again*, 740.

CHAPTER II

1 Philip Rahv, *Literature and the Sixth Sense* (Boston, 1969), 32.
2 Mark Schorer, *World We Imagine* (New York, 1968), 17.
3 Louis D. Rubin, Jr., *Thomas Wolfe: The Weather of His Youth* (Baton Rouge, La., 1955), 27.
4 Floyd C. Watkins, *Thomas Wolfe's Characters: Portraits from Life* (Norman, Okla., 1957), 182.
5 Hayden Norwood, *The Marble Man's Wife: Thomas Wolfe's Mother* (New York, 1947); Mabel Wolfe Wheaton, with LeGette Blythe, *Thomas Wolfe and His Family* (Garden City, N.Y., 1961); Elizabeth Nowell, *Thomas Wolfe: A Biography* (Garden City, N.Y., 1960).
6 Ernest Hemingway, *Death in the Afternoon* (New York, 1932), 278, 1.
7 James Joyce, *A Portrait of the Artist as a Young Man*, ed. Richard Ellmann (New York, 1964), 215.
8 *Look Homeward, Angel*, page following dedication.
9 *The Story of a Novel* (New York, 1936), 21.
10 Bernard De Voto, "Genius Is Not Enough," in *Forays and Rebuttals* (Boston, 1936), 324–33. Originally published in *Saturday Review of Literature*, April 25, 1936, pp. 3–4, 14–15.
11 Carlos Baker, *Hemingway: The Writer As Artist* (3rd ed.; Princeton, N.J., 1963).
12 Hemingway, *Death in the Afternoon*, 2.
13 *The Story of a Novel*, 31–32.
14 Hemingway, *Death in the Afternoon*, 20.
15 *Look Homeward, Angel*, 583. The ellipses are in Wolfe's text.

CHAPTER III

1 *The Story of a Novel* (New York, 1936), 53.
2 Elizabeth Nowell (ed.), *The Letters of Thomas Wolfe* (New York, 1956), 336.

3 The most detailed examination of these efforts is in Richard S. Kennedy, *The Window of Memory: The Literary Career of Thomas Wolfe* (Chapel Hill, N.C., 1962), particularly Parts 4 and 7. It is worthy of note, however, that Joseph Warren Beach recognized and described non-novelistic organization efforts as early as 1940 in his *American Fiction, 1920–1940* (New York, 1941), 173–215.

4 Bernard De Voto, "Genius Is Not Enough," in *Forays and Rebuttals* (Boston, 1936), 324–33. Originally published in the *Saturday Review of Literature*, April 25, 1936, pp. 3–4, 14–15.

5 John Peale Bishop, "The Sorrows of Thomas Wolfe," in Edmund Wilson (ed.), *The Collected Essays of John Peale Bishop* (New York, 1948), 135. Originally published in *Kenyon Review*, I (Winter, 1939), 7–17.

6 Nowell (ed.), *Letters*, 330.

7 C. Hugh Holman and Sue F. Ross (eds.), *The Letters of Thomas Wolfe to His Mother* (Chapel Hill, N.C., 1968), 225.

8 *Of Time and the River* (New York, 1935), 104–11, 116–30, 132, 136–41, 141–50, 177–84, 185–86, 192.

9 A convenient listing of these publications in chronological order is given in Holman and Ross (eds.), *Letters to His Mother*, xxv–xxviii. Many other magazine publications have appeared since Wolfe's death.

10 *Of Time and the River*, 407–19; *The Web and the Rock* (New York, 1939), 441–49; *You Can't Go Home Again* (New York, 1940), 3–4.

11 Nowell (ed.), *Letters*, 631–32.

12 A copy of the salesman's dummy is in the Thomas Wolfe Collection, Pack Memorial Library, Asheville, N.C.

13 Kennedy, *The Window of Memory*, 247–48. He does not put it this bluntly, but he clearly implies this judgment.

14 *The Story of a Novel*, 13–17.

15 Perkins probably underestimated Wolfe's lack of self-confidence. See his account of their relationship in his introduction to *Look Homeward, Angel* (New York, 1962), Scribner Library Edition.

16 Howard Nemerov, "Like Warp and Woof: Composition and Fate in the Short Novel," *Graduate Journal*, V (Winter, 1963), 375.

17 *Ibid.*, 379–80.

18 C. Hugh Holman (ed.), *The Short Novels of Thomas Wolfe* (New York, 1961), reprints the magazine versions of *A Portrait of Bascom Hawke, The Web of Earth, No Door, "I Have a Thing to Tell You,"* and *The Party at Jack's.* The introduction and headnotes give the histories of these short novels. It is worth noting that in *You Can't Go Home Again*, a work whose formal shape Wolfe had little to do with, the separately published works undergo much less fragmentation, and George Webber is a more shadowy figure than the protagonists in the other novels.

19 R. P. Blackmur (ed.), *The Art of the Novel: Critical Prefaces by Henry James* (New York, 1934), 232–33.

20 Nemerov, "Like Warp and Woof," 375.

21 *The Story of a Novel*, 51–52. There have been several excellent studies of Wolfe's concept of time: Karin Pfister, *Zeit und Wirklichkeit bei Thomas Wolfe* (Heidelberg, 1954); Louis D. Rubin, Jr., *Thomas Wolfe: The Weather of His Youth* (Baton Rouge, La., 1955), 28–54; Margaret Church, "Thomas Wolfe: Dark Time," in *Time and Reality: Studies in Contemporary Fiction* (Chapel Hill, N.C., 1963), 207–26.

22 Blackmur (ed.), *The Art of the Novel*, 220.

23 Charles G. Hoffman, *The Short Novels of Henry James* (New York, 1957), 123.

24 Blackmur (ed.), *The Art of the Novel*, 220, 229.
25 *Scribner's Magazine*, LXXXVIII (September, 1930), 33 of front matter.
26 *Ibid.*, XCI (March, 1932), I of front matter.
27 *Ibid.*, LXXXVIII (December, 1930), 86 of back matter.
28 *Ibid.*, LXXXIX (February, 1931), 233.
29 *Ibid.*, XC (August, 1931), 19 of front matter.
30 *Ibid.*, LXXXVIII (July, 1930), 26 of front matter; XC (August, 1931), 18 of front matter.
31 *Ibid.*, LXXXIX (January, 1931), 26 of back matter.
32 *Ibid.*, LXXXVIII (August, 1930), 25 of back matter.
33 *Ibid.*, LXXXVIII (October, 1930), 345.
34 *Ibid.*, CX (August, 1931), 18 of front matter.
35 *Ibid.*, LXXXIX (March, 1931), 29 of front matter.
36 *Ibid.*, LXXXIX (February, 1931), 233.
37 *Ibid.*, CX (August, 1931), 18 of front matter.
38 *Ibid.*, XCII (August, 1932), 10 of back matter.
39 The New York *Sun*, March 31, 1932, quoted in Nowell (ed.), *Letters*, 338.
40 Nowell (ed.), *Letters*, 339.
41 Holman (ed.), *The Short Novels of Thomas Wolfe*, 76–77.
42 Alfred Dashiell (ed.), *Editor's Choice* (New York, 1934), 111.
43 Nowell (ed.), *Letters*, 339.
44 Rubin, *The Weather of His Youth*, 122–23.
45 Nowell (ed.), *Letters*, 378.
46 Holman and Ross (eds.), *Letters to His Mother*, 199.
47 Nowell (ed.), *Letters*, 365.
48 Kennedy, *The Window of Memory*, 259–62, disagrees with my judgment on this matter, arguing that *No Door* had little formative influence.
49 Kennedy, *The Window of Memory*, 261; Holman and Ross (eds.), *Letters to His Mother*, 213.
50 Robert Penn Warren, "The Hamlet of Thomas Wolfe," in Richard Walser (ed.), *The Enigma of Thomas Wolfe* (Cambridge, Mass., 1953), 126. Originally published in the *American Review*, V (May, 1935), 191–208.
51 Nowell (ed.), *Letters*, 631.
52 *Ibid.*, 333, 401, 406, 409. The editor, Charles Angoff, in "Thomas Wolfe and the Opulent Manner," *Southwest Review*, XLVIII (Winter, 1963), 81–84, describes the editing, which he now views as excessive and unfortunate.
53 Nowell (ed.) *Letters*, 700, 488.
54 *Ibid.*, 700.
55 *You Can't Go Home Again*, 729.
56 Nowell (ed.), *Letters*, 631, 652–53.
57 Holman and Ross (eds.), *Letters to His Mother*, 218.
58 *The Story of a Novel*, 51–52.

CHAPTER IV

1 F. K. Stanzel, *Die typischen Erzählsituationen ein Roman* (Vienna, 1955). This work has been translated by James P. Pusack, as *Narrative Situations in the Novel* (Bloomington, Ind., 1971).
2 Van Wyck Brooks, *The Ordeal of Mark Twain* (New York, 1920).
3 Wayne Booth, *The Rhetoric of Fiction* (Chicago, 1961), 323–36.
4 Elizabeth Nowell (ed.), *The Letters of Thomas Wolfe* (New York, 1956), 566.
5 See Francis E. Skipp, "The Editing of *Look Homeward, Angel*," *Papers of the Bibliographical Society of America*, LVII (1963), 1–13.

6 Richard S. Kennedy, "Thomas Wolfe's Fiction: The Question of Genre," in Paschal Reeves (ed.), *Thomas Wolfe and the Glass of Time* (Athens, Ga., 1971), 1–30.
7 *Look Homeward, Angel* (New York, 1929), 2.
8 *Ibid.*, 456.
9 Nowell (ed.), *Letters*, 254, 322, 566, 587, 700.
10 Nowell (ed.), *Letters*, 566.
11 *Look Homeward, Angel*, 625–26.
12 Kennedy, "The Question of Genre," 206.
13 Richard S. Kennedy and Paschal Reeves (eds.), *The Notebooks of Thomas Wolfe* (2 vols.; Chapel Hill, N.C., 1970), II, 468.
14 In the *American Mercury*, August, 1935.
15 In the *New Republic*, March 10, 17, and 24, 1936.
16 In *Scribner's Magazine*, June, 1937.
17 *Saturday Evening Post*, September 11, 1937.
18 *Harper's Bazaar*, October, 1937.
19 Richard S. Kennedy, *The Window of Memory: The Literary Career of Thomas Wolfe* (Chapel Hill, N.C., 1962), 259–75; Nowell (ed.), *Letters*, 219–26.
20 Elizabeth Nowell, *Thomas Wolfe: A Biography* (Garden City, N.Y., 1960), 13.
21 Maxwell Perkins, "Thomas Wolfe," *Harvard Library Bulletin*, I (Autumn, 1947), 272.
22 Kennedy and Reeves (eds.), *Notebooks*, II, 622–38.
23 Perkins, "Thomas Wolfe," 272.
24 Robert Penn Warren, "The Hamlet of Thomas Wolfe," in Richard Walser (ed.), *The Enigma of Thomas Wolfe* (Cambridge, Mass., 1953), 129.
25 John Peale Bishop, "The Sorrows of Thomas Wolfe," in Edmund Wilson (ed.) *The Collected Essays of John Peale Bishop* (New York, 1948), 132–33. Originally published in the *Kenyon Review*, I (Winter, 1939), 7–17.
26 Joseph Warren Beach, *American Fiction, 1920–1940* (New York, 1941), 178–79
27 Kennedy, "The Question of Genre," 25.
28 C. Hugh Holman, "The Loneliness at the Core," *New Republic*, CXXXIII (October 10, 1955), 16–17.
29 *Of Time and the River* (New York, 1935), 53, 90, 853, 856.
30 *You Can't Go Home Again* (New York, 1940), 505–508.
31 *Ibid.*, 741, 737.
32 Nowell (ed.), *Letters*, 641–45.
33 Kennedy and Reeves (eds.), *Notebooks*, II, 832.
34 Nowell (ed.), *Letters*, 211.

CHAPTER V

1 Henry James, "Ivan Turgénieff," *Library of the World's Best Literature* (1897), reprinted in M. D. Zabel (ed.), *The Portable Henry James* (New York, 1968), 457.
2 *Of Time and the River* (New York, 1935), 265.
3 *Ibid.*, 327.
4 Richard S. Kennedy and Paschal Reeves (eds.), *The Notebooks of Thomas Wolfe* (2 vols.; Chapel Hill, N.C., 1970).
5 *Of Time and the River*, 853.
6 I have discussed this aspect of Wolfe's work at length in my essay, "Thomas Wolfe" in William Van O'Connor (ed.), *Seven Modern American Novelists* (Minneapolis, 1964), 189–225. The essay is reprinted in modified form as Chapter I in this volume.

7 Northrop Frye, *Anatomy of Criticism* (Princeton, 1957).
8 Richard Kennedy, "Thomas Wolfe's Fiction: The Question of Genre," in Paschal Reeves (ed.), *Thomas Wolfe and the Glass of Time* (Athens, Ga., 1971), 1–44.
9 *You Can't Go Home Again* (New York, 1940), 14.
10 *Ibid.*, 385.
11 Elizabeth Nowell (ed.), *The Letters of Thomas Wolfe* (New York, 1956), 714.
12 *You Can't Go Home Again*, 393.
13 Hamilton Basso, review of *You Can't Go Home Again*, *New Republic*, September 23, 1940, pp. 422–23.
14 Richard S. Kennedy, *The Window of Memory: The Literary Career of Thomas Wolfe* (Chapel Hill, N.C., 1962), 403–11.
15 *The Story of a Novel* (New York, 1936), 59–60.
16 *You Can't Go Home Again*, 77.
17 *Ibid.*, 633.
18 *Ibid.*, 139.
19 *Ibid.*, 195, 118.
20 Marcel Proust, *Sodome et Gomorrhe I* (1921) and *Sodome et Gomorrhe II* (1922), translated together as *Cities of the Plain*, trans. C. K. Scott Moncrieff (New York, 1927).
21 *You Can't Go Home Again*, 260, 263.
22 Henry Steele Commager, *The American Mind* (New Haven, Conn., 1951), 267–69.
23 Alfred Kazin, "John Dos Passos: Inventor in Isolation," *Saturday Review*, March 15, 1969, p. 17.
24 See, for example, Nowell (ed.), *Letters*, 370–71.
25 See William Braswell and Leslie A. Field (eds.), *Thomas Wolfe's Purdue Speech: "Writing and Living"* (West Lafayette, Ind., 1964), 36–37.
26 See C. Hugh Holman and Sue F. Ross (eds.), *The Letters of Thomas Wolfe to His Mother* (Chapel Hill, N.C., 1968), 94.
27 John Dos Passos, *The 42nd Parallel* (New York, 1937), 81.
28 John Dos Passos, *The Big Money* (New York, 1937), 461–63.
29 Robert Penn Warren, "The Hamlet of Thomas Wolfe," in Richard Walser (ed.), *The Enigma of Thomas Wolfe* (Cambridge, Mass., 1953), 132.
30 *Hamlet*, I, ii, 135–37.
31 *The Story of a Novel*, 30–31, 31–32.
32 *You Can't Go Home Again*, 395–96, 189, 249, 467–68, 111.
33 *Ibid.*, 145–46.
34 *Ibid.*, 728, 729–30, 263, 321, 262–63.
35 *Ibid.*, 434–36.
36 *Ibid.*, 508, 741.
37 *Ibid.*, 741.
38 Max Lerner, *America as a Civilization* (New York, 1957), 791.
39 J. B. Priestley, *Literature and Western Man* (New York, 1960), 440.

CHAPTER VI

1 Maxwell Geismar, *Writers in Crisis* (Boston, 1947), 196.
2 *Look Homeward, Angel* (New York, 1929), 155.
3 *The Web and the Rock* (New York, 1939), 14, 242, 243.
4 Elizabeth Nowell (ed.), *The Letters of Thomas Wolfe* (New York, 1956), 235.
5 *The Story of a Novel* (New York, 1936), 39.
6 *The Web and the Rock*, 246–47.

7 Nowell (ed.), *Letters*, 226, 284.
8 *You Can't Go Home Again* (New York, 1940), 327.
9 William Gilmore Simms, *The Wigwam and the Cabin* (New York, 1856), 4–5.
10 Henry David Thoreau, *Walden*, ed. J. Lyndon Shanley (Princeton, N.J., 1971), 3.
11 Nowell (ed.), *Letters*, 487, 446–47.
12 *Ibid.*, 489.
13 *Look Homeward, Angel*, 3.
14 *The Story of a Novel*, 51.
15 Louis D. Rubin, Jr., and Robert D. Jacobs (eds.), *South: Modern Southern Literature in Its Cultural Setting* (Garden City, N.Y., 1961), 43.
16 *Of Time and the River* (New York, 1935), 93.
17 Robert Penn Warren, *Segregation: The Inner Conflict in the South* (New York, 1956), 15.
18 Virginia Rock, "Agrarianism in Southern Literature," *Georgia Review*, XI (Summer, 1957), 157.
19 Allen Tate, "The New Provincialism," in *Essays of Four Decades* (Chicago, 1968), 543.
20 *Of Time and the River*, 90.
21 Alfred Kazin, *On Native Grounds* (New York, 1942), 468; Wilbur J. Cash, *The Mind of the South* (New York, 1941), 386–87; Joseph Warren Beach, *American Fiction, 1920–1940* (New York, 1941), 211.
22 *The Web and the Rock*, 245–46.
23 C. Hugh Holman and Sue F. Ross (eds.), *The Letters of Thomas Wolfe to His Mother* (Chapel Hill, N.C., 1968), 42–43.
24 *You Can't Go Home Again*, 396.
25 *I'll Take My Stand: The South and the Agrarian Tradition*, by Twelve Southerners (New York, 1930), xx.
26 *You Can't Go Home Again*, 393.
27 *Ibid.*, 741.
28 *Ibid.*, 742.
29 *Of Time and the River*, 83.
30 *The Story of a Novel*, 59.
31 Louis D. Rubin, Jr., and Robert D. Jacobs (eds.), *Southern Renascence: The Literature of the Modern South* (Baltimore, 1953), 65.
32 Ellen Glasgow, *The Woman Within* (New York, 1942), 42.
33 Ellen Glasgow, *A Certain Measure* (New York, 1943), 155.
34 William Faulkner, *Go Down, Moses* (New York, 1942), 345.
35 *The Story of a Novel*, 60.
36 *You Can't Go Home Again*, 434–36.
37 *The Story of a Novel*, 63–64.
38 *You Can't Go Home Again*, 328.
39 Charles Woodmason, *The Carolina Back Country on the Eve of the Revolution: The Journal and Other Writings of Charles Woodmason, Anglican Itinerant*, ed. Richard J. Hooker (Chapel Hill, N.C., 1953).
40 *The Web and the Rock*, 13.
41 *Ibid.*, 14.
42 *Ibid.*, 15, 16–17.
43 Jonathan Daniels, "Wolfe's First Is Novel of Revolt," Raleigh (N.C.) *News and Observer*, October 20, 1929.
44 *Look Homeward, Angel*, 626.
45 *Ibid.*, 53.
46 *The Web and the Rock*, 246.
47 *Of Time and the River*, 866.

48 *The Story of a Novel*, 39.
49 *You Can't Go Home Again.*
50 *The Web and the Rock*, 83.
51 *Ibid.*, 90.
52 *Ibid.*, 262, 695.

CHAPTER VII

1 Nathalia Wright, *American Novelists in Italy, The Discoverers: Allston to James* (Philadelphia, 1966); Van Wyck Brooks, *The Dream of Arcadia: American Writers and Artists in Italy, 1760–1915* (New York, 1958).
2 George M. Reeves, Jr., *Thomas Wolfe et l'Europe* (Paris, 1955), 83, 142. Another monograph, Daniel L. Delakas, *Thomas Wolfe, la France, et les romanciers français* (Paris, 1950), also takes this view. Neither Reeves nor Delakas sees the issue as a simple one, and both put Wolfe's work apart from that of the expatriates. Reeves, for example, while he asserts that Wolfe's experience is like that of "La Génération Perdue," declares his work to lie "en dehors du principal courant littéraire de son époque" (p. 83).
3 Malcolm Cowley, *Exile's Return: A Literary Odyssey of the 1920s* (New York, 1951), 9, 291–92.
4 William Braswell and Leslie A. Field (eds.), *Thomas Wolfe's Purdue Speech: "Writing and Living"* (West Lafayette, Ind., 1964), 36–37.
5 These biographical data are assembled from C. Hugh Holman and Sue F. Ross (eds.), *The Letters of Thomas Wolfe to His Mother* (Chapel Hill, N.C., 1968); Elizabeth Nowell, *Thomas Wolfe: A Biography* (Garden City, N.Y., 1960); Richard S. Kennedy, *The Window of Memory: The Literary Career of Thomas Wolfe* (Chapel Hill, N.C., 1962); Delakas, *Thomas Wolfe, la France, et les romanciers français*, 143–47, whose useful "Tableau Chronologique de la Vie de Wolfe" is very detailed on Wolfe's European travels; and Andrew Turnbull, *Thomas Wolfe* (New York, 1967).
6 An almost unbelievable listing of the cities Wolfe visited is given in Delakas' "Tableau Chronologique" (see Note 5 above). The postcards listed in Holman and Ross (eds.), *Letters to His Mother*, xvii–xx, also give an idea of Wolfe's coverage of Europe.
7 Kennedy, *The Window of Memory*, 97–106, has a good account of this work.
8 *Of Time and the River* (New York, 1935), 858–59.
9 *The Story of a Novel* (New York, 1936), 31.
10 *The Web and the Rock* (New York, 1939), 692–93.
11 *The Story of a Novel*, 30–31, 35–36, 37–38.
12 Richard S. Kennedy and Paschal Reeves (eds.), *The Notebooks of Thomas Wolfe* (2 vols.; Chapel Hill, N.C., 1970), II, 460.
13 *Of Time and the River*, 329.
14 Elizabeth Nowell (ed.), *The Letters of Thomas Wolfe* (New York, 1956), 240–45. This very important letter of July 17, 1930, to Maxwell Perkins deserves examination in its totality and is too richly instructive to be reduced to the brief summary I have given of it.
15 Braswell and Field (eds.), *Purdue Speech*, 68.
16 *Ibid.*, 67.
17 Martha Dodd, *Through Embassy Eyes* (New York, 1939), 91.
18 *You Can't Go Home Again* (New York, 1940), 622.
19 *Ibid.*, 631.
20 *Ibid.*, 626, 635.
21 *Ibid.*, 626, 627.
22 *Ibid.*, 728, 704.
23 The work can be found in C. Hugh Holman (ed.), *The Short Novels of Thomas*

Wolfe (New York, 1961), 233–78, in the form in which it was published in the *New Republic*, LXXXX (March 10, 17, 24, 1937), 132–36, 159–64, 202–207. A longer version appears in *You Can't Go Home Again*, 634–704.

24 Bella Kussy, "The Vitalist Trend and Thomas Wolfe," in C. Hugh Holman (ed.), *The World of Thomas Wolfe* (New York, 1962), 110. The essay originally appeared in *Sewanee Review*, L (July–September, 1942), 306–24.

25 See the comments of Bruce R. McElderry, Jr., *Thomas Wolfe* (New York, 1964), 64–66, on similarities between Wolfe and Mark Twain. See also Bruce R. McElderry, Jr., "The Durable Humor in *Look Homeward, Angel*," *Arizona Quarterly*, XI (Summer, 1955), 123–28.

26 Cowley's *Exile's Return* is excellent on the ideals of this group.

27 *Of Time and the River*, 135. The material on Hatcher's class—almost all of it satiric—is on pp. 130–35, 167–75, 282–304, 309–24.

28 *Ibid.*, 698–99.

29 *The Hills Beyond*, 186.

30 See, among many possible sources, Nowell (ed.), *Letters*, 262–66, particularly Wolfe's description of Fitzgerald "in the Ritz Bar where he was entirely surrounded by Princeton boys, all nineteen years old, all drunk and all half-raw" (p. 263).

31 *Ibid.*, 67: "I'm going to Heaven in September [1924]. That is, to England."

32 *Ibid.*, 71, 74.

33 *The Web and the Rock*, 302–303.

34 Nowell (ed.), *Letters*, 92.

35 *Ibid.*, 93.

36 *You Can't Go Home Again*, 703–704.

37 Nowell (ed.), *Letters*, 192–93.

38 Holman and Ross (eds.), *Letters to His Mother*, 94.

39 *The Story of a Novel*, 92–93.

40 Kathleen Hoagland, "Thomas Wolfe: Biography in Sound, An NBC Radio Broadcast," *Carolina Quarterly*, VII (Fall, 1956), 9.

CHAPTER VIII

1 Robert Scholes and Robert Kellogg, *The Nature of Narrative* (New York, 1966), 58, 208.

2 Seymour M. Pitcher, "Epic," in Alex Preminger *et al.* (eds.), *Encyclopedia of Poetry and Poetics* (Princeton, N.J., 1965), 243.

3 R. R. Purdy (ed.), *Fugitives' Reunion: Conversations at Vanderbilt, May 3–5, 1956* (Nashville, Tenn., 1959), 34.

4 Benjamin T. Spencer, *The Quest for Nationality: An American Literary Campaign* (Syracuse, N.Y., 1957), 328.

5 Roy Harvey Pearce, *The Continuity of American Poetry* (Princeton, N.J., 1961), 61.

6 Joel Barlow, "Preface," *The Columbiad* (Philadelphia, 1807), viii–xvi.

7 Hector St. John de Crévecoeur, *Letters from an American Farmer* (London, 1782), Letter III.

8 Pearce, *The Continuity of American Poetry*, 61.

9 Alexis de Tocqueville, *Democracy in America*, trans. Henry Reeves, ed. Phillips Bradley (2 vols.; New York, 1957), II, 80–81, 78.

10 James Fenimore Cooper, *Notions of the Americans* (Philadelphia, 1828), Letter XXIII.

11 Nathaniel Hawthorne, *The Marble Faun* (Boston, 1883), 15.

12 John Morton Blum, *The Promise of America: An Historical Inquiry* (Boston, 1966), 3.

13 Stephen Vincent Benét, "Invocation," *Western Star* (New York, 1943), vii.
14 Tocqueville, *Democracy in America*, II, 77.
15 Jacques Barzun, "Byron and the Byronic in History," in *The Energies of Art* (New York, 1962), 57.
16 Walt Whitman, "Song of Myself," *Leaves of Grass*, ed. H. W. Blodgett and Sculley Bradley (New York, 1965), 28, 11. 1–3.
17 Pearce, *The Continuity of American Poetry*, 134–35.
18 Robert F. Sayre, in *The Examined Self: Benjamin Franklin, Henry Adams, Henry James* (Princeton, 1964), 200, reached a similar conclusion after a sophisticated study of American autobiography; he says, "From Whitman to Hart Crane and Ezra Pound there is good precedent for the author as epic hero. As the American Epic has tended to be autobiographical, so in the *Education* [of *Henry Adams*] does autobiography become epic."
19 Spencer, *The Quest for Nationality*, 328.
20 William Gilmore Simms, "Preface," *The Yemassee*, ed. C. Hugh Holman (Boston, 1961), 5.
21 Herman Melville, *Moby-Dick*, ed. L. S. Mansfield and H. P. Vincent (New York, 1952), 114.
22 John Braine, "A Novelist Should Stick to His Last," *New York Times Book Review*, January 10, 1965, p. 1.
23 Walt Whitman, "A Backward Glance O'er Travel'd Roads," *Leaves of Grass and Selected Prose*, ed. John Kouwenhoven (New York, 1950), 558.
24 Elizabeth Nowell (ed.), *The Letters of Thomas Wolfe* (New York, 1956), 587.
25 *The Story of a Novel* (New York, 1936), 30–31.
26 John Livingston Lowes, *The Road to Xanadu: A Study in the Ways of Imagination* (Boston, 1930). The footnote is on p. 477 (where *Wolfe* is spelled *Wolf*); the passage is on p. 188.
27 Thomas Wolfe, "The Supernatural in the Poetry and Philosophy of Coleridge" [MS in Harvard College Library, Accession No. HCL*46AM–8(9)].
28 Lowes, *The Road to Xanadu*, Chapters 1–3.
29 *Ibid.*, 390, 396.
30 Wolfe, "The Supernatural in Coleridge," 9.
31 *Of Time and the River* (New York, 1935), 91–92.
32 *The Story of a Novel*, 42–43. These "ledgers" are gathered in Richard S. Kennedy and Paschal Reeves (eds.), *The Notebooks of Thomas Wolfe* (2 vols.; Chapel Hill, N.C., 1970).
33 See C. Hugh Holman (ed.), *The Thomas Wolfe Reader* (New York, 1962), in particular, "The Return of the Far-Wanderer," 61–71; "Angel on the Porch," 77–84; "Love in the Enchanted Wood," 139–71. The headnotes in *The Thomas Wolfe Reader* and in C. Hugh Holman (ed.), *The Short Novels of Thomas Wolfe* (New York, 1961), give detailed information about much of Wolfe's fragmenting of his work.
34 *Of Time and the River*, 130–35, 167–75, 282–304, 309–24.
35 *Ibid.*, 440–47, 454–68, 491–97.
36 *The Web and the Rock* (New York, 1939), 132–56; *You Can't Go Home Again* (New York, 1940), 109–40, 196–322, 634–40, 641–51, 655, 663–704; and compare with Holman (ed.), *The Thomas Wolfe Reader*, 498–99, 574–75, and with Holman (ed.), *The Short Novels of Thomas Wolfe*, 233–323.
37 S. H. Butcher, *Aristotle's Theory of Poetry and Fine Arts* (London, 1911), 91, 65, 111.
38 *Look Homeward, Angel* (New York, 1929), 589.
39 *Of Time and the River*, 732.
40 *You Can't Go Home Again*, 505–508.
41 *Ibid.*, 508.

Index

Aeneid, The, 155, 157
Agrarians. *See* Nashville Agrarians
American hero: defined by Crèvecoeur,
  157; defined by Tocqueville, 157–58
American Mercury, 64, 171
Anderson, Sherwood, 2, 59; his *Mill
  Girls*, 59
Angoff, Charles, 171
Aristotle, 165–66
Asheville, N.C.: as a New South town,
  7–8, 94, 152; its reaction to *Look
  Homeward, Angel*, 11, 40
Aswell, Edward, xiv, 16–19, 77, 88–89,
  150, 165
Autobiography: in American fiction, 37

Baker, Carlos, 42
Baker, George Pierce, 6, 10, 107
Balzac, Honoré, 55, 111
Barlow, Joel, 156. Works: *The
  Columbiad*, 156; *The Vision of
  Columbus*, 156
Barzun, Jacques, 159
Basso, Hamilton, 49, 63, 93
Beach, Joseph Warren, 81, 115
Benét, Stephen Vincent, 156, 158.
  Works: *John Brown's Body*, 156;
  Western Star, 156, 158
Bergson, Henri, 27, 30, 112
Berlin, Germany: Wolfe's visits to, 15,
  143–48
Bernstein, Mrs. Aline, 10–11, 12. Works:
  "Eugene," 10; *The Journey Down*, 10;
  Three Blue Suits, 10
Bishop, John Peale, 48, 58, 81; his *Many
  Thousands Gone*, 58
Blake, William, 111

Blum, John Morton, 158
Booth, Wayne, 40, 73; his *The Rhetoric
  of Fiction*, 40
Bourget, Charles Joseph Paul, 55
Braine, John, 160
Brooks, Cleanth, 116
Brooks, Van Wyck, 73
Burgum, E. B., 33, 34
Burnett, W. R., 58
Butler, Samuel, 37; his *The Way of All
  Flesh*, 37, 75
Byrd, William, 127; his *A History of
  the Dividing Line*, 127

Cabell, James Branch, 112, 113
Caldwell, Erskine, 127
Calhoun, John C., 116
Camus, Albert, 55
Capote, Truman, 56
Carolina Playmakers, 6, 9
Cash, Wilbur J., 115
Cather, Willa, 56, 58. Works: *A Lost
  Lady*, 56, 58; *My Mortal Enemy*, 56
Chapel Hill. *See* University of North
  Carolina
Charles Scribner's Sons, 11, 14, 15, 20,
  41, 62, 78–79, 141; Wolfe's break with,
  15, 65
Chekhov, Anton, 55
Church, Margaret, 27
Clemens, Samuel L., 22, 55–56, 73, 149.
  Works: *The Adventures of Huckle-
  berry Finn*, 73, 84; *The Innocents
  Abroad*, 149; *The Man That Cor-
  rupted Hadleyburg*, 56; *The
  Mysterious Stranger*, 55
Coleridge, Samuel Taylor, 162–63

Index ※ ※ ※ ※ ※ ※ ※ ※ ※ ※ ※ ※ ※ ※ ※ ※ ※

Commager, Henry Steele, 98
Conrad, Joseph, 55, 58, 73. Works:
 Heart of Darkness, 73; Youth, 58
Cooper, James Fenimore, 55, 158, 160;
 his The Leatherstocking Tales, 160
Cowley, Malcolm, xv, 58, 139
Cozzens, James Gould, 58; his S.S. San
 Pedro, 58
Craddock, Charles Egbert. See Murfree,
 Mary N.
Crane, Hart, 159; his The Bridge, 159
Crane, Stephen, 55
Crèvecoeur, Hector St. John de, 157
Cummings, E. E., 99

Daniels, Jonathan, 130
Dashiell, Alfred, 57, 60, 63, 71; his
 Editor's Choice, 60
Davidson, Donald, 119
De Maupassant, Guy. See Maupassant,
 Guy de
Depression, 94, 95, 99
De Tocqueville, Alexis. See Tocqueville,
 Alexis de
De Voto, Bernard, xv, 15, 41, 48, 86; his
 "Genius is Not Enough," 41
Dickens, Charles, 37, 51, 136; his David
 Copperfield, 73, 84
Dodd, Martha, 144, 145
Dodd, William E., 144, 145
Dorman, Marjorie, 62
Dos Passos, John, 99, 160, 161; com-
 pared with Wolfe, 98, 100–101, 102;
 his U.S.A., 100, 160, 161
Dostoevski, Feodor, 136
Dramatic scene: defined, 86

Eliot, George, 55; her Silas Marner, 55
Eliot, T. S., 138
Emmons, Richard, 156; his The
 Fredoniad, 156
Epic: defined, 155–56, 165–66; American
 efforts at, 156–61, 164, 177
Epiphany: in short story, 52

Faulkner, William, 20, 22–23, 56, 68, 76,
 112, 113, 115, 116, 120, 121, 122, 126,
 128, 130–31, 132, 133, 134, 137. Works:
 The Bear, 56, 122; "Delta Autumn,"
 121; Knight's Gambit, 56; The Sound
 and the Fury, 122; "That Evening
 Sun," 76

Fielding, Henry, 160; his Tom Jones, 72
Fitzgerald, F. Scott, 35, 84, 151, 176; his
 The Great Gatsby, 73
Flandrau, Grace, 58; her The Way of
 Love, 58
Flaubert, Gustave, 152
"47 Workshop," 6, 9, 107
France, Anatole, 55
Frye, Northrop, 88
Fugitives. See Nashville Agrarians

Galsworthy, John, 55. Works: The
 Apple Tree, 55; The Forsyte Saga, 55;
 Indian Summer of a Forsyte, 55
Garland, Hamlin, 128
Geismar, Maxwell, 107
Germany, 18, 31, 65, 92, 95, 96, 102,
 104, 141, 143–48, 151
Gide, André, 55
Glasgow, Ellen, 112, 113, 120, 121, 126,
 128, 131, 132
Goethe, Johann Wolfgang von, 55.
 Works: Sorrows of Werther, 84;
 Wilhelm Meister, 75
Guggenheim Memorial Foundation, 12,
 20, 84, 141
Gulliver's Travels, 84

Harland, Henry, 56
Harper and Brothers, 66
Harper's Bazaar, 78
Harris, George Washington, 127
Harvard University, 6, 9, 13, 19, 42, 80,
 107, 132, 149
Hawthorne, Nathaniel, 73, 158; his The
 Scarlet Letter, 73
Hemingway, Ernest, 56, 65, 73, 99;
 compared with Wolfe, 2–3, 38–45.
 Works: Across the River and Into the
 Trees, 39; Death in the Afternoon, 39,
 44; A Farewell to Arms, 38, 42; In
 Our Time, 40; The Old Man and the
 Sea, 39, 56; The Sun Also Rises, 38–39,
 40–41, 42
Herbst, Josephine, 59; her A New
 Break, 59
Hermann, John, 59; his The Big Short
 Trip, 59
Hesse, Herman, 144
Heyward, DuBose, 56; his Porgy, 56
Hitler, Adolf, 65, 92, 144, 145, 147
Hoagland, Kathleen, 154

Homer, 157
Howe, E. W., 128
Howells, William Dean, 55

I'll Take My Stand, 118–19

James, Henry, 53–54, 55, 56, 71, 86, 138, 152. Works: *The Ambassadors*, 72; *The Aspern Papers*, 56; *The Author of Beltraffio*, 53; *The Beast in the Jungle*, 56; *Daisy Miller*, 56, 73; *The Lesson of the Master*, 56; *Madame de Mauves*, 56; *The Turn of the Screw*, 56
Jefferson, Thomas, 116
Johnson, Lyndon B., 126
Johnson, Pamela Hansford, 33
Joyce, James, xiii, 10, 37, 39, 49–50, 52, 60, 64, 73, 74, 90, 134. Works: "Anna Livia Plurabelle," 60; *Finnegans Wake*, 60; *A Portrait of the Artist as a Young Man*, 37, 39, 49–50, 73, 74–76; *Ulysses*, 10, 60, 74

Kafka, Franz, 55
Kazin, Alfred, 98, 115
Kellogg, Robert, 155
Kennedy, Richard S., 19, 42, 74, 76, 79, 81, 88, 93. Works: "Thomas Wolfe's Fiction: The Question of Genre," 81; *The Window of Memory*, 42
Kirkland, Joseph, 128
Knickerbocker Magazine, 110
Koch, Frederick, 6
Kussy, Bella, 31, 148

Lanier, Sidney, 119
Lawrence, D. H., 37, 75; his *Sons and Lovers*, 37, 75
Ledig-Rewohlt, Heinz, 145
Lerner, Max, 106
Lewis, Sinclair: his influence on Wolfe, 10, 32, 91, 128; praises Wolfe, 11, 64; as Lloyd McHarg, 18, 95, 97
Lindbergh, Charles A., 145
Lockridge, Ross, 161; his *Raintree County*, 161
Loeb, Harold, 39; his *The Way It Was*, 39
Longfellow, Henry Wadsworth, 110, 156; his *Hiawatha*, 156

Longstreet, Augustus Baldwin, 127; his *Georgia Scenes*, 127
Lost Generation, 99, 138–39, 149, 175
Lowes, John Livingston, 6, 10, 161–63; his *The Road to Xanadu* 6, 162
MacKaye, Percy, 61
Mann, Thomas, 55, 67. Works: *Buddenbrooks*, 67; *Death in Venice*, 67; *The Magic Mountain*, 67; Tonio Kröger, 67
Mansfield, Katherine, 58; her *Prelude*, 58
Maugham, W. Somerset, 37–38; his *Of Human Bondage*, 37–38, 75
Maupassant, Guy de, 55, 58; his *Boule de Suif*, 58
Mauriac, François, 55
Maurois, André, 58; his *The Weigher of Souls*, 58
Melville, Herman, 55, 160; compared with Wolfe, 90–91. Works: *Benito Cereno*, 55; *Billy Budd*, 55; *Mardi*, 90; *Moby-Dick*, 55, 72, 73, 84, 90, 160, 161; *Pierre*, 90–91; *Redburn*, 90; *White-Jacket*, 90
Metro-Goldwyn-Mayer, 12
Modern Monthly, 78
Muller, Herbert, 69
Murfree, Mary N., 127

Narrative point of view, 72–73
Nashville Agrarians, 107, 109, 116, 117–19
Nathan, Robert, 56
Naziism: Wolfe's reaction to, 15, 18, 31, 65, 104, 144, 148
Nemerov, Howard, 51–54
New Republic, xv, 65
New York *Sun*, 59
New York University, 10, 12, 13, 81
North Carolina: people of, 108–109; compared to South Carolina by Wolfe, 129–30
Norwood, Hayden, 38; his *The Marble Man's Wife*, 38
Nouvelle. See Short novel
Novel: defined, 52–54
Novella. *See* Short novel
Nowell, Elizabeth, 38, 49, 64, 78

O'Connor, Flannery, 127
Odyssey, The, 165–66
Of Time and the River: summarized,

xiii; reception of, xv, 13–14; myth in, 4; editing of, 21–22, 78–79, 111; form of, 81–82. *See also* Wolfe, Thomas

Page, Thomas Nelson, 126
Pearce, Roy Harvey, 157, 159
Pearson, Norman Holmes, 74
Perkins, Maxwell, 4, 11, 12–13, 20, 21, 25–26, 32, 33, 49, 50, 59, 62, 65, 67, 74, 78–80, 84, 108, 111
Pfister, Karin, 30
Pitcher, Seymour M., 155
Poe, Edgar Allan, 52
Porter, Katherine Anne, 56, 59. Works: *The Cracked Looking-Glass*, 59; *Noon Wine*, 56; *Pale Horse, Pale Rider*, 56
Pound, Ezra, 159; his *Cantos*, 159
Priestley, J. B., 106
Proust, Marcel, 27, 30, 38, 98, 112. Works: *Remembrance of Things Past*, 38, 84; *Sodome et Gomorrhe (Cities of the Plain)*, 98
Purdue University, 84, 139

Rahv, Philip, 38
Raleigh (N.C.) *News and Observer*, 130
Ransom, John Crowe, 116, 155–56
Roscoe, Burton, 59
Rawlings, Marjorie Kinnan, 58; her *Jacob's Ladder*, 58
Raynolds, Robert, 61
Redbook Magazine, 64
Reeves, George M., Jr., 138–39; his *Thomas Wolfe et l'Europe*, 138–39
Reeves, Paschal, 19, 79
Revolt from the Village, 128
Rhetoric: defined, 86
Robb, Carroll E., 58
Roberts, J. M., 9
Roberts, Margaret, 5–6, 9
Robinson Crusoe, 84
Rock, Virginia, 114
Roosevelt, Franklin D., 126
Rousseau, Jean-Jacques, 84; his *Confessions*, 84
Rowohlt, Ernst, 145
Rubin, Louis D., Jr., 22, 38, 60, 112
Ryan, Pat M., 19

Saturday Evening Post, The, 3, 78, 149

Sayre, Robert F., 177; his *The Examined Self*, 177
Schiebelhuth, Hans, 144
Scholes, Robert, 155
Schorer, Mark, xiii, xiv-xv, 38
Scribner's. *See* Charles Scribner's Sons
Scribner's Magazine, 12, 56–60, 61, 62, 63, 71, 77, 78
Seldes, Gilbert, 58
Shakespeare, William, 101. Works: *As You Like It*, 34; *Hamlet*, 34, 101
Shirer, William L., 145; his *Berlin Diary*, 145
Short novel, 51–56, 57–58
Short Novel Contests, 57–60
Short story: defined, 51–55
Simms, William Gilmore, 55, 110, 111, 127, 160; his *Guy Rivers*, 127
Smith, Lillian, 127
Soskin, William, 59
South, the: writers of, 107–23; characteristics of, 123–31; Piedmont region of, 124–26; Piedmont writers of, 126–28
Stallings, Laurence, 59
Stanzel, F. K., 72
Stein, Gertrude, 56
Steinbeck, John, 56, 89. Works: *Of Mice and Men*, 56; *The Pearl*, 56; *The Red Pony*, 56
Sterne, Laurence, 27, 55, 82. Works: *A Sentimental Journey*, 55; *Tristram Shandy*, 27, 82, 84
Stevenson, Robert Louis, 55; his *Dr. Jekyll and Mr. Hyde*, 55
Stribling, T. S., 127. Works: *The Forge*, 127; *The Store*, 127; *Teeftallow*, 127; *Unfinished Cathedral*, 127
Styron, William, xiv, 113; his *Lie Down in Darkness*, 113

Tate, Allen, 113, 114, 116, 122. Works: "Ode to the Confederate Dead," 113; "The Wolves," 122
Thoreau, Henry David, 110
Tocqueville, Alexis de, 131, 157–59
Tolstoy, Leo, 111
transition, 60
Turgenev, Ivan, 55
Twain, Mark. *See* Clemens, Samuel L.
Twelve Southerners. See *I'll Take My Stand*

University of North Carolina, 6, 9, 42, 107, 109

Vanderbilt University, 109
Vanity Fair, 78
Virgil, 155, 157, 159
Vision of Columbus, The, 156
Voltaire, 55

Wallace, George, 62
Warren, Robert Penn, 15, 63, 81, 101, 112–13, 114, 116, 120, 122, 156. Works: *The Ballad of Billie Potts*, 113; *Brother to Dragons*, 156; "Original Sin," 122; *World Enough and Time*, 113
Watkins, Floyd C., 5, 38
Wells, H. G., 10; his *The Undying Fire*, 10
Welty, Eudora, 56, 113. Works: *Losing Battles*, 113; *The Optimist's Daughter*, 56; *The Ponder Heart*, 56; *The Robber Bridegroom*, 56
West, Nathanael, 56
Wharton, Edith, 56, 58, 59. Works: *Ethan Frome*, 56, 58; *False Dawn*, 56; *Her Son*, 59; *The Old Maid*, 56
Wharton, James, 58
Wheaton, Mabel Wolfe, 8–9, 38; her *Thomas Wolfe and His Family*, 38
Wheelock, John Hall, 20, 38, 62, 78–79
Whitman, Walt, 2, 13, 24–25, 33, 34–35, 67–68, 80, 92, 101, 105, 106, 131, 132, 134, 153, 159, 161, 165. Works: *Democratic Vistas*, 33, 92; *Leaves of Grass*, 24, 84, 153; *Song of Myself*, 159, 165
Wilder, Thornton, 56; his *The Bridge of San Luis Rey*, 56
Williams, Horace, 6, 7
Williams, William Carlos, 159; his *Paterson*, 159
Willis, Elizabeth, 58
Wilson, Edmund, 59, 99
Wolfe, Ben, 8, 9, 82
Wolfe, Julia Elizabeth Westall, 8, 59–60, 118
Wolfe, Thomas: and America, 8, 33, 91, 93, 98–99, 109–10, 149, 161–67; his attitude toward evil, 33–34, 119–21; and autobiography, 4–5, 14, 22, 30, 35–36, 37–46, 61, 82, 134, 135, 152–53,

161, 163–64; biography of, 7–17; his break with Scribner's, 15, 65; catalogues of, 132–33; characterization in his works, 30–31, 102–103, 132–33; compared with Faulkner, 134–35; death of, 19–23, 69, 123; his use of dramatic scene, 3–4, 14, 86, 88–106; and editors, 15, 41–42, 111, 171; education of, 5–7, 9–10, 162–63; his epic impulse, 2, 101–102, 104–106, 109–10, 137, 153, 161–67; in Europe, 139–53, 162; his failure discussed, 35–36, 69, 106, 167; and history, 112–13; and industrialism, 32, 116–19; his lack of organizing principle, 4–5, 35, 42–43, 47–48, 69–71; and language, 23–27, 35, 43, 44, 153–54; and loneliness 2, 9, 25–27, 62, 68, 102, 132, 134, 140, 141–42, 150; and the Lost Generation, 99, 138–39, 175; his lyric qualities, 2–3, 86–106, 113–14; his use of myth, 4, 13, 135; and narrative point of view, 74–85; his use of opposites, 1–7, 23, 26–27, 88, 116; his use of protagonists, 42–43, 48–49, 55, 67–71, 111, 164–65, 171; as a radical, 32–33, 66, 119; realism in his works, 5, 24, 113–14, 150; his use of rhetoric, 2–3, 13, 14, 44, 86–106, 114–16, 134; as a Romantic, 5–7, 23, 34, 162–64; scope of his planned work, 47, 110–12; his search for a father, 25–26, 134; his sense of guilt, 121–23; his short novels and stories, 3–4, 14, 35–36, 43–44, 48–51, 53–54, 55, 59–71, 97, 165; as social critic, 31–33, 64, 65–66, 89–106, 166–67; as a southerner, 7–8, 33–34, 91, 93, 107–23, 128–37; and success, 36, 69, 167; his use of symbolism, 30, 62, 66, 103–104, 135–36; and the theme of self, 2, 89–90; his use of time and memory, 27–30, 44–45, 54–55, 69–70, 112; his tragic sense of life, 34; vitalism in, 31, 148. Works: "An Angel on the Porch," 59; "The Bell Remembered," 77; *Boom Town*, 64, 165; "The Bums at Sunset," 78; "Chickamauga," 3, 19, 113; "The Child by Tiger," 3, 43, 78, 136, 165; *Death the Proud Brother*, 14, 61, 62, 64, 68, 77; "The Doaksology," 16; "The Face of War," 78; "The Four Lost Men," 77; *From Death to Morning*, xiii, 14, 43, 49, 60,

61, 62, 68, 82; "God's Lonely Man," 9, 150; "The Hills Beyond," 19, 49; *The Hills Beyond*, xiv, 4, 18–19, 113; "The Hound of Darkness," 21; "The House of the Far and the Lost," 62, 63; "*I Have a Thing to Tell You*," 43, 65, 68, 77, 148, 165; "In the Park," 14, 43; *K-19*, 50, 67, 77, 79; "Katamoto," 78; *Look Homeward, Angel*, xiii, xv, 6, 8, 10, 11, 12, 13, 14, 20, 22, 25, 30, 36, 39–40, 42, 43, 45–46, 47, 48, 49, 50, 59, 67, 74–76, 77, 78, 79, 80, 82, 89, 91, 94, 99, 107, 115, 130, 131, 133, 139, 140, 141, 144, 162, 164, 166; "The Lost Boy," 3, 19, 28–29, 64; *Mannerhouse*, 19, 130; *The Mountains*, 19, 130; "No Door," 62; *No Door*, 62–63, 64, 67, 68, 77, 79; *Notebooks*, 19, 79, 87, 110, 142, 164; "The October Fair," 12, 20, 59, 65; *Of Time and the River*, 10, 14, 16, 17, 25, 26, 29, 30, 31, 32, 42, 43, 49, 62, 63, 64, 78, 79, 80, 84, 86–88, 113, 114, 120, 132, 142, 143, 144, 150, 164; "Oktoberfest," 77–78; "Only the Dead Know Brooklyn," 3, 14, 54; *The Party at Jack's*, 32, 43, 55, 63–64, 66, 68, 71, 165; "Passage to England," 140; *A Portrait of Bascom Hawke*, 12, 48–49, 50–51, 55, 57, 59, 61, 64, 67, 70, 77; "The Promise of America," 83; *The Short Novels of Thomas Wolfe*, 67; *The Story of a Novel*, xiii, xiv, 12, 14, 41, 42, 44, 50, 69, 94, 101, 108, 110, 120, 121, 122, 141, 143, 153–54, 164; "The Sun and the Rain," 78; "The Supernatural in the Poetry and Philosophy of Coleridge," 163; "The Train and the City," 49, 61, 67, 77; "The Vision of Spangler's Paul," 16; *The Web and the Rock*, xiv, 1–2, 3, 13, 17, 21, 24, 30, 31, 42–43, 49, 78, 79, 84, 107, 108, 117, 128, 130, 132, 133, 136, 141, 165; *The Web of Earth*, 14, 24, 26, 59–61, 64, 67, 68, 70, 77; *Welcome to Our City*, 19, 130; *You Can't Go Home Again*, xiv, 7, 12, 17–18, 21, 31, 32, 33, 34, 42, 49, 68, 77, 78, 83–84, 89–106, 119, 121, 122, 133, 135, 137, 148, 165, 166

Wolfe, William Oliver, 8
Woodmason, Charles, 126
Woodward, C. Vann, 34, 120
Woolf, Virginia, 55
Wordsworth, William, 27, 132

Yellow Book, 56, 71
"Young America" group, 110

Zola, Emile, 111

76877